Structural Transformation and Economic Development

This book examines long-term structural changes and the broad impact on economic development in regional comparative perspectives. The book analyses data across Africa, Asia and Latin America. It looks at key variables of productivity growth, industrialization, poverty, urbanization and employment. This book is concerned with understanding structural change dynamics and how it affects job creation, living standards and the efficiency of productive cities through manufacturing productivity growth that benefits majority of citizens.

With empirical evidence from a selected number of developing countries, including China, India, Brazil, Nigeria and South Africa, the book attempts to present the considerable structural changes of these countries over the last few decades. It highlights that growth without the expected job creation is one of the distinct features in emerging and developing countries. It suggests that countries may well record economic growth, whether through within sector productivity increase or through structural change, but this may not necessarily lead to employment, an important concern for long-term development.

Banji Oyelaran-Oyeyinka is currently Director of Regional Office for Africa, and previously Chief Scientific Advisor at UN-HABITAT. He is a professor in the fields of economic development, industrial policy and technology management. He has provided leadership in the fields of political economy and technology development, and continues to break new grounds uniting ideas in social sciences, engineering and technology policy.

Kaushalesh Lal is a development economist with emphasis on technical change. He earned his PhD from Erasmus University Rotterdam, The Netherlands. He has held faculty positions in various national and international institutions, namely, University of Delhi; Institute of Economic Growth, Delhi; and United Nations University-MERIT, The Netherlands. He has widely published research articles and books with renowned international publishers.

Routledge Studies in Development Economics

For a complete list of titles in this series, please visit www.routledge.com/series/SE0266

Structural Transformation and Economic Development

Cross regional analysis of industrialization and urbanization

Banji Oyelaran-Oyeyinka and Kaushalesh Lal

with contributions from
Shampa Paul and Oluyomi Ola-David

Routledge
Taylor & Francis Group

LONDON AND NEW YORK

First published 2017
by Routledge
2 Park Square, Milton Park, Abingdon, Oxon OX14 4RN

and by Routledge
711 Third Avenue, New York, NY 10017

First issued in paperback 2017

Routledge is an imprint of the Taylor & Francis Group, an informa business

British Library Cataloguing in Publication Data
A catalogue record for this book is available from the British Library

Library of Congress Cataloging-in-Publication Data
A catalog record for this book has been requested

ISBN 13: 978-0-8153-5086-6 (pbk)
ISBN 13: 978-1-138-67337-3 (hbk)

Typeset in Galliard
by Apex CoVantage, LLC

Contents

Figures

Tables

Preface

This book examines long-term structural transformation and its broad impact on economic development in regional comparative perspectives. It provides new insights into the mechanisms driving the structural transformation. Furthermore, it links structural transformation with different drivers of development, namely employment, productivity growth, urbanization, industrialization and poverty. This book through in-depth analysis and creation of new knowledge is a more nuanced understanding into the structural transformation dynamics. It gives insights into how it affects per capita income, economic structures, and how it is as well influenced by institutions and state policies that promote development. Specifically, the book analyses the relationships of industrialization and urbanization with structural transformation and how these foster employment and reduce poverty. We conclude that sustainable urbanization and industrialization are not just closely connected, but are key drivers of economic change.

To our knowledge, little or no empirical analysis has been conducted to quantify the relationships between structural transformation with the myriad and complex drivers of economic growth. This book aims to contribute to the literature by drawing on rich sources of data by which it carried out very robust empirical analysis to provide evidence-based policy recommendations. It relies heavily on value-added data from Groningen Growth and Development Centre (GGDC), University of Groningen, The Netherlands to understand long-term behaviour of a sample of economies of selected African, Asian and Latin American countries. Additional data came from World Development Indicator database to complement the GGDC data.

Most importantly, the book findings shed light on unconventional patterns of growth particularly in almost all African and in few Asian countries. Notably, significant economic growth goes in tandem with jobless growth as one key feature of certain developing and emerging economies. It suggests that countries may record economic growth through sector productivity increase or structural change, but this may not necessarily lead to employment. Second, we found the predominance of services at the expense of manufacturing industry; that is, while the pace of manufacturing is reduced or skipped – a phenomenon we refer to as 'jumping manufacturing' or premature de-industrialization – the services sector grows progressively. Third, structural transformation tends to occur in African countries without improvements in labour productivity, leading to increasing urbanization without structural change.

All these findings put conventional wisdoms on the known pathway of structural transformation into question, thus posing important challenges to our understanding of long-term development and calling attention of policymakers to the need to adopt a new approach to development. To this end, the book attempts to understand the role of governments and policies in the contribution and premature dominance of the services sector and the regress of Africa's industrial sector. Finally, it provides policy recommendations to achieve sustained process of successful industry-led structural transformation which will in turn drive economic development.

Acknowledgements

The authors would like to place on record our deep appreciation of the International Ecological Safety Collaborative Organization (IESCO) for financial support of the research project leading to this book. We also express our gratitude to our research associates, particularly Drs. Shampa Paul and Oluyomi Ola-David. Both these scholars contributed research materials on policy initiatives taken by selected governments of Asia and Africa. Our special thanks to Dr. Paul who made substantial academic inputs related to analytical issues. We would also like to acknowledge the contributions of Victoria Chebet, Gbemisola Adetoro and Gulelat Kebete. In addition, we thank our research assistants, namely, Adedoyin Luwaji, Tumaini Bulere, Shruti Vasudev, Charlotte Albin, Adeleke Emmanuel for their valuable research and editorial contributions. We also appreciate the administrative support of Jacqueline Macha, Mary Dibo, Anne Muchiri and Pamela Odhiambo.

Acronyms and abbreviations

ADB	African Development Bank
AEO	African Economic Outlook
AU	African Union
CAGR	Compound Annual Growth Rate
CCPIT	Council for the Promotion of International Trade, China
DTI	Department of Trade and Industry, South Africa
DU	degree of urbanization
EPC	Export Promotion Council
EPZ	Export Processing Zones
EU	European Union
FAO	Food and Agriculture Organization
GDP	gross domestic product
GGDC	Groningen Growth and Development Centre
GVA	gross value added
HDI	human development index
HPE	high-performing economies
HVA	high value added
ICT	Information and Communications Technology
ISI	Import Substitution Industrialization
LA	Latin America
LP	labour productivity
MENA	Middle East and North Africa
MFA	Multi-Fibre Arrangement
MFP	multi-factor productivity
MDG	Millennium Development Goal
MNC	multi-national corporation
MVA	market value added
NIEs	Newly Industrializing Economies
ODA	Official Development Aid
OECD	Organization for Economic Cooperation and Development
OLS	Ordinary Least Square
PPP	Purchasing Power Parity
RNFE	rural nonfarm employment

RNFI	rural nonfarm income
SAP	Structural Adjustment Programme
SD	standard deviation
SDG	Sustainable Development Goal
SIDA	Swedish International Development Agency
SME	small and medium enterprises
ST	structural transformation
TFP	total factor productivity
UNECA	United Nations Economic Commission for Africa
UNIDO	United Nations Industrial Development Corporation
UNRISD	United Nations Research Institute for Social Development
UNCTAD	United Nations Conference on Trade and Development
WDI	World Development Indicators
WFP	World Food Programme
WTO	World Trade Organization

1 Structural transformation in developing countries

1.1 Introduction

Structural transformation is defined as the transition of an economy from low-productivity and labour-intensive economic activities to higher-productivity and skill-intensive activities. The driving force behind structural transformation is the change of productivity in the modern sector which is dominated by manufacturing and services. It is also characterized by the movement of workforce from labour-intensive activities to skill-intensive ones. The movement of labour is severely affected by the existence of opportunities in skill-intensive sector because, even if the opportunities exist, labour may not necessarily move to a new sector unless the labour force is properly trained to be absorbed in the sector. If that be the case, then existing labour force would require requisite training before they move to the new sector. Another scenario could be that existing skills of labour force was used inefficiently. The labour force was already trained for skill-intensive activities, but was engaged in sectors where their skill was not fully utilized. Given the opportunities in the new sector, the labour force would move without any additional training. The later scenario may be considered the case of inappropriate allocation of human resources. In both cases, productivity of labour force would change resulting in changes in structure of the economy.

One aspect of structural change is labour, and the other is the opportunities in modern sector. The new opportunities are created by industrial policies of a nation. The growth and development of a modern sector depends on both the institutional environment and availability of appropriate human resources. The relationship among them is bidirectional and mutually re-enforcing. The growth of the modern sector would result in structural change. Hence, it can be argued that the causal relationship between labour productivity (LP) and structural transformation is bidirectional and is quantifiable. As mentioned earlier, industrial policies also play an important role in structural change. The relationship between institutional environment and structural change is not quantifiable, although it can be identified by content analysis.

It is clear from the above discussion that analysis of changes in productivity is of utmost importance to understand the causes of structural transformation. Although total factor productivity might be a better instrument to analyse structural change, analysis in this study would be based on single-factor productivity, that is, labour due to lack of data on other factors. The Groningen Growth and Development Centre of Groningen University maintain a sector-wide database on gross value added in national currency and total employment for selected countries. This study intends to use the same data and a ratio of value added to total employment in a particular sector as a measure of labour productivity. Subsequently, labour productivity would be divided into two components: (1) change in productivity due to structural change and (2) intra-sectoral productivity growth. Such analysis would help in quantifying the association between labour productivity and structural transformation.

The empirical evidence also suggests that structural change can take place without much change in labour productivity. The pattern of Structural Change observed in many African countries is a case in point. In that scenario, changes in economic structure are driven largely by the export of natural resource-based products. A study by de Vries *et al.* (2013) analysed structural transformation in 11 sub-Saharan African countries and its implications for productivity growth during the past 50 years. They found that the expansion of manufacturing activities during the early post-independence period led to a growth-enhancing reallocation of resources, but the process of structural change was stalled in the mid-1970s and 1980s. However, when growth rebounded in the 1990s, workers mainly relocated to services industries rather than manufacturing. This study analyses the reasons for stagnant or declining productivity in the modern sector on the African continent.

1.1.1   *Structural change and urbanization dynamics*

Urbanization is one of the most significant global trends in the 21st century. More than 50 per cent of the world population now lives in urban areas, while about 5 billion people or 60 per cent of world population will live in urban areas by 2030. Approximately, 90 per cent of world urban population growth between now and 2030 will take place in developing countries. Hence, cities are the locus of significant global challenges.

Urbanization is known to be a vehicle for national economic and social transformation. Planned urbanization is expected to bring about rapid economic progress and prosperity, with industrialization as its end-result. Therefore, planned urbanization will lead to higher productivity and, eventually, rising living standards and better quality of life. Cities are known to be centres of change and innovation, mainly because the concentration of people, resources and activities are expected to favour innovation. However, research has shown that there are a number of countries that are highly urbanized without having seen a large shift of economic activity towards manufacturing and services in most developing countries. These countries, as would be discussed later in this study, were identified to be natural resource exporters and do not conform to the standard model of urbanization (Gollin *et al.* 2013). For example, in 2010, Asia and sub-Saharan Africa were both at the same level of urbanization; the former has recorded the fastest-growing nations (which are South Korea and China), while the latter has seen very little growth in income per capita over the years (this will be discussed in the appropriate chapter). Generally, in developing countries urbanization has taken place in cities of all sizes.

Across regions, the distribution of city size is quite similar. For instance, in 2010, there were 257 Asian and 60 African "megacities" with over 750,000 inhabitants. Asia and Africa have approximately the same number of megacities per capita. These megacities represent around 40 per cent of the population in both continents. Asia is an example of the standard story of urbanization with structural transformation. The successful Asian economies typically went through both a green revolution and an industrial revolution, with urbanization following along as their economic activity shifted away from agricultural activities. In contrast, Africa offers a perfect example of urbanization without structural transformation. This is because there has been little evidence of a Green Revolution in Africa. Its food yields have remained low. Also, there has been no industrial revolution in Africa. Its manufacturing and services were 10 per cent and 26 per cent, but 24 per cent and 35 per cent for Asia, and African labour productivity was 1.7 and 3.5 times lower in industry and services, respectively.

1.1.2   Urbanization and employment

Employment creation and structural economic transformation are amongst the two major challenges at the forefront of current African growth and development strategies. At the micro level, employment creation provides opportunities for earnings and underpins increases in household expenditures and secure livelihoods. At the macro level, development occurs through the reallocation of labour across sectors toward sectors with the greatest growth potential and the highest productivity. Jobs also facilitate social (e.g. female wage employment) and political (seeking identity) transformations. However, it is not easy to achieve sustained employment generation (World Bank 2013a).

African countries will achieve high and sustained economic growth rates, alongside improved levels of social development only if productivity changes are based on widespread economic diversification (United Nations Economic Commission for Africa [UNECA] and AU 2011). The achievement of development goals and higher living standards will therefore depend on the ability of countries to foster entrepreneurship and promote innovation, including the spread, adaptation and adoption of pre-existing know-how and techniques, services, processes and ways of working. Unfortunately, much of the economic growth in low-income countries over the last decade has not led to structural changes.

1.1.3   Poverty and urbanization

About 70 per cent of the total population in large metropolis lives in slum communities. Research revealed that there is a negative correlation between informal employment and gross domestic product (GDP) per capita; hence, informal growth tends to be growth-reducing in developing countries. Thus, informal workers tend to be less well-off than those who work and live in more formal settings. The formation of cities in developing countries is taking the shape of informality, illegality and slums. Therefore, urban growth in most developing countries is strongly associated with slum growth due to the lack of appropriate planning and affordable housing. Urban Inequality has grown due to differentiated wealth concentration in cities. For example, in Africa, statistics show that about 81.7 per cent of Africans live on less than USD 4 per day, with 60.8 per cent falling below the USD 2 per day mark. There is also the problem of high costs of informal services provision and the absence of social safety net.

African economies today are facing nothing less than the formidable challenge of creating more and better jobs, not just by sustaining the pace of growth, but by making it more inclusive. Emerging economies such as Brazil, China and India among others, have been more successful than most African countries in this respect, achieving impressive reductions in poverty for more than two decades. How are they different from Africa? One answer is that they have undergone a more rapid structural transformation; that is, the process by which new, more productive activities arise and resources move from traditional activities to newer ones. A higher proportion of labour thus moved from low-productivity to high-productivity sectors (Organization for Economic Cooperation and Development [OECD] 2013a). The countries that manage to pull out of poverty and get richer are those that are able to diversify away from agriculture and other traditional products. As labour and other resources move from agriculture into modern economic activities, overall productivity rises and incomes expand. The speed with which this structural transformation takes place is the key factor that differentiates successful countries from unsuccessful ones.

In Latin America about 40 per cent of the population lived in the urban centres in 1950, but by 1990, it was up to 70 per cent. Today, an estimated 80 per cent of the region's population lives in cities, making Latin America the world's most urbanized region. In comparison, the European Union (EU) is 74 per cent urbanized, whereas East Asia and Pacific region are 50 per cent urbanized. By 2050, UN-Habitat predicts Latin America's cities will include 90 per cent of the region's population. This growth came at a cost; it was traumatic and at times violent because of its speed, marked by the deterioration of the environment and, above all, by a deep social inequality (UN-HABITAT 2012, 2014). By 2050, 90 per cent of Latin America's population will be in towns and cities. Brazil and the southern cone may reach this level by 2020. Inequality and violence are the main problems cited. Latin American cities are the most unequal and often most dangerous places in the world, with social divisions hardwired into the urban fabric. Some 111 million Latin Americans (out of a total of 588 million) live in shanty towns. Improving such dwellings and their surroundings has contributed to their stability, all the more necessary given the considerable housing shortage.

Despite efforts in the past 10 years to redistribute wealth, 122 million city residents still live in poverty. The informal economy, with the associated lack of welfare coverage, hits young people and women particularly hard. As at 2014,

260 million people live in the region's 198 large cities (populations of more than 200,000 people) and generate 60 per cent of Latin America's GDP. This is more than 1.5 times the contribution expected from large cities in Western Europe. Brazil and Mexico, the region's urban leaders, are home to 81 of the region's large cities. These two countries are projected to contribute 35 per cent of Latin America's overall growth by 2025. By 2025, 315 million people will live in Latin America's large cities where the per capita GDP is estimated to reach USD 23,000 – more than that of Portugal in 2007.

Growing cities will have to revamp public infrastructure expenditure to increase citizens' living standards, but these transformations also offer a unique opportunity for city leaders to shape an emerging global dialogue on urban development. Latin America's working-age population is projected to expand until it peaks in the 2040s at around 470 million potential workers. These young, urban workers are critical for creating wealth and raising regional living standards, but policies must be in place to provide access to quality education and opportunities to enter the formal workforce through channels that maximize their know-how and ability to unleash new generators of economic development.

1.2   Industrialization in the developing world: a selected review

In analysing the remote and current industrialization challenges in the developing world, the section that follows provides a selected review of what the academic literature tells us about the Asian, Latin American and African industrial conditions. Attempts at industrialization by all regions of the world hacks back to the success first of Great Britain, followed by Western Europe and thereafter North America during the 19th and early 20th centuries (Adebowale *et al.* 2014). The literature on the experiences of these countries seems to agree that although the early industrializing countries started out at different stages of growth, they followed more or less a similar format of change that led to their transformation. Marked by the shift from a subsistence/ agrarian economy towards more industrialized/mechanized modes of production, hallmarks of industrialization include technological advance, widespread investments into industrial infrastructure and a dynamic movement of labour form agriculture into manufacturing (Romer 1986; Lewis 1978; Rapley 1996; Todaro 1989).

Agreement exists on the fact that a dynamic process of industrialization is fundamental to overall economic development of countries, given that it promotes growth-enhancing structural change, which is the gradual movement of labour and other resources from agriculture to manufacturing, as accompanied by productivity increases. Manufacturing is construed as critical in most such expositions because of the empirical correlation between the degree of industrialization and the per capita income in countries (Szirmai 2012). Given that productivity is higher in the case of manufacturing than agriculture, transfer of resources into manufacturing should normally provide a basis for higher rates of productivity-induced growth structures.

1.3   Nature and sources of structural transformation: the convergence of urbanization and structural change

Structural transformation is defined as the shift of an economy's structure from low-productivity, labor-intensive activities to higher-productivity, capital- and skill-intensive activities (Szirmai *et al.* 2012). It is a long-term shift in the fundamental institutions of an economy, and this explains the pathways of economic growth and development (Etchemendy 2009; McMillan, Rodrik and Verduzco-Gallo 2014). In technical terms, four essential and interrelated processes define structural transformation in any economy: (1) a declining share of agriculture in GDP and employment; (2) a rural-to-urban migration underpinned by rural and urban development; (3) the rise of a modern industrial and service economy; and (4) a demographic transition from high rates of births and deaths (common in underdeveloped and rural areas) to low rates of births and deaths – associated with better health standards in developed and urban areas (Timmer 2012; Africa Focus 2013; Oyelaran-Oyeyinka 2015). In summary, it can be defined as the reallocation of economic activity across three broad sectors (agriculture, manufacturing and services) that accompany the process of modern economic growth (Herrendorf *et al.* 2013).

1.4   Why structural transformation?

Structural transformation is essential as not only a source of higher-productivity growth and rising per capita income, but as mechanism that helps to achieve greater diversity of the economic structure, which creates a country's resilience to vulnerability to poverty and external shocks (United Nations Research Institute for Social Development [UNIDO] 2009). Structural transformation is underpinned in large part by institutions and policies that promote the development, adoption and use of technologies to change what an economy produces and how it does so. Specialization, productivity and growth trigger further processes of agglomeration, specialization and technological advances.

The rise of new economic powers has generally been driven by the rapid structural transformation of their economies, featured by the shift from primary production, such as mining and agriculture to manufacturing; and in manufacturing from natural resource-based to more sophisticated, skill- and technology-intensive activities. With urbanization, labor-intensive manufacturing activities grow faster than primary activities, generating new jobs, income and demand. Capital accumulation leads to a more sophisticated manufacturing structure, and the economy gradually moves to skill- and technology-intensive sectors (UNIDO 2009).

While structural change can be defined as an alteration in the relative importance of economic sectors, the interrelated processes of structural change that accompany economic development are jointly referred to as economic transformation. These transformation patterns can be observed in newly industrializing countries in Asia and Latin America, yet also relate to the experiences of European countries during the 19th and early 20th centuries. During the transformation period, the economic structure changes significantly, while industrialization triggers a rapid increase in the share of manufacturing in the economy, and a concomitant decline in agriculture's share.

Furthermore, the share of the total labour force employed in the agricultural sector falls, while that of other economic sectors rises. However, that does not imply an absolute decline in the number of labourers employed in the agricultural sector, as the share of agricultural employment in the total labour force could decline relatively slowly compared with declines in the agricultural sector's GDP share in the economy. Within this process, the centre of the country's economy shifts from rural areas to cities, and the degree of urbanization significantly increases (Stern *et al.* 2005).

Therefore, transformation involves the modernization of a country's economy, society and institutions. Economic transformation has fundamental impacts on human life, and sociologists emphasize the important role of changing values, norms, beliefs and customs in the transformation from a traditional to a modern society. Kuznets describes the necessary adjustments in society and institutions during transformation as a "controlled revolution" (Kuznets 1973: 252). Shifts in production structure lead to changes in incentive structures, educational requirements, and the relative positions of different groups in the society. Urbanization leads to shifts in family formation, gender relations and personal status. Changes in transport and communication services open up less favoured areas and connect factor and commodity markets. The management of these fundamental changes requires legal and institutional innovations, in which the state and other institutions play key roles (Breisinger and Diao 2008).

Rich countries by definition produce more output per worker than poor countries. But they also produce different, presumably more challenging products. Therefore, the process of development involves moving from simple poor-country goods to more complex rich-country goods. This process is often called structural transformation. Part of this transformation is related to changing factor endowments as physical, human and institutional capital is accumulated (Hausmann and Klinger 2006; Rodrik 2012).

According to Rodrik (2013), two traditions exists side-by-side within growth economics. The first has its origin in development economics, and it is based on the dual economy approach which was initially developed by Lewis (1954) and Ranis and Fei (1961). The second tradition has its origin in macroeconomics, and it stems from the neoclassical growth model of Solow (1956). The first tradition (dual economy) draws a sharp distinction between the traditional and modern sectors of the economy, typically characterized as agriculture and industry, respectively. The neoclassical model (second tradition) differs in its view and presumes that different types of economic activity are structurally similar enough to be aggregated into a single representative sector. Dual economy models are built on structural heterogeneity. They assume there are different economic logics at work in traditional and modern parts of the economy, so these two cannot be lumped together. Accumulation, innovation and productivity growth all take place in the modern sector – often in unexplained ways – while the traditional sector remains technologically backward and stagnant. Economy-wide growth therefore depends in large part on the rate at which resources – principally labour – can migrate from the traditional to the modern sectors. In neoclassical models, by contrast, growth depends on the incentives to save, accumulate physical and human capital, and (in subsequent variants that endogenize technological change) innovate by developing new products and processes (Rodrik 2013).

In large part, most countries have been able to sustain a rapid transition out of poverty because of increase in productivity in its agricultural sector. This process points to successful structural transformation, where agriculture through higher productivity provides food, labour and even savings to the process of urbanization and industrialization. Clearly, a vibrant agriculture raises labour productivity in the rural economy, pulls up wages, and gradually eliminates the worst dimensions of absolute poverty. However, the process lead to a gradual decline in the relative importance of agriculture to the overall economy, as the industrial and service sectors grow even more rapidly, partly through stimulus from a modernizing agriculture and migration of rural workers to urban jobs (Timmer 2007; Timmer and Akkus 2008).

In developed industrial economies, structural transformation proceed in such a way that agriculture as an economic activity has no distinguishing characteristics from other sectors, at least in terms of the productivity of labour and capital (Timmer and Akkus 2008). Furthermore, the gap in labour productivity between agricultural and non-agricultural workers approaches zero when incomes are high enough and the two sectors have been integrated by well-functioning labour and capital markets.

Increase in productivity of an economy will help to achieve and sustain higher standards of living. The processes required to achieve this includes utilization of improved technologies, investment in higher educational and skill levels for the labour force, lower transactions costs to connect and integrate economic activities, and more efficient allocation of resources. The process of actually implementing these mechanisms over time leads to economic development. When successful and sustained for decades, it leads to the structural transformation of that economy (Timmer 2007; Timmer and Akkus 2008).

Structural transformation divides the economy into sectors such as rural versus urban, agricultural versus industry and services; for the purpose of understanding how to raise productivity levels. Unless the non-agricultural economy is growing, there is little long-run hope for agriculture. At the same time, the historical record is very clear on the important role that agriculture itself plays in stimulating the non-agricultural economy (Timmer 2007).

1.5   Structural change by region

The studies have established that countries and regions vary in their structural transformation experiences (McMillan 2012; Rodrik 2012; Timmer 2012). A recent cross-sectional study on sampled advanced economies, emerging market economies and low- income countries, indicating the country's fundamentals explains the significant proportion of the real value-added shares by all sectors (Dabla-Norris *et al.* 2013). They found that natural resource dominance was associated with lower structural change, while there are large and systematic differences in the gap between actual and predicted shares within countries, groups and regions. Hence, sectoral shifts are not mechanical processes; their speed and extent reflect the willingness and ability of labour and capital to move toward higher-productivity sectors, all of which are strongly influenced by the policy and institutional environment.

Therefore, this section presents a literature review on structural transformation experiences of the countries and regions of interest to this study. Furthermore, the comparative perspectives of their experiences are identified and discussed.

1.5.1 *Africa*

In Africa, structural transformation will only materialize when there is a concomitant investment in skill development, particularly in areas that have kept the continent behind other developing regions. In this regard, Africa needs to harness its natural resources to build skills for its youthful population in order to achieve its development objectives and secure a place in the global value chain. Developing skills has a lot of benefits; it will unleash the dynamism of Africa's untapped entrepreneurship potential, creating opportunities for increased job and wealth creation. An enlightened population is important to Africa's global engagement in trade and commerce. Structural transformation also pre-supposes a transformed relationship between state and citizens. Except for the brief period in many African countries following de-colonization, the experience of political governance has been largely negative, fraught with corruption and nepotism, human rights violations, military or one-party dictatorships and poor stewardship of the economy (Timmer 2012; AfricaFocus Bulletin 2013).

African countries have been growing at a relatively fast rate since the beginning of the new millennium, which in turn has led to improvements in several areas such as trade, mobilization of government revenue, infrastructure development, and the provision of social services. Within the period of 2001–2008, Africa became one of the fastest-growing regions in the world economy, and this increase in growth performance has been widespread across countries (OECD 2013a).

Historically, much of sub-Saharan countries adopted a package of policies aimed at either stimulation of economic growth or stabilization and adjustment in return for multilateral and bilateral loans. During the two decades of Structural Adjustment Polices in Africa, several studies raised questions related to the appropriateness and efficacy of such measures such as trade liberalization and their lasting impact on African industrial development (Stein 1992; Stewart *et al.* 1992; Lall 1995). On the contrary to the poor industrial performance in African countries, we do know that economic growth, driven by various industrial development strategies, has been considerable in several developing countries over the past decades. The "Asian Tigers" namely Taiwan, Hong Kong, South Korea and Singapore, as well as China, have set such considerable standards of dynamic growth, showing that catching up with the traditionally viewed industrial leaders is possible (Amsden 1989; Vogel 1991; World Bank 1993; Stiglitz 1996; Wade 2004). Other Newly Industrializing Economies (NIEs) like Indonesia, Malaysia, Thailand and the Philippines (to a lesser degree) have also emerged as "a second-generation of Asian Tigers" (OECD 2013: 21). Howbeit, we can summarize the state of African industry as follows; First, these economies are dominated by low-productivity agriculture and petty service activities. However, there is a clear rise of certain consumer-based industrial activities and services, albeit at the expense of manufacturing. Others include mining, the exploitation of crude oil and services which are however limited to petty trading and basic commercial services.

Second, the share of manufacturing value-added in total GDP has been low on the average in Africa, for example in Sierra Leone, Nigeria, Mali, Djibouti, Rwanda and Ethiopia. In Nigeria, between 1990 and 1994, the share of manufacturing value-added in total GDP fluctuates between 5 per cent and 7 per cent, while between 2000 and 2004 it declined and fluctuated between 4 per cent and 3 per cent (World Bank 2015). Examples of countries that experienced decline in the share of market value added (MVA) in total GDP within the period of 1990–1994 and 2000–2004 were South Africa, Mauritius, Cameroon, Zambia, Zimbabwe, Côte d'Ivoire and Kenya. South Africa recorded 24 per cent MVA in 1990 and 19 per cent in 2004, while Zambia reported 36 per cent MVA in 1990, but it declined to 11 per cent in 2004 and Kenya reported 12 per cent in 1990, but the share declined to 11 per cent in 2004. Botswana, Ghana, Burundi, Rwanda, South Africa and Tanzania experienced a stagnant share of 6 per cent, 10 per cent, 12 per cent, 7 per cent, 19 per cent and 9 per cent MVA in total GDP between 2000 and 2004 respectively (World Bank 2015). In countries like Ethiopia, Kenya, South Africa, Swaziland, Madagascar, Lesotho and Mauritius, there was an increase in the relative share of manufactures in total value added. This has generally been associated with the expansion of garments exports based on special preferences associated with the now-expired Agreement on Textiles and Clothing (Chemengich 2010; Páez *et al.* 2010).

Third, primary commodity exports accounted for approximately 14 per cent of Africa's merchandise exports during the period 2002–2012. During this period, the region's total merchandise exports (in value terms) grew at an average annual rate of 14 per cent, rising from USD 100 billion to USD 400 billion. Much of this impressive performance was driven by the region's natural resources, underpinned by the commodity price boom of 2003–2008. Oil, metal and other mineral exports increased from USD 56 billion in 2002 to USD 288 billion in 2012, and oil exports alone accounted for over half of goods exports in 2012. Together, these commodities have contributed to over two-thirds of total export growth during this period. While high commodity prices have helped the region in recent years, the heavy reliance on resource-based exports also makes the region highly vulnerable to shocks in commodity prices, as was observed during 2009 (World Bank 2013).

Although the region experienced notable economic growth over the last decade, the current pattern of growth is neither inclusive nor sustainable (OECD 2013a). The reason in large part could be the dependence by African countries on natural resources as drivers of economic growth which neither provides widespread employment nor inclusive wealth creation. Again, most of these commodities are non-renewable and are being depleted at a very rapid rate, because of high level of consumption. This poses a threat to future growth and sustainability. Another reason is that the region's agricultural per capita output and productivity still remains low compared to the global average. This has led to a dreadful effect on food security and social stability in the region (World Food Programme 2010). The African Development Bank estimates that Africa's per capita agricultural output is about 56 per cent of the global average, while 30 per cent of the region's total population is estimated to have been undernourished in 2010 (Food and Agriculture Organization 2010; World Food Programme 2010). The third reason is that Africa's current pattern of growth has been accompanied by de-industrialization.

There is continuous increase in the proportion of the African population living in urban areas. The current rate of 40 per cent of urban dwellers is projected to rise to 60 per cent by 2050. Over the years, urbanization in African cities have been driven by natural resources exports rather than by industrial or agricultural revolution (Jedwab 2012). The absolute number of workers in the agricultural sector in most African countries had continuously increased; this was the case for Nigeria, within 1990 to 2010 when the dominant sector was agriculture. This accounted for about half of all GDP across this period until towards the year 2010, when it fell to 40 per cent. Wholesale and retail trade is the next largest, accounting for just over 20 per cent of GDP. The predominance of these two industries reflected in the shares of the labour force they employed. Manufacturing has maintained a relatively constant share of GDP, roughly 5 per cent, while finance and business services have declined from around 10 per cent in 1996 to 7 per cent in 2009. Some of that loss is made up for by the expansion of transportation and communications from only 4 per cent to over 8 per cent in the same period (OECD 2013a).

In Ghana, the GDP and the employment shares of agriculture remained almost unchanged between 1960 and 2006, with the exception of the 1967–1984 period. During this period, the economy contracted, and the GDP and employment contributions of the industrial and services sectors decreased. Agriculture in Ghana consists of four sub-sectors: (1) agriculture, hunting and livestock; (2) cocoa; (3) forestry and logging; and (4) fishing. Ghana's economic development seems to take place without industrialization, contrary to what occurred in South East Asian Countries or China today. Further, the employment share of agriculture decreased from 61.8 per cent in 1960 to 54.3 per cent in 2006 and 41.6 per cent in 2010, while its GDP share decrease from 51.1 per cent to 43.2 per cent in 2006 and 43.0 per cent in 2010 (Jedwab and Osei 2012).

In South Africa, the drop in real GDP growth in 2014 reflected a recent downward trend with GDP growth declining from 3.2 per cent in 2011, to 2.2 per cent in 2012 and 2.2 per cent in 2013. Slow growth reflected continued feebleness in

South Africa's main trading partners, in particular the EU and China, as well as structural weaknesses, such as labour market rigidities, skills shortages and infrastructure gaps. The performance of the manufacturing sector was worsened by strong labour unrest; labour costs that were higher than productivity increases; a volatile rand within a 9.1 per cent band during the first three-quarters of 2014; and severe energy bottlenecks. Growth in 2015 is forecast to rebound at 2.0 per cent, benefiting from the gradual global economic recovery, stronger demand from emerging partners and lower oil prices. However, tighter domestic fiscal conditions, concerns over security of electricity supply, weak consumption and the future of the United States Federal Reserve's tapering policy are likely to act as a constraint on growth. Growth had a positive, although marginal, effect on job creation in 2014. In recent years, however, it has not created sufficient jobs to match the supply of low-skilled labour. The manufacturing sector, in particular, saw its share in GDP decline and capital intensity levels rise.

Unemployment, at 25 per cent in much of 2014, remains the most pressing social and economic challenge for South Africa. Youth unemployment remained extremely high at 51 per cent in that quarter, up from 50 per cent during the same period in 2013. Unemployment has a racial dimension, reflecting South Africa's unequal educational background and historical legacy, and disproportionately affects "Black African" and "Coloured" population groups at 29 per cent and 24 per cent respectively, compared to "Asian/Indian" and "White" population groups at 12 per cent and 7 per cent respectively. About 10.3 per cent of South Africa's population is considered multi-dimensionally poor (the Multidimensional Poverty Index value was 0.04 in 2014). Food security remains a pressing issue: in 2013, 23 per cent of households did not have adequate access to food and 13 per cent had experienced hunger. While the government is implementing important programmes reducing poverty and improving access to social services, high inequality levels profoundly affect social cohesion (OECD 2015).

In general, the share of manufacturing in Africa's GDP fell from 15 per cent in 1990 to 10 per cent in 2008. The most significant decline was observed in Western Africa, where it fell from 13 per cent to 5 per cent over the same period. Nevertheless, there has also been substantial de-industrialization in the other sub-regions of Africa. For example, in Eastern Africa the share of manufacturing in output fell from 13 per cent in 1990 to about 10 per cent in 2008, and in Central Africa, it fell from 11 to 6 per cent over the same period. Furthermore, in Northern Africa, it fell from about 13 to 11 per cent and in Southern Africa it fell from 23 to 18 per cent. The declining share of manufacturing in Africa's output is of concern because historically, manufacturing has been the main engine of high, rapid and sustained economic growth (UNIDO 2011; United Nations Conference on Trade and Development [UNCTAD] 2012).

Overall, economic transformation which is often known to be associated with the migration of labour out of rural agricultural sector into the urban industrial sector has not been strongly experienced in the African context during most of the first five decades of their independence. Driven by urbanization and decades of neglect of agriculture, most countries in the region have seen rapid labour migration out of a stagnating agriculture sector into an informal services sector, with even lower productivity levels. The contribution to overall economic productivity has therefore been negative.

The industrial sector has seen zero to negative growth, leaving the entire burden of absorbing the growing labour force to the informal services sector. The latter has expanded at an extremely rapid pace to a size that is currently not justified by the level of development of African economies. The agriculture sector, on the other hand, has shrunk faster than is normal under successful transformation (Badiane 2012). Overall, sub-Saharan Africa can be said to have benefited from structural change which has contributed positively to Africa's overall growth accounting for nearly half of the countries (McMillan *et al.* 2014). Findings also show that in over half of African countries, structural change coincided with some expansion of the manufacturing sector, although the magnitudes are small, indicating that these economies may be becoming less vulnerable to commodity price shocks.

1.5.2 Structural transformation in Latin America

In a study conducted by Ferreira and da Silva (2014), Latin American economies experienced a strong process of labour force reallocation, with steep decreases in the participation of agriculture and an increase in the share of labour in services. The region was reported to be at the early stage of structural transformation compared with developed economies, although, each country is going through different phases of labour reallocation process.

It is established that for most Latin American and sub-Saharan African countries, broad patterns of structural change have served to reduce rather than increase economic growth since 1990 (McMillan *et al.* 2014). Globalization in Latin America and sub-Saharan Africa appears not to have fostered the desirable kind of structural change. Labour has moved in the wrong direction, from more productive to less productive activities. This finding differs from other studies that reported the productivity-enhancing effects of trade liberalization. Labour pull effect was reported to be relatively weak compared to the effect it had in the Asian countries, while a similar decline in agriculture was experienced for Asia and Latin American countries (Lu 2012).

Latin America is far from solving its development problems, and it is still struggling in concurrently tackling inequalities and achieving economic transformation. But the region has been witnessing high growth, the emergence of a new middle class with new aspirations and demands and a renewed commitment of governments to promote science, technology and innovation as pillars of new development strategies more in line with the new global economic landscape. Like Africa, Latin America as a region vary widely with countries that differ in endowments, geography and institutions, as well as in size (Primi 2013).

In a sample study of 12 countries in Latin America, 10 in Asia and 12 in Africa, scholars reported differences between the paths followed by sub-Saharan Africa, Asia and Latin America. Asia tends to be following a path that is closest to that of developed countries. A key feature for Asian countries is high industrial output shares. African countries have low agricultural output shares and high service output shares at very low GDP per capita. Latin American countries on the other hand, have agricultural output shares similar to those of developed countries, but a key feature for these countries is that they move from the first to the second phase of structural transformation at a low GDP per capita and with low maximum industrial output shares. This led to high service output shares around the end of the period of interest of that study, that is year 2000. Another finding of the study was the presence of structural transformation during periods of economic stagnation or decline. Many African and Latin American countries experienced periods of significant sectoral output changes in the "wrong" direction, while GDP per capita was stagnant or even declining (Bah 2007).

Sub-Saharan African and Latin American countries were reported to have been growing since the late 1990s and are facing the challenge of sustaining this growth and reducing inequalities in the long run. Also, the two regions are both influenced by the new trends in their traditional Organization for Economic Cooperation and Development (OECD) trade partners and in their emerging partners, which are redefining their development opportunities. In addition, they are both profiting from a good global momentum in which windows of opportunity for new comers seems to be more accessible due to increased diffusion of Information and Communications Technology (ICT), emerging global challenges such as the search for new and renewable energy sources and greener production and consumption modes, and changes in the organization of production at a global level, with growing specialization opportunities.

In addition, countries in Latin America, as well as in Africa, are increasingly involved in developing new visions for their development in context of new societal demands and growing concern about equity. Most countries in the two regions have in fact suffered from a process of institutional weakening in the realm of science, technology and production in the aftermath of the structural reforms, and are now facing the challenge of design and implementing industrial policies with old or weak institutions. Since the Millennium began, Latin America has witnessed a resurgence of interest in industrial policies. Brazil has been the pioneer, with the Integrated Industrial, Technology and Trade Policy introduced in 2003, that then evolved into the Production Development Policy in 2008 and in the Plano Brazil Maior in 2012. Other countries in the region have had a shier approach towards explicitly using the term industrial policy but in practice sectoral technology initiatives and governments incentives to promote domestic scientific, technological and industrial development have been strengthened in most countries of the region. Argentina, for example, has created its Ministry for Science, Technology and Productive Innovation in 2007, signaling the willingness of the country to increasingly shift towards a more knowledge-based growth pattern.

Latin American countries are recognizing the importance of strengthening their production and innovation capacities. Despite the perceived risks of failure of industrial policy, there is renewed interest in the subject. The new context and the increased availability of information about countries' strategies are showing that state intervention is needed to back private sector efforts to foster development. In the last decade, several emerging and developing economies re-engaged in active industrial policies in Africa, Asia and Latin America. Latin America looks today like a region in motion that is increasingly acknowledging the relevance of science, technology and innovation for development and that is, in different ways, trying to foster production transformation and upgrading through different channels. From the recent experience of the return of industrial policies in Latin America, it is possible to identify some lessons for Africa.

Essentially, industrial policy is back in Latin America, but with different emphasis and nuances in the different countries. Brazil is the country that more openly speaks about its industrial policy, however most Latin American countries have reinforced in the last decade government actions to strengthen domestic entrepreneurial activities and/or to promote a better inclusion in global value. This is actualized by promoting new forms of FDI and by increasing support to science and innovation. Achieving structural transformation in Latin American countries means overcoming several barriers – low skills, poor infrastructure, low demand and poor financing, for example. Critics often argue that getting all these conditions right is difficult for most developing countries. However, clarifying the objectives of structural transformation helps in revealing the barriers and in creating a demand for articulating the necessary actions. Regardless of the specific country approach, the countries of the region are in addition facing a major governance challenge to rehabilitate the planning functions in countries where these capabilities had been reduced due to the extensive application of the structural reforms packages of the 1990s (Primi 2013).

1.5.3   *Structural transformation in Asia*

The benefits from, and consequences of globalization depend on the manner in which countries integrate into the global economy. China, India and some other Asian countries have fulfilled the globalization promise with high-productivity employment opportunities having expanded in these countries to enable structural change which has contributed to their overall growth (McMillan *et al*. 2014).

Asian countries have, during the same period, experienced productivity-enhancing structural change in contrast to the productivity-reducing structural change observed both in Latin America and Africa. It is therefore difficult to ascribe Africa and Latin America's performance solely to globalization or other external determinants; clearly, forces were at work particularly country-specific forces. Notably, differential patterns of structural change account for the bulk of Latin America's as well as Africa's underperformance relative to Asia. In other words, Asia outshone the other two regions not so much in productivity growth within individual sectors (where performance has been broadly similar), but rather in terms of the broad pattern of inter-sectoral shifts, whereby structural change contributes to, rather than detracts from, overall economic growth (McMillan 2012).

Since the 1970s, the composition of agricultural output in developing Asia has shifted dramatically. Although with country-specific differences, increasing global trade was a key driver behind these trends. The share of developing Asia in global agricultural exports increased from 12 per cent to 17 per cent since 1970. The composition of export trade has changed, away from traditional tropical products (coffee, cocoa, tea, sugar, spices and nuts) towards products such as horticulture and seafood, as well as toward processed products (Jongwanich 2009).

The change in agricultural output composition occurred within a broader diversification, known as the agribusiness transition, involving input providers (farm equipment producers, logistics firms and other business service providers) as well as agro-processors, distribution companies, and retailers (World Bank 2009). The share of agribusiness in GDP is substantially higher than that of agriculture, and the ratio of the share of agribusiness to that of primary agriculture, is typically higher leading it increased per capita income of the country. For example, the shares of agribusiness in GDP for Indonesia and Thailand are 33 per cent and 43 per cent respectively; the share of agribusiness as percentage of GDP in the Philippines is 15 per cent. Agricultural transformation thus involves a parallel development of industry (agro-processing) and services (finance, logistics, marketing, etc.) (Balisacan *et al.* 2011).

Agriculture represented the largest employer in many Asian countries including Bangladesh, Cambodia, the PRC, India, Pakistan, PNG, Thailand and Vietnam. Moreover, the bulk of the poor are still found in rural areas where the primary source of employment is agriculture. Thus, discussion of developing Asia's future structural transformation cannot neglect this sector. This is obvious for countries where the process of structural transformation remains shallow (e.g. in Bhutan, Cambodia, Myanmar and Nepal, where the share of agriculture in employment remains over 60 per cent). In the rest of developing Asia, even though the output and employment shares of agriculture have declined over time, the reduction in the employment share lags behind that in the output share, implying relatively low levels of labour productivity in agriculture (Briones and Felipe 2013).

The analysts predict that the region will conform to the traditional mode and that the past directions of structural transformation will likely continue over the next few decades. As per capita incomes in developing Asia continue to rise, the share of agriculture in GDP will continue to fall. The share of agriculture in total employment will also decline, but at a slower pace. Only at a mature stage of development will the employment share catch-up with the output share, and this will be accompanied by an acceleration of agricultural labour productivity growth (as seen in the experiences of Japan and the Republic of Korea). The pace of agricultural transformation will also be determined by other global drivers.

1.6   Patterns of structural change: empirical analysis

The following sub-sections present the analysis of value-added share changes of various sectors during 1991 to 2012. The sectors included in the analysis are the following: agriculture, mining, manufacturing, utilities, construction, "trade, restaurants and hotels," "transport, storage and communications," and "finance, insurance, real state and business services." The value-added data have been taken from Groningen Growth and Development Centre (GGDC), University of Groningen, The Netherlands, for sample economies of all the three continents. The data for Uganda and Sri Lanka are taken from World Development Indicator database as GGDC did not have data for these countries.

1.6.1 Comparative structural change in regional perspective

Perhaps for the first time, the study uses advanced statistical technique to quantify structural change. In the estimation of composite score of structural change sectors namely: agriculture, mining, manufacturing, utilities, construction, "trade, restaurants and hotels services," "transport, storage and communication services," and "finance, insurance, real estate and business services" are included. The exceptions are Sri Lanka and Uganda where three sectors, namely, agriculture, industry, and services, are considered. It was done due to non-availability of a breakdown of industry and services sector data.

Estimation of structural change was done in three stages. In the first stage, composite score of the share of all sectors was generated. This was done by using Factor Analysis technique, an advanced statistical tool used for variable reduction situations. After obtaining the composite score, the next step was to measure the variability of the score over the sample period. Standard deviation was used to estimate variability. In the third stage, these deviations were standardized on a 100-point scale. The structural change witnessed by sample economies on a 100-point scale are presented and discussed in the following sub-section. The structural transformation in African countries is depicted in Figure 1.1.

In Uganda, the share of agriculture declined from 52.82 per cent in 1991 to 25.26 per cent in 2013 (Compound Annual Growth Rate [CAGR]: –4.03 per cent). At the same period, share of the services sector changed from 34.82

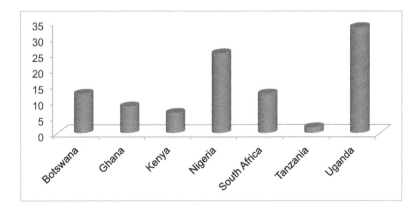

Figure 1.1 Comparative analysis of structural change in African countries

to 53.98 per cent (CAGR: 2.32 per cent). Such a drastic change in structure is captured by showing the highest structural change. On the other hand, agriculture share in Tanzania witnessed declining trend from 36.07 to 29.15 per cent during 1991 to 2011 (CAGR: –1.36 per cent), and other sectors with reasonable percentage of share did not experience much change, which is shown as lowest structural change.

Nigeria experienced second highest structural change due to the share of mining sector which declined from 52.61 per cent in 1991 to 28.17 per cent in 2011 (CAGR: –3.14 per cent); and the share of agriculture which increased from 24.88 to 37.69 per cent (CAGR: 2.66 per cent) during the same period. The share of trade services sector also grew at the rate of 2.54 and attained the value of 21.25 per cent in 2011. Such a major change in shares of mining, agriculture and trade services resulted in second highest change in the structure of the Nigerian economy. Figure 1.2 depicts the structural transformation in Asia.

Comparative analysis of structural change experienced by Asian economies shows that variability of the change is not as high as in case of African continent. In fact, Chinese and Indian economies have witnessed similar levels of structural change which is highest among the sample countries. The share of Chinese agriculture sector sharply declined from 30.21 per cent in 1991 to 9.14 per cent in 2010 (CAGR: –5.82 per cent), while share of manufacturing sector has grown from 22.29 to 36.53 per cent during the same period. On the other hand, the share of Indian agriculture sector declined at the rate of –3.58 per cent from 30.58 to 15.35 per cent, while manufacturing share remained more or less unchanged. The share of trade related services declined in China, while in India the sector recorded positive growth rate of 1.70 per cent annually. Its share changed from 13.22 in 1991 to 18.87 per cent in 2012. The decline in agriculture sector and positive growth in Chinese manufacturing and trade related services in India are similar. Hence, the structural change observed in both the countries are similar.

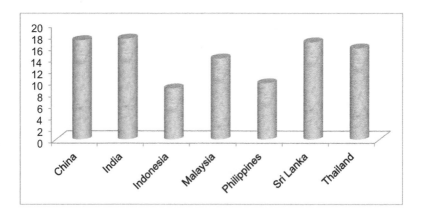

Figure 1.2 Comparative analysis of structural change in Asian countries

Sri Lankan economy also experienced similar change as that of China and India. Unlike India and China, the agriculture sector recorded positive growth rate of 1.30 per cent. Its share changed from 14.76 to 18.00 per cent. On the other hand, share of manufacturing sector drastically declined (CAGR: –4.80 per cent) from 26.75 to 12.81 per cent in 2010. The services sector share changed from 47.68 to 57.76 per cent by realizing positive annual growth rate of 1.16 per cent. It is clear that structural change in Sri Lankan economy has been similar to that of China and India.

Among the Asian economies, the Indonesian economy realized the lowest structural change. The mining sector recorded sharpest decline (CAGR: –1.98 per cent) from 16.52 to 10.07 per cent during 1991 to 2012. Although the growth of share of utilities and transport services (4.61 and 4.60 per cent respectively) is very high, the magnitude is small resulting in very little contribution to structural change. Consequently, the structural change witnessed by Indonesian economy is lowest.

The extent of structural change observed in Latin American economies, depicted in Figure 1.3 shows that Venezuela recorded the highest change. The mining sector contributed the highest share in 1991 (29.94 per cent) which declined at the rate of –0.96 per cent annually leading to its share of 26.67 per cent in 2012. Similarly, manufacturing sector contributed second highest (20.34 per cent) in 1991, experiencing a negative growth rate of –1.32 per cent. It is clear that both sectors which contributed more than 50 per cent recorded declining trend. Hence the structural change is very high.

The Brazilian economy experienced lowest structural change. The share of financial services was 21.48 per cent in 1991 followed by 17.45 per cent of manufacturing in the same year. Share of both sectors changed marginally (CAGR: –0.45 per cent in financial services and 0.27 per cent in manufacturing). Trade services that recorded share of 15.65 in 2011 recorded CAGR of 0.53 per cent. In view of the very little changes in the share of substantially contributing sectors, the Brazilian economy can be regarded as the one with the lowest structural change.

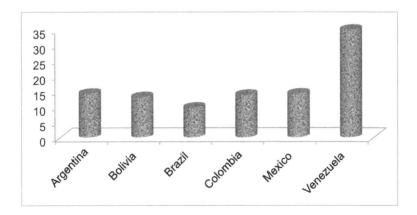

Figure 1.3 Comparative analysis of structural change in Latin American countries

1.7   Analysis of African economies

The analysis in this sub-section is based on the contribution of value added by various sectors and presented separately for each country.

1.7.1   Botswana

Figure 1.4 depicts the analysis of Botswana economy. It can be seen from the figure that the share of the mining sector in Botswana had substantial contribution to GDP (41.57 per cent) in 1991 but experienced the sharpest decline (CAGR: –2.58 per cent) resulting in a mere 18.56 per cent contribution in 2010. On the other hand, three service sectors, namely, trade, finance and transport performed well and increased their contribution during 1991 and 2010.

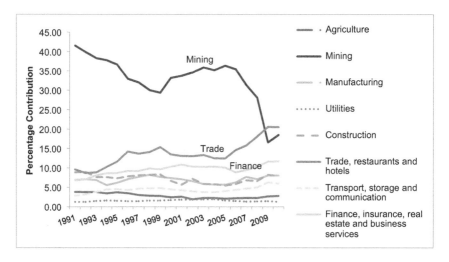

Figure 1.4 Structural change in Botswana

Source: Figure is based on GGDC Structural Transformation Data

The contribution of trade sub-sector increased from 9.65 to 20.56 with CAGR 3.46 per cent, while that of finance witnessed a change from 6.79 to 11.70 with CAGR 1.98 per cent during the same period. It is worth noting that transport service sector experienced a growth rate of 1.97 per cent, but at the base year, its contribution to GDP was just 2.86 per cent. The structure of other sectors by and large remains unchanged. The analysis of structural change suggests that the services sectors has assumed pre-eminence over the last two decades, while manufacturing has remained relatively stagnant.

1.7.2   Ghana

The structure of the Ghanaian economy during 1991 and 2010 presented in Figure 1.5 reveals that although contribution of agriculture sector witnessed a

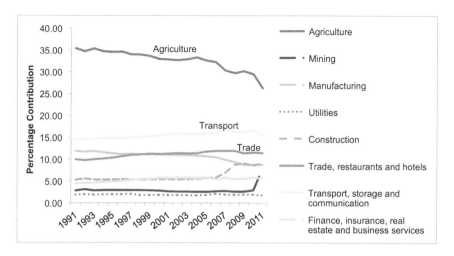

Figure 1.5 Structural change in Ghana

Source: Figure is based on GGDC Structural Transformation Data

decline (CAGR: –1.07 per cent) from 35.41 in 1991 to 26.24 per cent in 2011, the decline in manufacturing sector (CAGR: –1.40 per cent) has experienced the decrease highest.

The contribution of manufacturing sector declined from 11.86 in 1991 to 8.76 in 2010. On the other hand, the construction sector recorded the highest growth (CAGR: 2.54 per cent) with 9.14 per cent level of contribution in 2010. Like Botswana, contribution of all the services subsectors experienced positive growth at 0.90, 0.64 and 1.19 per cent in trade, transport and financial services respectively. We can infer from the results that in addition to services, construction sector made the highest contribution.

1.7.3 Kenya

The structural transformation of the Kenyan economy depicted in Figure 1.6 reveals that the share of agriculture declined at the annual rate of –0.66 per cent resulting in 23.33 in 2011 from 29.24 per cent in 1991; although the sector remained largest contributor to value added in 2013. The share of manufacturing sector also declined more or less at the same rate (–0.71 per cent).

On the other hand, two components of the services sector that is; trade and transport experienced a positive growth rate of 0.91 and 2.66 per cent annually. Although share of financial sector services also grew at the rate of 1.33 per cent, its contribution to value added remained much lower than trade and transport services. Lack of opportunities and poor attention to agriculture and manufacturing could be one of the possible reasons for decline in their share. Labour productivity aspect of structural change will be analysed in Chapter 3.

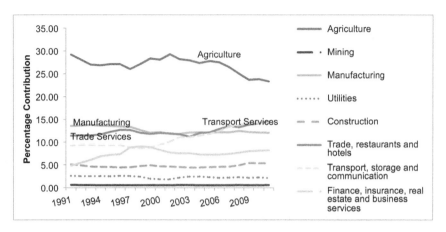

Figure 1.6 Structural change in Kenya

Source: Figure is based on GGDC Structural Transformation Data

1.7.4   *Nigeria*

Figure 1.7 presents the structure of the Nigerian economy during 1991 and 2010. It shows that the mining sector which had highest contribution (52.61 per cent) to value added in 1991 experienced sharpest decline (CAGR: –3.14 per cent) and lost its position as the highest contributor to agriculture which witnessed positive growth (CAGR: 2.66 per cent).

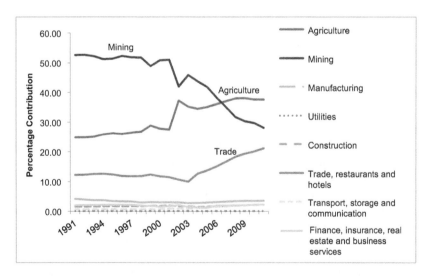

Figure 1.7 Structural change in Nigeria

Source: Figure is based on GGDC Structural Transformation Data

In 2010, contribution of agriculture was the largest at 37.69 per cent level. Like several other sample countries, services sector recorded continuous positive growth rate. The transport and trade services achieved CAGR of 7.08 and 2.54 per cent respectively, while share of financial services has been fluctuating with overall CAGR of –0.45 per cent. It may be worth mentioning that the contribution of the transport sector was at the level of 2.14 per cent in 2010, which is lowest among services sector. Structural change of Nigerian economy suggests that the services sector is dominant, while due attention is being given to agriculture, at the expense of manufacturing.

1.7.5 South Africa

The structural change analysis of the South African economy presented in Figure 1.8 is very different from other sample countries. In most of the other sample countries, the contribution of agriculture was highest in 2010, but the highest contributing sector in South Africa was financial services. With 18.42 per cent level of contribution in the same year, the sector has experienced the highest growth contribution (CAGR: 4.34 per cent).

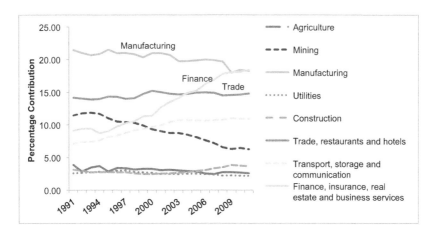

Figure 1.8 Structural change in South Africa

Source: Figure is based on GGDC Structural Transformation Data

The contribution of trade and transport services was 0.30 and 2.34 per cent with level of contribution in 2010 as 14.82 and 10.91 per cent respectively. Like the other sample countries, contribution of agriculture witnessed a negative growth rate of –1.50 per cent with level of contribution at just 2.62 per cent in 2010. Notably, the level of contribution of agriculture in South Africa had historically been much less compared to other African countries. Although, contribution of construction sector experienced a positive growth rate of 1.37 per cent, its level of contribution is similar to that of agriculture with 3.68 per cent in 2010. Analysis of the structural change of the South African economy suggests that the country has been experiencing de-industrialization with a strong rise of the services sector for a long period.

1.7.6 Tanzania

The structural transformation of the Tanzanian economy is depicted in Figure 1.9. It shows clearly that the transformation is different from that of many African economies. For instance, while the share of manufacturing sector declined in South Africa, its share in Tanzania experienced a positive growth rate of 1.11 per cent. Similarly, the share of mining sector declined sharply in South Africa, while the contribution of the sector in Tanzania witnessed a positive growth, although the magnitude of the share was not very large.

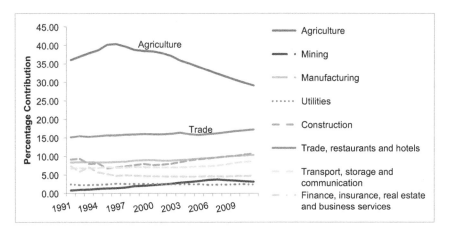

Figure 1.9 Structural change in Tanzania

Source: Figure is based on GGDC Structural Transformation Data

Structural transformation in Tanzania suggests that share of services sector did not improve much, a phenomenon very different from many developing economies. In fact, financial services declined at the rate of −1.61 per cent resulting in its contribution of 4.73 per cent in 2011. Trade and transport related services witnessed a positive annual growth rate of 0.49 and 1.02 per cent respectively.

1.7.7 Uganda

The structural transformation of Uganda is depicted in Figure 1.10. The data have been taken from World Development Indicator (WDI) online. This database is incompatible with GGDC as it provides data for industry as a whole and not component-wise. The analysis of Uganda is treated as industry level rather than manufacturing. The Ugandan economy experienced wide fluctuations in the last two decades and the overall picture is very different from other sample African

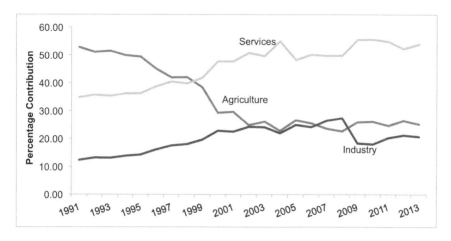

Figure 1.10 Structural change in Uganda

Source: Figure is based on World Development Indicators Online

countries.[1] The agriculture sector's contribution was the highest (52.82 per cent in 1991) among other sample countries, but it declined to 25.26 per cent in 2013 with CAGR −4.03. The contribution of agriculture was highest among all other sectors in the economy in the base year.

The services sector although growing, also experienced considerable upheavals as the base year contribution was 34.82 per cent; that is, second position, but moved to first in 2013 at 53.98 per cent, although the economy touched more than 55 per cent during 2004, 2009 and 2010 with a CAGR 2.32 per cent. Thus, it is a very dominant sector of the economy. The industrial sector has the highest CAGR (2.55 per cent) among all the three sectors, but could not contribute much as the share was lowest. Its share was 12.36 per cent in 1991 and achieved 20.76 per cent in 2013.

1.8 Analysis of structural change of Asian economies

The analysis for sample countries in Asia is presented in this section.

1.8.1 China

Figure 1.11 indicates structural changes in China. The figure indicates that the agriculture sector of the Chinese economy did not contribute much as exemplified by its declining trend since 1991 when it experienced largest contribution (30.21 per cent) which slid to fourth position in 2013 (7.64 per cent). On the other hand, manufacturing that was 22.29 in 1991 achieved first position by 2013 at 38.65 per cent. The services sector namely transport (from 6.52 in 1991 to 8.34 in 2013), finance (from 7.37 in 1991 to 8.26 in 2013), and construction (from 6.07 in 1991 to 6.74 in 2013) showed an increasing growth trend, thus contributing substantially to the economy.

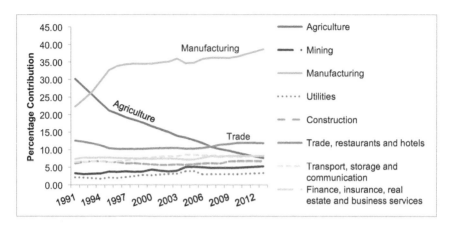

Figure 1.11 Structural change in China

Source: Figure is based on GGDC Structural Transformation Data

Also, share of the mining sector grew positively with a CAGR of 2.61 per cent. It can be inferred from the analysis that the growth of the Chinese economy has been driven by the manufacturing sector, unlike the pattern observed in the African economies.

1.8.2   India

The structural transformation in India is depicted in Figure 1.12. The services sector shows a positive impact on the economy with a CAGR of trade, transport and business services being 0.085, 0.092 and 0.115 per cent respectively; thereby suggesting that the strength of the Indian economy has grown on services sector during the last two decades.

Trade increased from 15.45 in 1991 to 22.37 in 2013, transport also experienced increasing growth from 7.35 in base year to 11.38 per cent in concluding year and business increased from 6.27 to 14.78 per cent. Thus, business services emerged the most dynamic among the three components of the services sector. Another sector showing positive growth trend is construction, which increased from 8.80 to 10.42 per cent with CAGR 0.081. The manufacturing sector in the country was in this period largely stagnant with CAGR 0.066 and the contribution being just about 19 per cent during the entire two decades. The agriculture sector behaved very similarly to that of China with a declining trend from 35.74 in 1991 to 17.25 per cent in 2013. The mining sector also shows a declining trend during the period from 4.49 to 2.63 per cent, although with positive CAGR of 0.044.

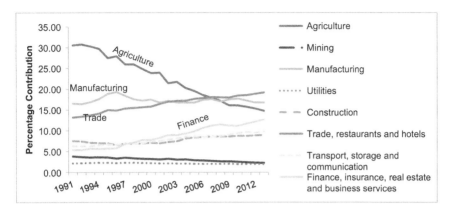

Figure 1.12 Structural change in India

Source: Figure is based on GGDC Structural Transformation Data

1.8.3   *Indonesia*

Figure 1.13 presents the transformation in Indonesia. The structural transformation of the Indonesian economy reveals that the manufacturing sector experienced high fluctuations during the sample period from 27.85 in 1991 to 31.60 per cent in 2001, but slightly declined to 28.28 per cent in 2013. The transport services performed very well since it was the lowest contributor to value added in 1991

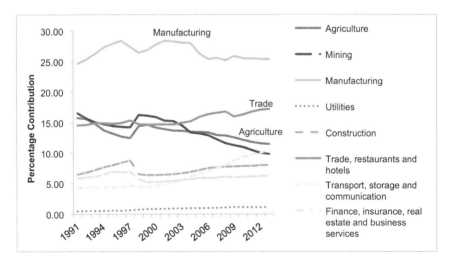

Figure 1.13 Structural change in Indonesia

Source: Figure is based on GGDC Structural Transformation Data

with 4.86 per cent, but achieved the fourth position by 2013 with 11.77 per cent as the most dynamic sector.

It can be seen from the figure that the manufacturing sector of the Indonesian economy experienced high fluctuations during the sample period from 27.85 in 1991 to 31.60 in 2001, but slightly declined to 28.28 per cent in 2013. The transport services performed very well since it was the lowest contributor to value added in 1991 with 4.86 per cent, but achieved the fourth position by 2013 with 11.77 per cent thereby indicating that this is the most focussed sector. Among the other components of the services sector, trade also showed a slight positive trend with CAGR 0.042 per cent (from 16.42 in base year to 19.21 per cent), while business services was almost stagnant but recorded a positive CAGR of 0.033. The agriculture (from 17.79 in 1991 to 12.83 in 2013) and mining sectors (18.66 to 11.00 per cent in 2013) showed a declining trend.

1.8.4 Malaysia

Figure 1.14 presents the transformation in Malaysia. As experienced in other countries, manufacturing sector of the Malaysian economy grew positively, but with much fluctuation and CAGR 0.059. In 1991, it was 26.09 per cent then shot to 31.96 in 2000 and slightly lower in 2013 at 29.60 per cent. The trade and business services also showed a promising growth. The trade services that was fourth in 1991 (15.27 per cent) jumped to second position in 2013 (19.89 per cent). The business sector followed with even better trajectory from 8.09 per cent to 18.20 per cent, thereby contributing much to the GDP and thus showing that Malaysian economy grew on the strong trade and business services relative to other sectors.

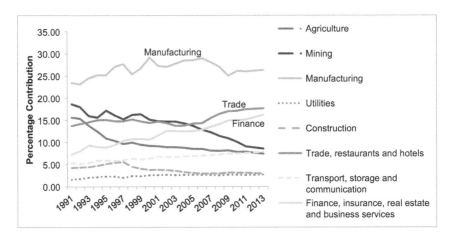

Figure 1.14 Structural change in Malaysia

Source: Figure is based on GGDC Structural Transformation Data

There are also indications that the contribution of transport services is quite substantial at 0.072 per cent CAGR. The growth of the sector was positive from 5.91 per cent in 1991 to 8.91 in 2013. The performance of agriculture and mining sectors showed a declining trend. The agriculture sector slid from 17.38 per cent in 1991 to 8.38 per cent in 2013, while mining declined from 20.76 to 9.67 during the same period.

1.8.5 Philippines

Figure 1.15 depicts the structural change in Philippines. Unlike other economies of Asia, structural change in the Philippines shows manufacturing sector in a declining trend from 32.34 per cent in 1991 to 27.38 per cent in 2013, with CAGR 0.036. The agriculture sector also recorded a declining trend as well from 18.62 to 12.75 during the same period. The mining and construction sectors remained almost stagnant. The services sector on the other hand showed a positive upward growth contributing quite substantially to the economy.

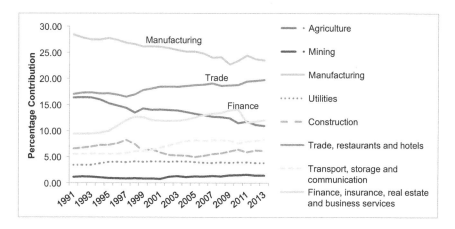

Figure 1.15 Structural change in Philippines

Source: Figure is based on GGDC Structural Transformation Data

Trade services grew from 19.38 in 1991 to 22.61 in 2013 with CAGR 0.053 per cent. The transport services also saw an upward trend from 6.26 to 9.43 per cent and the business services sector was 10.73 to 14.68 during the same period. From the analysis, the Philippines services sector was dominant during the last two decades; a pattern similar to that of African economies.

1.8.6 Sri Lanka

In case of Sri Lanka, the data have been taken from WDI online. This database is incompatible with GGDC in the sense that it provides data for industry as a whole and not component-wise. Therefore, analysis of Sri Lanka should be treated as

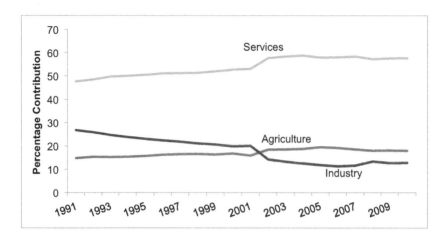

Figure 1.16 Structural change in Sri Lanka
Source: Figure is based on WDI online Data

industry rather than manufacturing. Another difference for Sri Lanka is that data have been taken up to 2010 rather than 2013 due to data limitation. Figure 1.16 presents the transformation that has taken place in Sri Lanka.

It is evident that the Sri Lankan economy relied more on services sector rather than industry which had a positive growth rate (from 14.76 per cent in 1991 to 18.00 per cent in 2010) with CAGR 1.16. This sector contributed quite substantially to value added. Very much like some of the African economies, the agriculture sector of this country shows a positive growth rate (CAGR: 1.30 per cent) from 14.76 per cent in base year to 18.00 per cent in 2010. The industry sector however indicates a declining trend with CAGR –4.80 per cent.

1.8.7 *Thailand*

The structural transformation in Thailand is depicted in Figure 1.17. The pattern of structural transformation in Thailand reveals that the agriculture sector shows a declining trend from 15.14 per cent in 1991 to 11.56 per cent in 2013. The contribution of manufacturing sector to the economy is very high; from 30.39 in 1991 to 43.13 per cent in 2013. Among the services sector, transport services showed a positive upward trend (from 6.25 to 8.74 during the sample period), while trade (from 29.03 to 22.89) and business services (5.05 to 3.85) showed a slight declining trend. Also, business services experienced fluctuations during the sample period with the peak 8.35 per cent in 1994.

The mining sector showed a slight positive trend with CAGR 0.056 per cent, while construction sector experienced a declining trend from 8.86 per cent in 1991 to 2.76 per cent in 2013. It is however evident that Thailand economy did not pay much attention to construction sector.

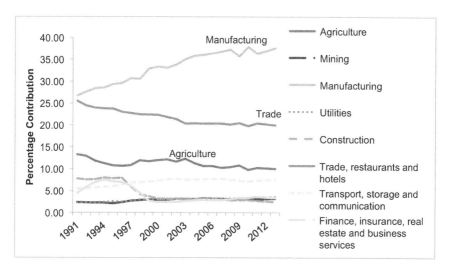

Figure 1.17 Structural change in Thailand

Source: Figure is based on GGDC Structural Transformation Data

1.9 Analysis of Latin American economies

1.9.1 Argentina

Figure 1.18 depicts the structural change of Argentina. The contribution towards value added of manufacturing sector was highest in 2013 accounting for 27.08 per cent. The growth of trade and transport services has also been quite high with 18.55 and 14.20 per cent respectively. The growth of transport services has been quite exceptional from 7.35 in 1991 to 14.20 in 2013. The business services could not do much good to the economy with CAGR 0.038, growing from 5.03 in 1991 to 7.17 per cent in 2013.

The agriculture sector in the country witnessed negative growth like other countries in Africa. It dropped from 11.19 in 1991 to 8.59 per cent in 2013. The mining sector also experienced a slight negative trend to 4.45 in 2013. On the other hand, construction sector indicated a slight positive growth from 4.96 in 1991 to 5.83 per cent in 2013 and business sector experienced growth from 5.03 in base year to 7.17 per cent in 2013.

1.9.2 Bolivia

The structural change in Bolivia is presented in Figure 1.19. The analysis of structural change in Bolivia reveals that the business and mining sectors in the country experienced much upheaval during the sample period. The growth in mining sector was significant from 14.41 in 1991 to 17.27 per cent in 2013; it jumped from fifth position to second in 2013.

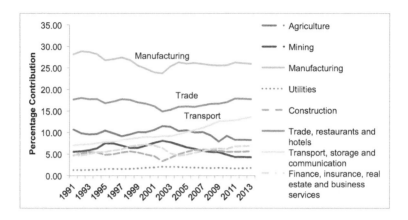

Figure 1.18 Structural change in Argentina

Source: Figure is based on GGDC Structural Transformation Data

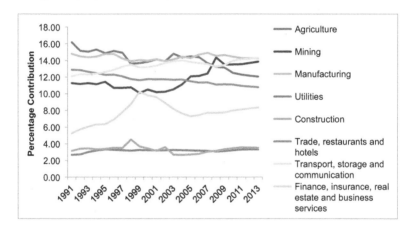

Figure 1.19 Structural change in Bolivia

Source: Figure is based on GGDC Structural Transformation Data

The business sector also grew from 6.72 in base year to 10.41 per cent in 2013. It showed maximum growth in 1999 at 12.80 per cent. Similar to this is the growth of the transport sector from 15.42 in the base year to 17.81 per cent. Other sectors namely, agriculture, manufacturing and trade services have experienced a declining trend of 15.00, 17.77 and 13.42 per cent respectively in 2013. The construction sector remained almost stagnant during the sample period.

1.9.3 *Brazil*

The structural transformation in Brazil, like Argentina and Bolivia, has experienced higher percentage towards value-added growth from 22.76 in 1991 to 26.80 in 2004, although it slightly declined to 22.87 in 2013. The business services that achieved first position in 1991 with 28.02, declined slightly to 22.33 per cent in 2013. Figure 1.20 indicates the structural transformation in Brazil.

The figure also depicts that trade services grew from 17.47 in base year to 20.50 per cent in 2013 thereby contributing substantially to the value added. The other sectors, namely, agriculture (from 6.74 to 8.31 per cent) and mining (from 2.87 to 3.67 per cent) showed slight positive growth. The CAGR of mining (0.042) is highest across the sectors in the sample period. However, construction and transport services in the country remained almost stagnant. The construction sector in the country remained almost stagnant at 7.50 per cent of share.

1.9.4 Colombia

The structural behaviour of various sectors of the economy in Colombia is presented in Figure 1.21. It shows that the agriculture sector contribution started

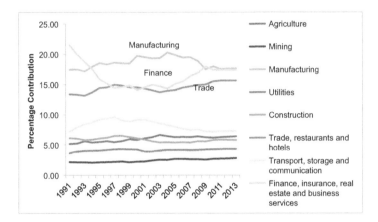

Figure 1.20 Structural change in Brazil

Source: Figure is based on GGDC Structural Transformation Data

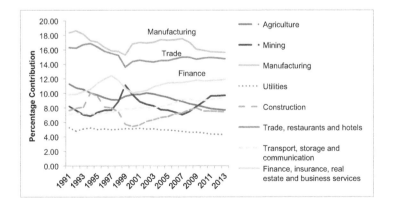

Figure 1.21 Structural change in Colombia

Source: Figure is based on GGDC Structural Transformation Data

(13.44 per cent) at third highest position, but declined to 9.54 per cent. The construction sector experienced much upheaval during the entire period (with CAGR 0.024), but remained stagnant at almost 9 per cent.

As seen from the figure, manufacturing contributed highest to the value added with CAGR 0.028. Among the services sector, the contribution of trade services is the highest at 19.42 in 1991 to 18.28 per cent in 2013. The business services performed quite well, the contribution increased from fourth position (11.68) to third position (14.72) with a positive CAGR of 0.038. The mining sector contribution also witnessed high fluctuation from 9.78 per cent in 1991 to 14.08 in 1999 and then came down to 12.03 per cent in 2013. The contribution of construction sector remained at the bottom of the graph with CAGR 0.024.

1.9.5 Mexico

The transformation in Mexico is depicted in Figure 1.22. It followed the broad pattern evident in other Latin American economies where the manufacturing, trade and business services have outpaced that of agriculture and construction. The contribution of manufacturing and trade services were almost same in 1991 at around 24 per cent. Both experienced huge fluctuations and trade services emerged first with 25.85 per cent contribution followed by manufacturing (22.10 per cent) in 2013.

The business services remained at the third position with CAGR 0.024 and positive stagnant growth of almost 15 per cent during the entire sample period. The agriculture and construction showed a slight declining trend from 5.17 to 4.06 per cent and 9.70 to 8.56 respectively. The mining sector contribution

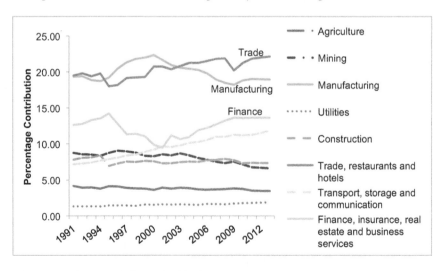

Figure 1.22 Structural change in Mexico

Source: Figure is based on GGDC Structural Transformation Data

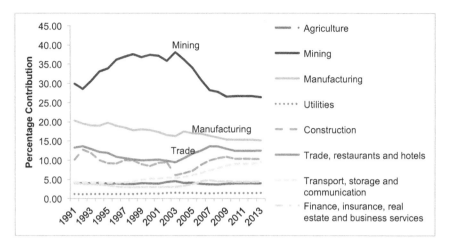

Figure 1.23 Structural change in Venezuela

Source: Figure is based on GGDC Structural Transformation Data

started at fourth position in 1991, but observed a declining trend from 10.87 in the base year to 7.74 per cent in 2013.

1.9.6 Venezuela

The trend of structural transformation in Venezuela was very different compared to other economies in the region and is depicted in Figure 1.23. The major contributor to value added is the mining sector due to its oil exploration with the highest percentage in 2003 at 45.05 per cent.

The manufacturing sector remained the second contributor to value added with 23.29 in 1991 to 18.11 per cent in 2013. Trade services maintained third (15.20 in 1991 to 14.96 per cent in 2013) position, with CAGR 0.022. The transport services also grew remarkably from 4.96 in 1991 to 11.33 in 2013, with highest CAGR 0.063 while the agriculture and construction sectors almost remained stagnant.

1.10 Conclusions

1.10.1 Comparative regional perspective

Growth-reducing structural change was observed for Latin America and African countries. Although in general, Africa's economic development level is much lower than that of Latin America. It was expected that flow of labour from traditional to modern sectors of the economy would be an important driver of growth in Africa; rather, labour seems to have moved from a high-productivity activity, which reduced Africa's growth. In general, Africa exhibits a lot of heterogeneity, but the sector with the largest relative loss in employment is formal wholesale and retail trade, where productivity is higher than the economy-wide average.

We concluded that Asian countries have, during the same period, experienced productivity-enhancing structural change, in contrast to the productivity-reducing structural change observed both in Latin America and Africa. It is, therefore, difficult to ascribe Africa's and Latin America's performance solely to globalization or other external determinants. Clearly, country-specific forces have been at work as well. We noted that differential patterns of structural change account for the bulk of Latin America as well as Africa's underperformance relative to Asia.

1.10.2   *"Jumping" the manufacturing phase*

Comparison with other developing regions confirms the underperformance of the agriculture sector and bloated nature of the services sector in Africa. For example, the average GDP share of agriculture in African countries is significantly smaller than that of South Asian countries with similar levels of income. It hardly exceeds the average share of agriculture in the GDP of countries in East Asia, the Middle East and North Africa, although the latter regions have per capita incomes that are three times higher than that of sub-Saharan African countries. Africa also has the highest average GDP share for services among developing regions. The GDP share of the services sector in Africa is only slightly lower than the average share of Latin American countries, which have an average per capita income that is nearly eight times higher than the African average. This imbalance in sectoral growth has delayed structural transformation and slowed productivity and income growth across Africa. There is a need for renewed industrialization strategies to sustain and broaden the recovery within and beyond the agriculture sector (Badiane 2012).

1.10.3   *Rent kills structural transformation*

Rents from natural resources are spent on urban goods and services which are not available in the rural areas. The region needs to engage in growth paths that generate jobs on a large scale to cater for marginal labour supply. This is essential because Africa has a young and a progressive population. This region is projected to account for 29 per cent of the world's population between ages 15 to 24 years. Therefore, there is need to move away from jobless growth strategies and towards inclusive growth paths that are labor-intensive and create learning opportunities for young people.

The new industrial strategies in African countries will have to address premature industrialization through technology, infrastructure and macroeconomic policies. New industrial policies would have to target enterprise creation and growth, not only in manufacturing, but also in the agribusiness sector and the informal services sector (Badiane 2012). The bulk of the difference between Asia's growth, Latin America and Africa's growth can be explained by the variation in the contribution of structural change to overall labour productivity (McMillan *et al.* 2014). While

Asian countries have tended to experience productivity-enhancing structural change, both Latin America and Africa have experienced productivity-reducing structural change.

1.11 The missing link

This study identifies the pattern of shift that has taken place in each country and region in general over the period. We seek to know the contributions each sector has made to the GDP of each country by the reason of the shift. The study will also examine the determinants of these contributions and policies that have affected activities in each sector. The study is interested in measuring the extent to which the shift has affected productivity, urbanization, poverty level and standard of living of the people. This has a direct bearing on the inclusive growth agenda, which increasingly has gotten traction within the global discourse, and currently a focus within the post-2015 debate and goal-setting process. Inclusive growth demands not just high economic growth, but also that benefits those in the lower income percentile, and the number and quality of jobs are key determinants and channel of achieving it.

Jobless growth constitutes a serious concern because leaving large swathes of society in the mire of unemployment is costly to economies and societies. It leads to lower growth, lower productivity and throws the economy into an inefficiency cycle. In a recent study', a strong association was established between lower levels of inequality in developing countries and sustained periods of economic growth. Developing countries with high inequality have "succeeded in initiating growth at high rates for a few years," but "longer growth spells are robustly associated with more equality in the income distribution." In other words, long-run sustainability is closely connected to sustain equality. Therefore, job-rich growth and structural change is fundamental to addressing inequality over the long term. Evidently, other factors are also necessary such as the role of the state in long-run growth, governance, state capacity and skills, but low inequality is still a necessary condition.

Note

1 The data have been taken from World Development Indicator (WDI) online. This database is incompatible with GGDC as it provides data for industry as a whole and not component-wise.

Bibliography

Adebowale, B., Diyamett, B., Lema, R. and Oyelaran-Oyeyinka, B. (2014). "Innovation Research and Economic Development in Africa." *African Journal of Science, Technology, Innovation and Development*, vol. 6(5): v–xi.

AfricaFocus Bulletin. (2013). *Structural Transformation in the African Context: Reflections on Priorities for the Post-2015 Development Agenda*, online, available at http://www.africafocus.org/docs13/econ1304.php (accessed on July 14, 2015).

Amsden, A. H. (1989). *Asia's Next Giant: South Korea and Late Industrialization.* New York and Oxford: Oxford University Press.

Badiane, O. (2012). *Beyond Economic Recovery: The Agenda for Economic Transformation in Africa*, online, available at http://wca.ifpri.info (accessed on July 21, 2015).

Bah, E. (2007). *Structural Transformation in Developed and Developing Countries.* Munich Personal RePEc Archive (MPRA Paper No. 10655), online, available at http://mpra.ub.uni-muenchen.de/10655/ (accessed on June 22, 2015).

Balisacan, A., Fuwa, N., Mapa, D., Piza, S., Sombilla, M. and Santos, C. (2011). *Inclusive Agribusiness Growth in the Philippines: The Role of Direct and Indirect Channels with a Focus on the Labor Market.* Quezon City: Asia Pacific Policy Center.

Breisinger, C. and Diao, X. (2008). "Economic Transformation in Theory and Practice: What are the Messages for Africa?" ReSAKSS Working Paper 21, International Food Policy Research Institute (IFPRI), Washington.

Briones, R. and Felipe, J. (2013). "Agriculture and Structural Transformation in Developing Asia: Review and Outlook." ADB Economics Working Paper Series 363, 1–39, Asian Development Bank, Philippines, online, available at www.adb.org/economics (accessed on June 22, 2015).

Chemengich, M. (2010). "Impact of AGOA on the Textile and Apparel Industry of Kenya." Online, available at http://pdf.usaid.gov/pdf_docs/PA00K1MS.pdf (accessed on June 23, 2015).

Dabla-Norris, E., Thomas, A., Garcia-Verdu, R. and Chen, Y. (2013). "Benchmarking Structural Transformation across the World." IMF Working Paper, WP/13/176, online, available at https://www.imf.org/external/pubs/ft/wp/2013/wp13176.pdf (accessed on July 4, 2016).

de Vries, G., Timmer, M. and de Vries, K. (2013). "Structural Transformation in Africa: Static Gains, Dynamic Losses." GGDC Research Memorandum 136, University of Groningen.

Etchemendy, S. (2009). "Models of Economic Liberalization: Regime, Power and Compensation in the Iberian-American Region." APSA 2009 Toronto Meeting Paper, online, available at http://ssrn.com/abstract=1449085 (accessed on June 24, 2015).

Ferreira, P. C. and da Silva, L. F. (2014). "Structural Transformation and Productivity in Latin America." Online, available at http://hdl.handle.net/10438/11889 (accessed on July 01, 2015).

Food and Agriculture Organization. (2010). "Global Forest Resources Assessment 2010: Main Report." FAO Forestry Paper 163, FAO, Rome.

Gollin, D., Jedwab, R. and Vollrath, D. (2013). "Urbanization with and without Structural Transformation." The Society for Economic Dynamic Meetings, 1–33, online, available at https://www.economicdynamics.org/meetpapers/2013/paper_344.pdf (accessed on July 03, 2015).

Hausmann, R. and Klinger, B. (2006). "Structural Transformation and Patterns of Comparative Advantage in the Product Space." John F. Kennedy School of Government – Harvard University. Faculty Research Working Papers Series RWP06-041.

Herrendorf, B., Rogerson, R. and Valentinyi, A. (2013). "Growth and Structural Transformation." CEPR Discussion Paper No. DP9370, online, available at https://www.imf.org/external/np/seminars/eng/2013/SPR/pdf/rrog2.pdf (accessed on July 4, 2016).

Jedwab, R. (2012). *Why is Africa So Urbanized? Evidence from Resource Exports in Ghana and Ivory Coast.* Unpublished Manuscript, George Washington University, Department of Economics.

Jedwab, R. and Osei, R. D. (2012). "Structural Change and Development in Ghana." Report Prepared for the Project *Structural Change in Developing Countries*, online, available at https://www.gwu.edu/~iiep/assets/docs/papers/Jedwab_IIEPWP2012-12.pdf (accessed on July 4, 2016).

Jongwanich, J. (2009). "The Impact of Food Safety Standards on Processed Food Exports from Developing Countries." *Food Policy*, vol. 34: 447–457.

Kuznets, S. (1973). "Modern Economic Growth: Findings and Reflections." *American Economic Review*, vol. 63(3): 247–258.

Lall, S. (1995). "Structural Adjustment and African Industry." *World Development*, vol. 23(12): 2019–2031.

Lewis, W. A. (1954). "Economic Development with Unlimited Supplies of Labor." *Manchester School of Economic and Social Studies*, vol. 22: 139–191.

Lewis, W. A. (1978). *Growth and Fluctuations 1870–1913*. London: Allen and Unwin.

Lu, S. (2012). *Why Have Asia and Latin America Grown differently?* Online, available at http://mx.nthu.edu.tw/~sslu/files/Lu_ShuShiuan_2012.pdf (accessed on June 25, 2015).

McMillan, M. (2012). *Global Patterns of Structural Change*, online, available at http://wca.ifpri.info (accessed on June 25, 2015).

McMillan, M., Rodrik, D. and Verduzco-Gallo, I. (2014). "Globalization, Structural Change, and Productivity Growth, with an Update on Africa." *World Development*, vol. 63: 11–32, online, available at http://drodrik.scholar.harvard.edu/files/dani-rodrik/files/globalization_structural_change_productivity_growth_with_africa_update.pdf?m=1435002696 (accessed on July 4, 2016).

OECD. (2013). Innovation in Southeast Asia. *OECD Reviews of Innovation Policy*, 307–345.

———— (2013a). *African Economic Outlook 2013*, online, available at http://dx.doi.org/10.1787/aeo-2013-en (accessed on June 15, 2015).

———— (2015). *African Economic Outlook 2015*, online, available at http://dx.doi.org/10.1787/aeo-2015-en (accessed on June 16, 2015).

Oyelaran-Oyeyinka, B. (2015). "The State and Innovation Policy in Africa." *African Journal of Science, Technology, Innovation and Development*, vol. 6(5): 481–496.

Páez, L., Karingi, S., Kimenyi, M. and Paulos, M. (2010). *A Decade of African-US Trade under the African Growth and Opportunity Act (AGOA): Challenges, Opportunities and a Framework for Post-AGOA Engagement*, online, available at http://ti.au.int/en/documents/au-conference-ministers-trade-6th-ordinary-session (accessed on June 20, 2015).

Primi, A. (2013). "The Return of Industrial Policy: (What) can Africa Learn from Latin America?" Working Paper Prepared for JICA/IPD Africa Task Force Meeting, 1–30, OECD Development Centre, Yokohama, Japan.

Ranis, G. and Fei, J. C. (1961). "A Theory of Economic Development." *American Economic Review*, vol. 51: 533–558.

Rodrik, D. (2012). *Industrial Policy and the Promotion of Structural Transformation*, online, available at http://wca.ifpri.info (accessed on July 09, 2015).

———— (2013). *Structural Change, Fundamentals and Growth: An Overview*, online, available at https://www.sss.ias.edu/files/pdfs/Rodrik/Research/Structural-Change-Fundamentals-and-Growth-An-Overview_revised.pdf (accessed on July 17, 2015).

Romer, P. M. (1986). "Increasing Returns and Long-Run Growth." *Journal of Political Economy*, vol. 94(5): 1002–1037.

Solow, R. M. (1956). "A Contribution to the Theory Economic Growth." *Quarterly Journal of Economics*, vol. 70: 65–94.

Stein, H. (1992). "Deindustrialization, Adjustment, the World Bank and the IMF in Africa." *World Development*, vol. 20(1): 83–95.

Stern, N., Dethier, J. J. and Rogers, F. H. (2005). *Growth and Empowerment, Making Development Happen.* Cambridge, MA: MIT Press.

Stewart, F., Lall, S. and Samuel, W. (eds.). (1992). *Alternative Development Strategies in Africa.* London: St. Martin's Press.

Stiglitz, J. (1996). "Some Lessons from the Asian Miracle." *World Bank Research Observer*, vol. 11(2): 151–177.

Szirmai, A. (2012). "Industrialization as an Engine of Growth in Developing Countries, 1950–2005." *Structural Change and Economic Dynamics*, vol. 23(4): 406–420.

_____ Naudé, W. and Haraguchi, N. (eds.). (2012). *Structural Change, Poverty Reduction and Industrial Policy in the BRICS.* Vienna: UNIDO.

Timmer, P. (2007). "The Structural Transformation and the Changing Role of Agriculture in Economic Development: Empirics and Implication." Wendt Lecture, October 30, 1–146.

_____ (2012). *The Mathematics of Structural Transformation*, online, available at http://pages.au.int/sites/default/files/IFPRI%20WCAO%20TRN2%20 Structural%20Change_0.pdf (accessed on May 15, 2015).

_____ and Akkus, S. (2008). *The Structural Transformation as a Pathway out of Poverty: Analytics, Empirics and Politics*, online, available at www.cgdev.org (accessed on July 16, 2015).

Todaro, M. P. (1989). *Economic Development for the Third World.* New York: Longman.

UNCTAD. (2012). *Innovation, Technology and South-South Collaboration: Technology and Innovation Report.* New York: United Nations Conference on Trade and Development.

UN-Habitat. (2012). *State of Latin American and Caribbean Cities Report 2012: Towards a New Urban Transition*, online, available at http://www.unhabitat.org/ (accessed on July 20, 2015).

_____ (2014). *Structural Transformation in Ethiopia: The Urban Dimension*, online, available at www.unhabitat.org (accessed on July 21, 2015).

UNIDO (2009). Structural Change in the World Economy: Main Features and Trends. Research and Statistics Branch Working Paper 24 / 2009). UNIDO: Vienna. https://www.unido.org/fileadmin/user_media/Publications/Pub_free/ Structural_change_in_the_world_economy.pdf

United Nations Economic Commission for Africa (UNECA) and African Union (AU). (2011). *Economic Report on Africa 2011: Governing Development in Africa – The Role of the State in Economic Transformation.* UNECA, Addis Ababa.

Vogel, E. (1991). *Four Little Dragons: The Spread of Industrialisation in East Asia.* Massachusetts, MA: Harvard University Press.

Wade, R. (2004). "Is Globalization Reducing Poverty and Inequality." *World Development*, vol. 32(4): 567–589.

World Bank. (1993). *The East Asian Miracle, Economic Growth and Public Policy.* New York: Oxford University Press.

_____ (2009). *World Development Report 2008 Agriculture for Development.* Washington, DC: World Bank.

_____ (2013). *Africa's Pulse: An Analysis of Issues Shaping Africa's Economic Future,* *8, 1–40*, online, available at WWW.Worldbank.org/africapulse (accessed on July 14, 2015).

_____ (2013a). *World Development Report 2013: Jobs.* Washington, DC: World Bank.

_____ (2015). *Manufacturing, Value Added (Current US$)*, online, available at http://data.worldbank.org/indicator/NV.IND.MANF.CD (accessed on June 17, 2015).

World Food Programme (WFP). (2010). *Fighting Hunger Worldwide: Annual Report 2010*, online, available at http://home.wfp.org/stellent/groups/public/documents/communications/wfp220666.pdf (accessed on June 21, 2015).

2 Employment

2.1 Introduction

This chapter demonstrates that employment and structural economic transformation are two interconnected phenomena that determine the growth and development trajectories of countries. At the micro level, employment creation provides opportunities for earnings and underpins the increases in household expenditures and secure livelihoods. At the macro level, development occurs through the reallocation of labour towards sectors with the greatest growth potential and the highest productivity. Jobs also facilitate social welfare such as female wage employment and rise in living standards. The analysis of structural transformation enables to unearth the historical evolutionary roots of long-term unemployment as well as the immediate causes of both rural and urban unemployment.

Both national and global development agendas have focused on creating employment due to the opportunities it holds for earnings, security of livelihood, and redistribution of labour amongst others. Employment creation is therefore positively associated not only with economic growth, but equally with investment opportunities and international openness. The global economy was estimated to grow by 3.1 per cent in 2015, and for 2016, the current estimation lies at 3.6 per cent. This is significantly lower than earlier predictions, which indicates a weakening of the world economy driven by the slowdown in emerging and developing economies. It greatly impacts employment with an increase in global unemployment which reached 197.1 million in 2015, approaching 1 million more than in the previous year and over 27 million higher than pre-crisis levels, with vulnerable employment accounting for 1.5 billion people, or over 46 per cent of total employment (IMF 2015; ILO 2016). This increase is considerably influenced by long-standing structural weaknesses coupled with unfavourable and unstable conditions in the global economy and is anticipated to grow further.

Generating jobs at a pace rapid enough to absorb the unemployed in the labour market remains an enormous challenge especially for developing economies. Youth unemployment and gender dimensions are examples of the wide variety of unemployment types forming the broader phenomenon confronting countries across the continents regardless of their level of socio-economic development, for instance, global unemployment increased from 170 million in 2007 to nearly

202 million in 2012, of which about 75 million were young women and men (United Nations 2016). This is due to the large turnout of the young, new entrants into the labour market every year, the lack of appropriate employment opportunities in poor economies and the low quality of education and training without a proper link to the labour markets. In view of the youth employment challenge, many governments are investing substantially in youth employment programmes, which complement general poverty reduction and employment policies.

The academic literature tells us that structural transformation (ST) is closely connected to employment because it is characterized by the transition of an economy from low-productivity and labour-intensive economic activities to higher-productivity and skill-intensive activities. The driving force behind structural transformation is the change of productivity in modern sector, which is dominated by manufacturing and services. Structural change is equally attended by the movement of the workforce from labour-intensive activities to skill-intensive urban-based ones. The key constraint to the movement of labour from rural to urban space is the lack of opportunities in skill-intensive sectors such as manufacturing. When labour migrates to cities with little or no opportunities, available labour is underemployed or employed inefficiently.

Therefore, productivity changes based on widespread economic diversification and structural transformation is critical towards achieving high and sustained economic growth rates with high levels of social development.

In addition, it underpins the achievement of the Sustainable Development Goal (SDG) 8, which is aimed at promoting sustained, inclusive and sustainable economic growth, full and productive employment and decent work for all. Also, other development gaps such as the provision of 470 million jobs needed globally for new entrants to the labour market between 2016 and 2030, and poverty eradication through stable and well-paid jobs, can be closed depending on the ability of countries to foster entrepreneurship and promote innovation. The spread, adaptation and adoption of pre-existing know-how and techniques, services, processes and ways of working can be incorporated to achieve the targets faster.

Trends in employment generation of the various sectors of the economy has implications for how policymakers and individuals prepare for the future of work, and for how efforts should be focused to bolster positive links between work and human development. A stable macroeconomic environment which boosts investment – both private and public – and thus growth, is fundamental to the creation of new formal jobs for all groups of workers. The sectoral policies in particular can promote job creation in the medium- to long-term, provided they are well designed and targeted to sectors with high potential for employment growth.

2.2 Review of literature

Growth in a sector of the economy may not necessarily translate into socio-economic benefits, because it is far more dependent on the profile of growth which encompasses employment or productivity-intensity, sectoral location and extent of mobility across sectors (UNDP 2015). The quality jobs are drivers of development and more broadly, human capital is a key factor in enhancing labour productivity, job quality, and hence, GDP growth.

Across regions, employment gaps remain prevalent with different levels of intensity ranging from high rates of unemployment in developed economies to prolonged vulnerable employment rates in many emerging and developing economies. Africa is one of the fastest-growing regions of the world with an average growth of 5 per cent per annum (UNECA 2015). In North Africa, economic growth has continued despite the ongoing political crises and instabilities, but has inhibited social progress particularly in employment creation. Youth unemployment rate stands at 30 per cent, reaching 45 per cent for female youth. In sub-Saharan Africa, economic growth has weakened, falling to 3.6 per cent in 2015 from 4.9 per cent in 2014 and influenced by the lack of economic diversification, leading to subdued labour. The unemployment rate increased slightly to 7.4 per cent in 2015, from 7.3 per cent in 2014 (ILO 2016).

In Latin America and the Caribbean, economic growth has continued to decelerate. The region registered sustained growth in the 2000s, but economic growth began to experience a downward trend since mid-2011 with estimated GDP growth of 0.3 per cent in 2015, the second lowest rate worldwide (IMF 2015). The unemployment rate for the region also took on a declining trend from 6.8 per cent in 2013 to 6.5 per cent in 2015, but may rise in 2016 (ILO 2016).

The Asia and the Pacific regions face the challenge of combining rapid growth with sufficient job creation in an environmentally sustainable manner despite having a third of the world's GDP and some of the highest economic growth rates in the world. In 2015, 21 million net new jobs were created, but total employment growth continues to fall short of working-age population growth. As a group, the emerging and developing economies continue to experience levels of growth above the global average, with projections close to 4 per cent in 2015, whereas growth in these economies reached 4.6 per cent in 2014 and 5.0 per cent in 2013 (ILO 2016). This slowdown is attributed to the effects of several long-standing drivers, notably the decline in long-term capital investment, population ageing, rising inequality and weakening productivity gains.

As employment trend varies between regions, it also varies between the developed and developing economies. Advanced economies moved from agriculture to industry to services during the past century, and the sectoral distribution of economic activity is reflected both in value added as a proportion of GDP and in employment by sector. The agricultural sector requires considerable efforts to improve productivity and working conditions to have notable impact on human development. Globally, about 1.34 billion people are working in the sector with 70–80 per cent of the world's agricultural land managed by more than 500 million family farms. Around 43 per cent of the agricultural labour force in developing countries are women, and about 50 per cent are women in Africa and Asia (UNDP 2015).

Reardon *et al.* (2001) studied that rural nonfarm employment (RNFE) and incomes (RNFI) in 11 Latin American rural households using 1990s data and showed that RNFI averages 40 per cent of rural incomes. Both RNFI and RNFE have grown quickly over the past three decades. The findings suggest nonfarm wage incomes exceed self-employment incomes; RNFI far exceeds farm wage incomes and local RNFI far exceeds migration incomes; the service sector RNFI far exceeds manufactures RNFI. They suggest the need for more development programme attention to wage employment in the service sector than traditional focus on small enterprise manufactures. Also, the RNFE of the poor tend to be the low-paid nonfarm equivalent of semi-subsistence farming.

In developed and developing economies, industry (particularly manufacturing) accounts for 23.2 per cent of global employment. Manufacturing as a share of total employment has however declined in many countries, even in strong exporting countries due to its capital-intensive nature, rise in the use of robots and skill intensiveness. Globalization and labour-saving technologies exerts pressure on manufacturing jobs, hence, many countries, particularly in sub-Saharan Africa, face untimely de-industrialization as opportunities in industry shrink with much lower levels of income than for early industrializers, posing huge consequences for employment creation and expanding opportunities (UNDP 2015).

On the other hand, the service sector has been the leading employment sector globally since 2002, and the sector accounted for 46 per cent of all jobs in 2013 (UNDP 2015). This is driven by the growth of knowledge-intensive work and low-skill work. A study on India's services sector to assess if trade is able to generate employment in the services sector reveals that international trade is not an important determinant of employment in this sector. The study was based on the time series macro data, the direct and indirect effects of exports and imports on employment and the overall growth on formal and informal services. On the whole, trade in the services sector may enhance growth, but this pattern of growth is less likely to be inclusive (Mitra 2011).

The growing dominance of the service sector requires policy attention to ensure that essential services for human development and technological progress are sustained, to enable workers providing these services to gain the requisite skills and to protect service workers against inadequate wages and exploitative work conditions.

2.3 Skill development and employment

Skill development is becoming increasingly crucial in the globalized economy for employment and inequality reduction. A study of the shortage of entrepreneurial skills with focus on entrepreneurship development and skill differences between young and adult entrepreneurs in Swaziland reveals that for young entrepreneurs facing high costs of search for business opportunities, support for training is more effective in stimulating productive start-ups than subsidies (Brixiová *et al.* 2015). Also, in an assessment of the level of financial literacy and its impact on youth entrepreneurship in Vhembe district in South Africa, it was discovered that financial literacy among youth entrepreneurs in the district appears to be above average and contributes meaningfully to their entrepreneurship skills (Oseifuah 2010).

Skill mismatch is evident by high vacancy rates amidst large scale unemployment. In Latin American Countries, firms have difficulties to find employees with desirable skills. An average of 31.5 per cent of businesses considers insufficient qualifications of employees as a major obstacle for the performance of the company, the percentage varies between 10 per cent in Mexico and 69 per cent in Brazil. A study conducted in Costa Rica, El Salvador and Peru indicated that skills problem is increasing due to a lack of soft skills mostly in new technologies and generic skills such as attitudes, values and learning capacity (Weller 2011). Furthermore, a survey from nine countries indicated that less than half of employers (43 per cent) were able to find the skills they needed in entry-level workers (Barton, Farrell and Mourshed 2013).

In Africa, despite the growing numbers of unemployed young people, many enterprises struggle to fill open positions. For example, an estimated 1.5 million young people are unemployed in Egypt, while at the same time private sector firms cannot fill 600,000 vacancies; in South Africa, 800,000 vacancies are not filled despite the presence of 600,000 unemployed graduates and 3 million young people not in education, employment or training (ILO 2011; The Economist 2012). A complete absence of skills is a problem too, a survey among experts on 36 African countries about the major challenges youth face in labour markets indicated that 54 per cent found a mismatch of skills between what job seekers have to offer and what employers require to be a major obstacle, while 41 per cent identified a general lack of skills among job seekers as a major obstacle (African Economic Outlook [AEO] 2012).

Technical and vocational skills development also has the potential to provide people with more applied skills and better chances in the labour market. Of the global youth who are not in education, training or employment, 62 per cent of them are in South Asia (101 million) and East Asia and the Pacific (119.4 million) (African Development Bank [ADB] 2013), despite labour market interventions implemented by governments and public-private sector partnerships to enhance self-help and self-employment initiatives.

There is therefore a need to improve education and skill acquisition based on the requirement of employers and the labour market entirely. This will narrow the skill and education gap to meet the needs of the labour market, improving education in technical fields and agriculture, and improving quality.

2.4   Youth, gender and employment

Despite the enormous potentials a youthful population presents for stimulating economic growth through productive employment, asset creation and investment, the task of creating decent employment opportunities is daunting, thus requiring policymakers to expand access to education at all levels and to adapt technical, vocational, and higher education to changing labour market requirements (ADB 2012).

After the period of rapid increase between 2007 and 2010, the global youth unemployment rate settled at 13.0 per cent for the period 2012 to 2014. At the same time, the number of unemployed youth declined by 3.3 million (76.6 million youth were unemployed in 2009 compared to an estimated 73.3 million in 2014). As of 2014, 36.7 per cent of the global unemployed were youth, while the youth share in total unemployment was 41.5 per cent in 2004. While the indicator marks an improvement over time, it is still worthy of note that the youth are strongly over-represented among the unemployed (ILO 2015).

Substandard education and training are pushing poor, young workers into informal sector jobs which are often characterized by low pay and miserable working conditions. A study was undertaken on the unique retrospective survey data collected in Burkina Faso in 2000 to examine the changes that urban youth employment has undergone over the last 20 years and the impact of the changing socio-economic context on young people's access to labour market, with particular reference to educated youth and young women. The analysis which was based on employment histories shows increasing unemployment and informal trend of youth employment in urban Burkina Faso. This illustrates strong evidence of a rupture between education and modern sector employment among young men, and the increased instability of employment among young women (Calvès and Schoumaker 2004).

Another study on the youth in informal sector in Egypt found that a large proportion of educated youth work within the realm of informality and there is a clear policy gap in addressing this issue, which is contrary to the expectations of young people who value access to social security and work stability. They face systemic hurdles related to access to such benefits (Barsoum 2015). Due to the legacy of guaranteed government hiring of the educated in Egypt, young people express a great appreciation of work in the government for virtually being the only employer offering job stability and social security in the labour market.

A review of the youth unemployment crisis in resource-rich sub-Saharan Africa, particularly Ghana, which is the region's top mineral-rich country, shows that although the region has experienced a continuous and a seemingly limitless flow of investment in all types of extractive industries in recent decades, this growth has not directly translated into significant job creation and poverty reduction. Its overdependence on natural resources economically had a negative impact on socio-economic development overall, generating very few jobs for the youth and exacerbating the existing unemployment crises (Ackah-Baidoo 2016).

Women constitute 40 per cent of the global workforce, and their active engagement in productive employment contributes not only to faster economic growth, but also its long-term sustainability (ILO 2008). Between 1980 and 2009, the global rate of female labour force participation rose from 50.2 per cent to 51.8 per cent, while the male rate fell from 82.0 per cent to 77.7 per cent. Consequently, gender differentials in labour force participation rates declined from 32 percentage points in 1980 to 26 percentage points in 2009 (World Bank 2012). In spite of the progress made in advancing towards gender equality in workplace during the last few decades, women continue to be over-represented in more precarious, informal and less remunerated work than men. This is largely due to slow progress in social change in many societies, burden of unpaid care work that mostly women continue to undertake, and gender blindness of macroeconomic and development policies (ILO 2008).

A study of the South Asian female employment suggests that the pervasive existence of structural and institutional barriers such as patriarchal ideologies are reinforced by gender in-egalitarian interpretations of holy texts; second, women's limited access to education and skill development; and third, lack of non-agricultural employment and economic resources resulting in economic dependence on men and sex-based division of labour (Pio and Jawad 2013).

Also, analyses of the positive role of the state in promoting women's employment since the founding of Communist China in 1949 identifies patterns of gender inequality, which exist throughout the process such as recruitment and retirement. It tries to analyse the major reasons for the occurrence of this gender discrimination, which ranges from inadequate social security for childbearing and ineffective legislative monitoring mechanisms to gender bias in the employment legislation. The study concludes that recent radical economic and social reforms in China have disrupted the context within which a level of equal opportunity has been achieved in the past few decades and demands a new legal framework under which greater equality between men and women in employment can be achieved (Cooke 2001).

In Latin American countries, labour participation of women has increased from 49.2 per cent in 2000 to 52.9 per cent in 2010, but still below that of men, which is 79.6 per cent. By contrast, the rate of female unemployment, at 9.1 per cent, remains higher than that of men, which is 6.3 per cent. Considering the level of education of economically active women, 53.7 per cent reached 10 or more years of formal education, compared with 40.4 per cent for men. In addition, 22.8 per cent of women in the workforce have college education, against 16.2 per cent for men. Yet, women still earn less than their male colleagues. In 2000, women earned 60 per cent of what men made, and in 2010, the figure was 68 per cent (ILO 2014).

Seven of 10 Latin American working women are in the services sector with precarious working conditions and of which 64.6 per cent do not have a contract. The same is true for 34.8 per cent of those working in commerce, and approximately 17 million women are employed in domestic work. Domestic work is the largest source of employment for women in Latin America, and although significant steps have been taken to improve the situation, it is a sector where informality prevails (70 per cent) (ILO 2014).

In Africa, male employment-to-population ratio was estimated at about 69.2 per cent, while female employment-to-population ratio is 39.2 per cent. Social exclusion of women in employment in Africa (especially in North Africa) is acute. In 2011, East Asia region had the highest average female employment ratio (at about 64 per cent) and highest gender equality in employment in the developing world at 75 per cent. While Africa's female employment ratio was low at 39 per cent, that of sub-Saharan Africa was about 59 per cent. Expanding economic opportunities has attracted new female entrants into the labour market, while average gender equality has increased from 70 per cent to 76 per cent; however, they still face other issues like being mostly employed in the informal sector (Anyawu and Augustine 2012).

In conclusion, integrating gender equality concerns into national, regional and international employment policies and dialogues, taking into account all thematic areas of employment, and the burden of unpaid work on women is pertinent to achieve gender equality in employment and economic growth.

2.5   Empirical evidence

We start this analytical section with an examination of structural transformation and its impact on wealth creation, and subsequently the links with labour productivity, employment, migration, urbanization and poverty. We know that the optimum allocation of resources resulting in structural transformation might lead to increase in wealth and higher productivity, but in some instances without any change in employment. Many countries are struggling with the problem of jobless growth. Jobless growth in an economy leads to skewed economic development and a development process that is the anti-thesis of inclusive growth and development. Therefore, it is crucial to investigate the consequences of structural transformation on all aspects of development that influence job creation. This chapter is therefore devoted to structural transformation and its consequences on wealth generation and employment.

2.5.1   Structural transformation and wealth

The analysis of wealth of sample countries in Asia, Africa and Latin America is presented in this section. The following figures provide the GDP per capita in USD (Constant 2005) of sample countries in the respective continents from 1991 to 2013. The growth of wealth in African countries is depicted in Figure 2.1.

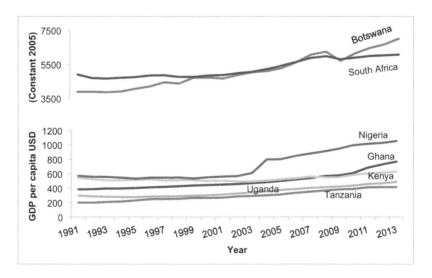

Figure 2.1 Growth of wealth in Africa

Source: World Development Indicator online

The sample countries in Africa can be divided into two categories depending upon their performance. The first category of countries is Botswana and South Africa, whose GDP per capita is much higher than other countries. Although base year income in South Africa (USD 4,914) and Botswana (USD 3,895) was substantially higher than other sample countries, CAGR in both the countries (South Africa, 1.38 and Botswana, 2.81 per cent) has been similar to that of other countries. In fact, GDP per capita in South Africa was higher than Botswana in 1991, but it decreased in 2013. The performance of Nigeria, Ghana, Kenya, Tanzania and Uganda was more or less similar. Among less GDP per capita economies, the highest growth rate has been achieved by Nigeria (3.65 per cent), while Kenya experienced the lowest with 0.76 per cent. The CAGR in Tanzania, Ghana and Uganda were 2.75, 2.93 and 3.57 per cent respectively.

Figure 2.2, shows the growth of wealth in Asia. It can be seen from the figure that the growth of income in four countries namely Sri Lanka, Philippines, India and Indonesia is very low, while that of China, Thailand and Malaysia was substantially high. The CAGR of China is highest (9.23 per cent) among all the sample countries, while the lowest is in Philippines at 2.25 per cent.

The GDP per capita in Malaysia was highest in 1991 at USD 3,356 and has maintained its position in 2013 at USD 6,998 although the growth of GDP per capita (2.99 per cent) during the study period has been similar to that of low-performing economies. On the other hand, GDP per capita in China in 1991 was lower than Malaysia, Thailand, Philippines and Sri Lanka, but it attained second position in 2013 by achieving an impressive growth rate of 9.23 per cent. Thailand that had second position in terms of GDP per capita in base year slid to third position in 2013 with marginal growth rate of 2.85 per cent. The CAGR of GDP per capita in Indonesia, Sri Lanka and India were 2.69, 4.39

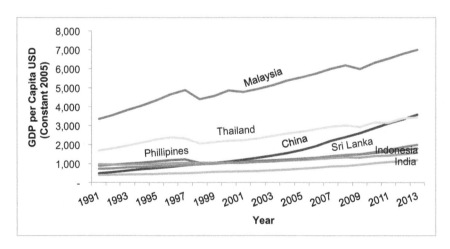

Figure 2.2 Growth of wealth in Asia

Source: World Development Indicator online

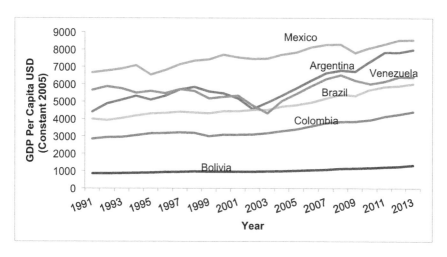

Figure 2.3 Growth of wealth in Latin America
Source: World Development Indicator online

and 5.19 per cent respectively. Figure 2.3 presents the growth of wealth in Latin American sample countries.

It can be seen from the figure above that all the sample Latin American economies grew at the same pace resulting in no change in their relative position by GDP per capita. The highest CAGR was experienced by Argentina (2.20 per cent), while in Venezuela, it was 0.58 per cent. The CAGR in Bolivia, Mexico, Brazil and Colombia were 1.80, 1.15, 1.89 and 1.79 respectively. Figure 2.3 also shows that the Venezuelan economy experienced wide fluctuations during 1991 and 2013.

By comparing growth of economies in the sample countries, it was found that the base year income in Latin American countries was much higher than other sample countries of Asia and Africa with few exceptions such as Botswana and South Africa in Africa; and Malaysia and Thailand in Asia. It was also noticed that Asian countries have experienced much higher CAGR than countries in the other two continents. The higher growth rate might have been achieved due to the structural transformation of Asian economies that will be discussed in subsequent sections.

2.5.2 *African economies*

Two aspects of structural change which are value added and employment in various sectors of the sample economies are discussed. Value-added data were taken from Groningen Growth and Development Centre (GGDC), University of Groningen, The Netherlands; for sample economies of all the three continents. GGDC data were not available up to 2013 for all the countries. Hence, in cases of non-availability of up to 2013, data for remaining years were extrapolated using growth rates of available years. The extrapolation exercise was limited to one or two years in any country. The structural change in terms of value added and employment in sample African economies (Botswana, Ghana, Kenya, Nigeria, South Africa and Tanzania) is discussed in the section. The share of agriculture in value added is very limited. Among other structural and macroeconomic reasons, the availability of abundant natural resources could be one of the causes of the lack of focus on agriculture.

2.5.3   Value added

The share of value added of core sectors, that is agriculture, manufacturing and services in sample economies in 1991 and 2013 are presented in Figure 2.4. It can be seen from the figure that the contribution of agriculture and manufacturing to Botswana's economy, which is dependent primarily on gold/diamond mines is almost negligible. The surprising fact is that share of agriculture in 1991 (3.89 per cent) declined to 2.59 per cent in 2013. On the other hand, services sector performed extremely well by increasing its share from 23.88 in 1991 to 50.17 per cent in 2013. The share of services sector grew at the rate of 2.66 per cent annually. The structural change of the Botswana economy suggests that the services sector has grown faster than the other two, a trend followed by most of the developing world.

The structure of the Ghanaian economy is different from Botswana in terms of its share of agriculture. Almost one-third of the contribution came from agriculture in 1991, but decreased at the rate of –1.07 per cent annually resulting in

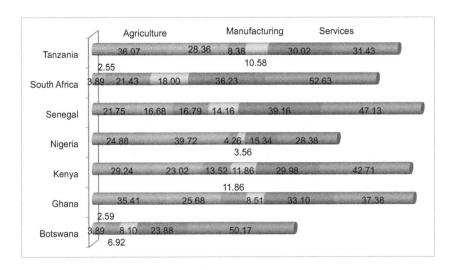

Figure 2.4 Shift of value-added share in main sectors (1991 to 2013)

Source: Figure is based on GGDC Structural Transformation Data.

25.68 per cent share in 2013. Although share of services sector increased during the sample period, its annual growth rate (0.73 per cent) was not very impressive. Consequently, its share increased from 33.10 to 37.38 per cent in 2013. At the same time, the share of manufacturing sector declined from 11.86 to 8.51 per cent during the sample period. One of the reasons for decline in the manufacturing sector could be availability of cheap Chinese products in the Ghanaian market. Another reason could be the complete abolition of quota system in 2005 by World Trade Organization (WTO) in garments manufacturing.

The structure of the Kenyan economy is more or less similar to that of Ghana and followed the similar structural shift. The agriculture sector share which was 29.24 per cent in 1991 declined at the rate of −0.66 annually. Highest growth was realized in the service sector, that is 1.39 per cent, while the share of the service sector rose from 29.98 to 42.71 per cent. Similar to that of Ghana, manufacturing sector share declined from 13.52 to 11.86 per cent. The abolition of quota system completely in apparel manufacturing could be one of the possible reasons for decline in share of manufacturing. The productivity aspect of the declining trend in agriculture and manufacturing are discussed in the next chapter.

The structure of the Nigerian economy is very different from other sample African countries. It is the only country where the share of agriculture experienced an increasing trend. The share of agriculture was 24.88 in 1991 and increased to 39.72 per cent in 2013 by growing at the rate of 2.66 per cent annually. The share of services sector also increased significantly with similar rate (2.59 per cent) than that of agriculture resulting in 28.38 per cent share in 2013. The share of manufacturing sector (4.26 per cent) was very low in 1991 and further declined to 3.56 per cent in 2013. Apparently, Nigeria followed the path of being self-reliant in agriculture, which provides considerable employment and food security to its citizens. A choice of agriculture over manufacturing might have been influenced by the law of comparative advantage. Due to the poor performance of the industrial manufacturing, the country has relied mainly on import of manufactured products for several years.

The share of agriculture contribution (3.89 per cent) in South Africa was negligible in 1991 and further reduced to 2.55 per cent in 2013. The share of manufacturing sector followed the trend of agriculture and changed from 21.43 to 18.00 per cent. On the other hand, services sector, which had 36.23 per cent share in the beginning of the study period, grew at the rate of 1.95 per cent annually, resulting in its increased share of 52.63 per cent in 2013. In the services sector, the finance sub-sector experienced the highest growth of 7.93 per cent followed by transport and communication. It can be inferred from the findings that like many developing economies in South Africa, services in general and financial sector in particular has been in ascendancy over the last few years. The extent of the superior performance of services sector can be judged from the fact that in 2013, 52.63 per cent of value added came from the services sector alone.

Structural transformation of the Tanzanian economy followed a somewhat different pattern than other economies in the region. Tanzania and Botswana are the only two countries where manufacturing sector experienced a positive growth, although its share is not very high. The share in Tanzanian manufacturing changed from 8.38 to 10.58 per cent with annual growth rate of 1.11 per cent. Although the share of agriculture in Tanzania declined over the study period, the rate of decline is not very high (−1.36 per cent annually). Its share changed from 36.07 to 28.36 per cent. Similarly, services sector experienced a moderate growth rate of 0.18 per cent, resulting in its shift of share from 30.02 to 31.43 per cent. The findings suggest that although the share of services surpassed that of agriculture in 2013, the policies of government have been focussing on all the sectors and not giving up on agriculture totally; a phenomenon witnessed in Botswana and South Africa. Self-reliance in agriculture might have been a driving force behind such policy regime.

The above sub-section presented the analysis for the three major sectors of the sample economies. The following sub-section examines other sub-sectors such as mining, utilities and construction. It was not possible to include all the sectors in one graph as the variability of share of various sectors is very large. Table 2.1 presents the analysis.

It can be seen from the table that share of mining in Botswana, predominantly gold/diamond mining, dropped its share drastically from 41.57 to 17.16 per cent in 2013. It is clear from the data that structural transformation of the Botswana economy has been from mining to services sector. The decline in share of mining (−2.58 per cent) is similar to that of growth in services sector (2.66 per cent). It can be inferred that Botswana has witnessed growth largely in the services sector. Consequently, the share of value added was 50.17 per cent in 2013, resulting in similar structure to that of South Africa.

The Nigerian structural transformation is also worth highlighting. The share of mining, predominantly oil exploration, was 52.61 per cent in 1991 and declined sharply (−3.14 per cent annually) resulting in its share of just 28.17 per cent in 2013. The decline in mining transformed to positive growth in agriculture (2.66 per cent) and services (2.59 per cent). Hence, in 2013, the structure is balanced in agriculture, mining and services with the highest share of agriculture. The share of utilities and construction sectors remained unchanged in most of the economies.

Table 2.1 Shift of value-added share in mining, utilities and construction

Country	MIN_91	MIN_13	UTI_91	UTI_13	CON_91	CON_13
Botswana	41.57	17.16	1.28	1.29	8.88	7.59
Ghana	2.90	8.06	1.90	1.74	5.34	9.61
Kenya	0.64	0.58	2.64	2.08	5.10	5.41
Nigeria	52.61	28.17	0.13	0.14	1.53	2.30
South Africa	11.44	5.86	2.63	2.14	3.15	3.78
Tanzania	0.83	3.70	2.44	2.40	9.15	11.03

Source: Based on GGDC Structural Transformation Data

2.5.4 Employment

The shifts in employment due to structural transformation are presented and discussed in this sub-section. The shares of employment in various sectors of the sample economies are presented in Figure 2.5.

As noticed earlier, value added by agriculture in Botswana declined over the study period and so did the share of employment; but the rate of decline of employment (–0.27 per cent) is much lower than that of value added (–2.95 per cent). The sector's share in total employment (37.78 per cent) remained largest in Botswana in 2013. On the other hand, the services sector made tremendous success in value added, but employment in the sector grew at the rate of 1.83 per cent and remained second highest employer (35.20 per cent) in 2013. In the manufacturing sector, although value-added share grew at the rate of 0.27 per cent annually, employment grew at the rate of 1.19 per cent. Clearly the country's growth as with much of Africa has not followed conventional wisdom that predicts faster shift from agriculture to industry.

The scenario in Ghana is similar to that of Botswana. The sharp decline of employment in agriculture (–1.64 per cent) resulted in loss of its position as the largest employer (55.43 per cent in 1991) of the services sector in 2013. The services sector employment grew at the rate of 2.45 per cent and became largest employer (39.22 per cent) in 2013. Among services sub-sector, employment in "finance, insurance, real estate and business services" recorded the highest growth (8.48 per cent), followed by "trade, restaurants and hotels services" (5.10 per cent). The productivity analysis presented in Chapter 3 would reveal to what extent augmentation of productivity has led to increase in employment in services sector.

It can be seen from Figure 2.5 that the agriculture sector in Kenya remained the largest employer (45.68 per cent) in 2013, although the employment

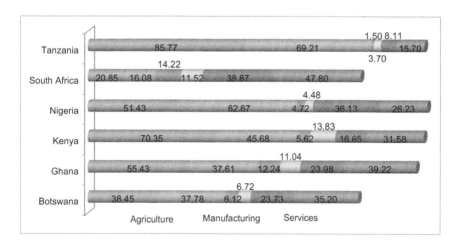

Figure 2.5 Change in employment share in main sectors (1991–2013)

Source: Figure is based on GGDC Structural Transformation Data.

declined at the rate of −1.92 per cent annually. At the same time, share of employment in manufacturing grew at the rate of 4.26 per cent and became triple in 2013 (13.83 per cent) to what it was in 1991 (5.62 per cent). Although employment share of services sector grew at the rate of 2.78 per cent, it remained as the second largest employer in 2013 (31.58 per cent). Within the services sector, "employment in trade, restaurants and hotels" and "transport, storage and communication services" achieved similar growth rate of 6.92 and 6.90 per cent respectively. The growth of employment in "finance, insurance, real estate and business services" has been moderate (3.26 per cent), a scenario different from many African countries.

Nigeria is the only sample economy where share of value added and employment in agriculture increased from 1991 to 2013. While the share of value-added growth is 2.66 per cent, the share of employment grew at the rate of 0.72 per cent resulting in its share of 62.67 per cent in 2013. The share of employment in other two sectors declined over the study period although the value-added share of services sector recorded positive growth rate. It can be inferred that productivity in agriculture and services increased, but the change was more rapid in services as the sector's value-added share increased, while employment share declined. It appears that the loss of employment in other sectors is compensated in agriculture, in fact, Nigeria is the only sample economy where the share of employment in services sector declined between 1991 and 2013.

Although value-added share of agriculture in South Africa is very small, the employment share was 20.85 per cent in 1991 and declined to 16.08 per cent in 2013. South Africa is another economy where employment share in manufacturing sector witnessed a negative growth rate of −0.43 per cent. The employment share of the services sector grew from 38.87 to 47.80 per cent in 2013 with annual growth rate of 1.05 per cent. The highest growth rate (5.22 per cent) was realized by "finance, insurance, real estate and business services" followed by "trade, restaurants and hotels services" (2.19 per cent).

In Tanzania, the agriculture sector emerged as the largest employer. Its share of employment changed from 85.77 to 69.21 per cent in 2013. The rate of decline in employment share in the sector was −1.06 per cent, whereas the employment share of the other two sectors recorded positive growth, that is manufacturing 4.97 per cent and services 3.28 per cent. Like other African economies, the employment in "finance, insurance, real estate and business services," "transport, storage and communication" and "trade, restaurants and hotels" grew at the rate of 10.56, 8.98 and 6.27 per cent, respectively. Although the services sector in Tanzania recorded a positive growth rate, its share in employment remained very low (15.70 per cent) in 2013.

The employment share in mining, utilities, and construction sectors are presented in Table 2.2. They are reported separately due to their low magnitude compared to other sectors.

Table 2.2 shows that despite the huge contribution of value added by mining share in Botswana, the employment share is very small. Similarly, the value-added share of Nigerian mining sector is very high, but employment share is less than

Table 2.2 Change in employment share in mining, utilities and construction (1991 to 2013)

Country	MIN_91	MIN_13	UTI_91	UTI_13	CON_91	CON_13
Botswana	2.96	1.81	1.43	0.51	12.90	2.20
Ghana	0.99	2.89	0.39	0.36	1.65	3.30
Kenya	0.09	0.71	0.32	0.18	1.46	3.17
Nigeria	0.29	0.28	0.42	0.26	1.03	1.95
South Africa	8.44	1.76	1.03	0.52	5.28	7.12
Tanzania	0.52	0.74	0.10	0.56	0.67	1.64

Source: Based on GGDC Structural Transformation Data

1 per cent, indicating that oil exploration is capital intensive and does not contribute much to employment. This could have been one of the reasons for sharp decline of value-added share in Nigeria. Apparently, Nigerian government paid more attention to the agriculture sector with twin objectives, that is self-reliance in agriculture and creation of mass employment.

2.5.5 *Comparative analysis of African economies*

On comparing the value-added share by various sectors in Africa, it was found that the pattern is not uniform across the region. For instance, the share of agriculture is very small (2.59 per cent in 2013) in Botswana and South Africa (2.55 per cent in 2013), while it is 39.72 per cent in Nigeria. The share of agriculture declined in all the countries except Nigeria, where it recorded a positive growth rate (2.66 per cent) during the sample period. In other economies, the value added declined from 1991 to 2013, although the rate of decline varied from one country to another. For instance, decline in Kenya was –1.92 per cent, whereas it was –1.36 in Tanzania. Statistically, decline is highest in Botswana (–2.95 per cent) but may not be assigned much importance as value-added share is very small.

The value-added share of the manufacturing sector in Botswana and Tanzania recorded a positive growth of 0.27 and 1.11 per cent respectively, whereas in other economies, the sector has witnessed a negative growth rate. They are Ghana (–1.40), Kenya (–0.71), Nigeria (–0.68) and South Africa (–0.70). The analysis suggests that rate of decline in manufacturing is less, compared to that in agriculture for several economies.

On the other hand, the services sector witnessed a positive growth rate in all the sample economies. Botswana is the only country where value-added share of services sector exceeded 50 per cent (50.17 per cent) in 2013. In fact, Botswana recorded the highest growth rate of 2.66 per cent in the sector, while the lowest was recorded in Tanzania (0.18 per cent). In 1991, the value-added share of mining was fairly large in Botswana and Nigeria but declined very sharply in 2013. The rate of decline was –2.58 and –3.14 per cent, respectively. The shares of employment in other sectors such as mining, utilities and construction are not very large, and they remained more or less static over the study period in all the economies.

As far as the shares of employment in the main sectors are concerned, they are not proportionate with value-added share, although they follow the same trend. For instance, value-added share in agriculture was very low in Botswana (2.59 per cent) and South Africa (2.55 per cent) in 2013, while share of employment was large, that is 37.78 per cent in Botswana and 16.08 per cent in South Africa in the same year. In other economies, the share of employment is much higher than the share of value added. It can be inferred that the sector cannot be totally neglected as it provides substantial employment.

On the other hand, value-added share of services sector is more, compared to agriculture, but the share of employment has been far less. Another distinguishing aspect of the sector is that except for Nigeria (−1.18 per cent), the share of employment registered a positive growth in all other countries. The annual growth rates are South Africa (1.05), Botswana (1.83), Ghana (2.45), Kenya (2.78) and Tanzania (3.28). From the analyses, the services sector, while being relatively low in productivity in African economies, could be a promising one for youth employment if sustainably managed, the sector has huge potential for expansion by creating new services. New technologies led by information and communication technologies have the ability to create new services in every sphere of life. Equipped with proper skills and training, today's youth is capable of creating and managing these services. Governments need to focus their policies towards proper training and skill formation in youths. Consequently, employment in the services sector has room to grow on the back of an industrializing Africa.

The growth and presence of the manufacturing sector in the region is very limited. As a result, the share of employment is very low compared to other sectors. Except Kenya, the share of employment remained static during the study period. In Kenya, it changed from 5.62 to 13.83 per cent. The employment share in construction sector changed from 12.90 to 2.20 per cent, while mining in South Africa witnessed shift of employment share from 8.44 to 1.76 per cent.

In summary, Africa has suffered largely from structural unemployment, a specific form of the problem of lack of demand. In Africa, the absence of the industrial sector means there is a lack of demand for industrial skills. Our analysis reveals deep-seated obstacles or inefficiencies in African urban labour markets, such as a mismatch between the characteristics of labour demand and supply in terms of necessary skill-sets. It may result from shifts in the composition of urban economies from industry to services, or from low-skilled to highly skilled occupations, and may require a combination of demand and supply-side policy responses.

2.6   Asian economies

The analysis of this section covers seven Asian economies, namely China, India, Indonesia, Malaysia, Philippines, Sri Lanka and Thailand. GGDC data were not available up to 2013 for all the countries. Hence, in cases of non-availability of up to 2013, data for remaining years were extrapolated using growth rates of available years. The extrapolation exercise was limited to one or two years in any country.

2.6.1 *Value added*

This section presents shift of value-added share of various sectors in the economy. The analysis of all Asian sample countries is presented in Figure 2.6. The figure shows the shift of value added share from 1991 to 1993 in agriculture, manufacturing and services. The data for Sri Lanka were taken from World Development Indicator (WDI) online. This database is incompatible with GGDC in the sense that it provides data for industry as a whole and not component-wise. Therefore, analysis of Sri Lanka may be treated as industry rather than manufacturing. Another difference for Sri Lanka is that the data were taken up to 2010 rather than 2013 due to data limitation. Figure 2.6 depicts value added by main sectors in sample countries for 1991 and 2013.

It can be seen from the figure that the agriculture sector in China experienced a drastic change in terms of value added. Its contribution shifted from 30.21 in 1991 to 7.64 per cent in 2013. On the other hand, the contribution of the manufacturing sector increased from 22.29 to 38.65 per cent in the same period. Services sector followed a similar trend to that of manufacturing by shifting its share from 28.48 to 31.11 per cent during 1991 to 2013. In terms of annual change of value-added share, agriculture, manufacturing and services sectors witnessed annual change of –5.82, 1.90 and 0.53 per cent, respectively.

The share of agriculture in India (30.58 per cent) was almost similar to that of China in 1991, which shifted to 14.80 per cent in 2013, resulting in less annual decline compared to China. The manufacturing sector's share was 16.56 per cent

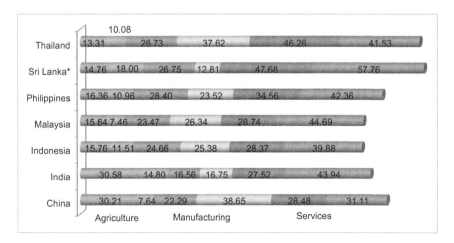

Figure 2.6 Shift of value-added share in main sectors (1991 to 2013)

Source: Figure is based on GGDC Structural Transformation Data; * Based on WDI online.

in 1991 and did not change much in 2013 (16.75 per cent). The value addition in Indian manufacturing sector could not keep pace with the Chinese counterpart that experienced a huge shift. As far as the services sector is concerned, the performance of India has been much better than that of China. Its value-added share shifted from 27.52 to 43.94 per cent during the sample period. Clearly, India seems to have focussed on services, while China concentrated more on the manufacturing sector. The annual change of value added in Indian agriculture, manufacturing and services sectors has been –3.58, –0.08 and 2.30 per cent respectively.

Indonesia followed similar trend to that of India. The share of agriculture declined from 15.76 to 11.51 per cent, while manufacturing sector share remained almost unchanged (24.66 in 1991 and 25.38 per cent in 2013). The share of services sector (28.37 per cent in 1991) was similar to that of China and changed with higher pace resulting in 39.88 per cent in 2013, suggesting that Indonesia followed a middle path compared to India and China with respect to focus on services sector. The value-added shares of agriculture and manufacturing declined at the rate of –0.94 and –0.20 per cent annually, while the services sector experienced a positive growth rate of 1.57 per cent annually.

Although the direction of shift of agriculture share in Malaysia followed a similar trend to that of Indonesia, its rate of change is very high. Agriculture share declined from 15.64 in 1991 to 7.46 per cent in 2013 resulting in –3.04 per cent decline annually. On the other hand, services sector made a big leap from its share of 28.74 to 44.69 per cent during the same period. In fact, services sector share became highest among all the sample countries in 2013. The annual growth of the service sector share was 1.74 per cent. As far as the share of the Malaysian manufacturing sector is concerned, it moderately changed from 23.47 to 26.34 per cent. Again, the services sector has been prominent in Malaysia.

The structural transformation of the Filipino economy has been different from that of other sample countries. For example, the share of agricultural sector followed a similar trend to that of the other Asian countries. It declined from 16.36 to 10.96 per cent during the study period, whereas share of manufacturing sector declined from 28.40 to 23.52 per cent, accounting for –0.92 per cent annual rate of decline, a trend different from other countries. The share of the services sector changed from 34.56 to 42.36 per cent, increasing annually at the rate of 1.16 per cent. Thus, the decline of share of manufacturing could be attributed to evolving dominance of the services sector.

From the figure, the share of agriculture in Sri Lanka increased from 14.76 to 18.00 per cent, a trend very different from India and China. Surprisingly, the share of industry declined from 26.75 in 1991 to 12.81 per cent in 2013. On the one hand, the growth of GDP per capita is comparable with many developing economies. Services sector share increased from 47.68 to 57.76 per cent. The pattern of growth of the Sri Lankan economy shows striking similarity to that of a number of African countries whereby stagnating industry and like the case of South Africa, premature de-industrialization is accompanied by an equally premature rise of the services sector that is largely of a low-productivity kind.

Clearly, the value-added share of services sector is the highest among sample Asian economies for Sri Lanka.

Thailand witnessed a type of structural change which is different from the other Asian countries. As far as the agriculture sector is concerned, Thai trend is similar to that of other sample countries. The share of agriculture declined from 13.31 to 10.08 per cent experiencing marginal rate of change of –0.87 per cent. The manufacturing sector share witnessed positive change from 26.73 to 37.62 per cent with annual rate of change being 1.74 per cent. However, the trend, followed by Thai services sector, is very different from other sample countries. It experienced a declining trend from 46.26 in 1991 to 41.53 per cent in 2013, with annual rate of –0.70 per cent. Apparently, Thailand found itself more competitive in manufacturing than services and hence concentrated on manufacturing rather than services sector. The productivity analysis chapter would reveal more on this aspect.

Figure 2.7 presents analysis of other sectors, namely, mining, utilities and construction. It was not possible to include these sectors in Figure 2.4, as magnitude of their share is very small compared to the main sectors. Hence, these sectors are analysed separately. It can be seen from the figure that in China, the share of these sectors has remained almost unchanged, although the share of construction is higher than the other two sectors. The trend in India is different from that of China as far as mining and utility sectors are concerned, the share of these sectors declined, although marginally. The mining sector in Indonesia and Malaysia had a fairly high share in 1991 (16.52 and 18.68 per cent respectively) but declined at the same pace, resulting in 9.87 and 8.60 per cent in 2013, respectively. The lack of productivity augmentation could be the main reason behind such a drastic drop in value-added share.

Philippines and Thailand also witnessed a declining trend in the mining sector, although the share of this sector in both countries is very small. Another

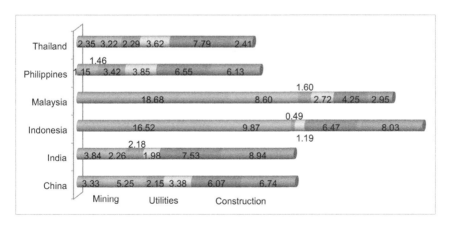

Figure 2.7 Shift of value-added share in mining, utilities and construction

Source: Figure is based on GGDC Structural Transformation Data

noticeable fact is that in Thailand, share of construction sector declined very sharply from 7.79 to 2.41 per cent in 2013.

2.6.2   Employment

Figure 2.8 presents the shift of employment share in various sectors of the sample economies. It can be seen from the figure that in most of the economies, share of employment in agriculture was very high in 1991, but declined sharply. For instance, in China, it declined from 59.24 to 26.86 per cent in 2013. On the other hand, services sector experienced a positive growth from 14.57 to 32.60 per cent in 2013, surpassing the employment share even in agriculture. In fact, services sector became the highest employer in 2013.

Employment share in India followed similar trend to that of China, but the rate of change is not comparable. Although the share of employment in agriculture declined from 66.97 to 45.64 per cent during the sample period, the sector remained the largest employer in 2013. Similarly, the services sector employment grew at the rate of 2.13 per cent, resulting in its share of 23.24 per cent in 2013. The employment in manufacturing sector almost remained static during the study period. It can therefore be inferred that focus of the Indian economy changed from agriculture to services, but could not match the rate of transformation of China.

The structural transformation of Indonesia with respect to employment was similar to that of China. In fact, employment in services sector has grown at a faster rate than China, resulting in being highest employer (36.38 per cent share) in 2013, whereas the share of employment in the Malaysian services sector was highest (34.70 per cent) in 1991 and increased to 45.64 per cent in 2013. On the other hand, share of employment in other two sectors in Malaysia declined. The

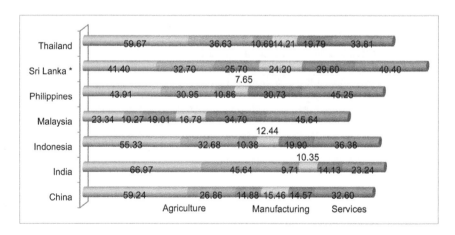

Figure 2.8 Change in employment share in main sectors (1991 to 2013)

Source: Figure is based on GGDC Structural Transformation Data; * Based on WDI online.

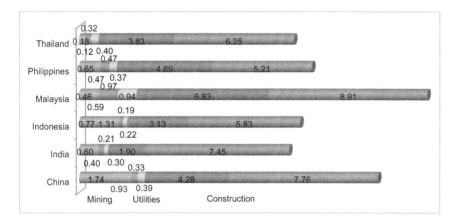

Figure 2.9 Change in employment share in mining, utilities and construction (1991 to 2013)

Source: Figure is based on GGDC Structural Transformation Data.

agriculture sector experienced the sharpest decline (–2.71 per cent). In Philippines, the services sector experienced highest growth of 1.80 per cent resulting in 45.25 per cent employment share; highest among all the sectors in the country, while the employment share in agriculture declined almost at the same rate (–1.48 per cent), leading to employment share of 30.95 per cent in 2013.

The share of employment in Sri Lanka followed a similar trend to that of China. The services and industry sectors experienced positive growth (1.01 and 1.07 per cent, respectively). It is worth mentioning that employment share of industry in 1991 was 25.70, but sharply declined to 19.40 in 1992, and has been on the rise since, leading to positive growth during 1991 and 2010. The shift in employment through structural transformation in Thailand followed a similar pattern to that of India, suggesting that the agriculture sector is the largest employer even in 2013. Figure 2.9 presents the employment structural transformation in mining, utilities and construction sectors.

From the figure, the construction sector experienced major employment change in China and India, but remained static in other countries. In fact, in India, employment share in construction changed from 1.90 to 7.45 per cent in 2013, while in China, the rate of change was relatively slower. The share of employment in mining and utilities compared to other sectors is very small.

2.6.3   Comparative analysis of Asian economies

In general, structural transformation in the region is marked by decline in share of value added in agriculture and increase in share of services, with few exceptions, such as Sri Lanka, where share of value added in agriculture also increased at the cost of industry. Thailand is another exception in the sense that the share of services sector declined from 46.26 to 41.53 per cent in 2013. However, the rate of change of shares varies among economies. For instance, in China, annual rate of decline of agriculture was –5.82 per cent, while in other economies, it was around –3.00 per cent. Similarly, the growth of services sector is not uniform across sample countries. For instance, share of Indian service sector grew at the rate of 2.30 per cent annually, while in other economies, it was around 1.50 per cent. The potential to augment labour productivity in a particular sector might have one reason to increase its share and opportunities in other sectors.

In the case of China, the transformation followed the classical route with continuous shifts from agriculture to industry to services and as such demand for skills in manufacturing ensured that the significant supply of educated graduates had jobs due to the ample opportunities in manufacturing and services sectors. Consequently, youth in the country found employment in the modern sectors and left behind the agricultural sector. In the Indian context, similar pattern was followed, but structural change is different from that of China. The major reason could be the lack of appropriate human development and economic policies. For augmenting productivity and generating employment in any sector, commensurable skill formation is extremely critical. It seems that India lacked appropriate skill, and consequently, the performance of services and manufacturing sectors have not met the potential. Similar argument is valid for other economies as well. In summary, while structural transformation is caused by several factors, a most important factor for the changes is rising productivity of the workforce. The productivity aspect of structural change is discussed and analysed in the following chapter of the book.

As far as the share of employment is concerned, the agricultural sector is found to be the major employment provider in all the economies, although its share in value added declined drastically over time. For instance, in China, share of value added of agriculture in 2013 was 7.64 per cent, while share of employment in the sector was 26.86 per cent. A similar situation persists in all the sample countries, except Malaysia, where shares of value added (7.46 per cent) and employment (10.27 per cent) in agriculture were almost identical.

The services sector has emerged the highest employer in all the sample economies, with the exception of India and Thailand, where the agriculture sector still leads. This might well be where the actual opportunities for the youth lie. With appropriate training and skill development, youth can be employed in various services sector activities. Keeping in mind the potential of the services sector, the Singaporean government has been encouraging youth to go for services sector training programmes rather than aspire to additional higher education degrees. New technologies led by information and communications technologies have also created significant opportunities in this sector. New technologies play an important role in quality of services. The countries need to tap the potentials of the services sector and focus on skill creation for youths.

The share of employment in manufacturing sector has almost been static in all the economies, suggesting limited opportunities for job creation in the sector. The manufacturing sector over the years has become capital and skill intensive, while automation has reduced employment opportunities. Although the employment share of the sector is comparatively low, value-added share is quite high. For instance, in China, employment share is just 14.57 per cent in 2013, while value-added share is 38.65 per cent. The scenario in Thailand is similar to that of China. Sri Lanka is the only one among sample economies to employ 24.20 per cent workforce, while in others, the employment share is around 10 per cent.

The comparative analysis of shares of value added and employment suggests that share of agriculture has declined and share of services sector increased over the sample period. The impact of this pattern of structural transformation on urbanization and industrialization will be analysed in relevant chapters.

2.7   Latin American economies

The six Latin American (LA) economies included in the study are – Argentina, Bolivia, Brazil, Colombia, Mexico and Venezuela. As earlier, two aspects of the structural change, that is value added and employment in various sectors of the economies, are discussed.

2.7.1   *Value added*

This section presents shift of value-added share of various sectors in the sample economies. The analysis of all LA countries is presented in Figure 2.10. It indicates the shift of value-added share from 1991 to 2013 in agriculture, manufacturing and services. The figure depicts value added by main sectors in sample countries from 1991 to 2013.

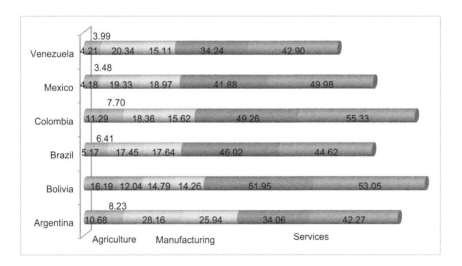

Figure 2.10 Shift of value-added share in main sectors (1991 to 2013)

Source: Figure is based on GGDC Structural Transformation Data.

It can be seen from the figure that performance in the agriculture sector changed marginally in terms of value added. Although its contribution in the sample countries did not change much from 1991 to 2013, Argentina, Bolivia, Colombia and Mexico indicate a decreasing trend. The contribution of the manufacturing sector across the countries also remained almost the same in the sample period. On the other hand, the services sector shows an increasing trend in Argentina, Bolivia, Colombia, Mexico and Venezuela. Brazil experienced a slight decrease in trend during the same period.

Share of agriculture in the sample countries except Bolivia indicates that it does not contribute much to the economy. In Argentina, 10.68 per cent share in 1991 declined to 8.23 per cent in 2013. Manufacturing sector share declined from 28.16 to 25.94 per cent, contributing significantly to the economy. As far as the services sector is concerned, the performance of Argentina was fairly good, its value-added share shifted from 34.06 to 42.27 per cent during the sample period, with annual growth rate of 0.74 per cent, thus suggesting that Argentina focussed on services sector. The annual rate of decline of value added in agriculture and manufacturing sectors was –0.49 and –0.53, respectively.

Bolivia concentrated more on the manufacturing sector than agriculture, the share of which experienced a slight decline from 16.19 to 12.04 per cent. At the same time, the manufacturing sector share remained almost unchanged (14.79 per cent in 1991 and 14.26 in 2013). On the other hand, the share of the services sector (51.95 per cent) was highest among the sample countries in 1991, but changed to 53.05 per cent in 2013. The annual growth rate in manufacturing and services sectors has been marginal, while the share of agriculture declined annually at the rate of –0.93 per cent.

Unlike Argentina and Bolivia, direction of shift of agriculture share in Brazil is slow but positive. It did not experience drastic change in any of the sectors during this period. Agriculture share grew from 5.17 in 1991 to 6.41 per cent in 2013, resulting in 1.05 per cent change annually. On the other hand, the services sector saw a decline of its share from 46.02 to 44.62 per cent during the same period. The annual decline of services sector share was –0.15 per cent. As far as the share of Brazilian manufacturing sector is concerned, it remained almost stagnant at around 17.50 per cent. The annual shift in share of manufacturing sector was positive at 0.27 per cent.

The structural transformation in Colombia has been almost similar to Argentina. As far as the share of agriculture sector is concerned, it declined from 11.29 to 7.70 per cent during the study period, and share of manufacturing sector also declined from 18.36 to 15.62 per cent, a trend similar to Argentina. The annual rates of decline in agriculture and manufacturing sectors were –1.21 and –0.35 per cent, respectively. The services sector share on the other hand showed positive change from 49.26 to 55.33 per cent; it increased annually at the rate of 0.44 per cent. Noticeable fact is that more than half of the value added comes from this sector alone, a unique distinction the country enjoys among other economies of the region. The decline of share of agriculture and manufacturing could be attributed to increased focus on the services sector.

It can be seen from the figure that Mexican economy showed similar trend as Bolivia. The share of agriculture in Mexico dropped from 4.18 to 3.48 per cent, a trend very similar to several sample LA countries. The share of manufacturing also declined from 19.33 in 1991 to 18.97 per cent in 2013. The rate of decline was −0.50 per cent in agriculture and −0.21 per cent in manufacturing. On the other hand, services sector share increased from 41.88 to 49.98 per cent, with annual growth of 0.85 per cent. On comparing the contribution of services sector, it can be seen that value-added share of the sector is very close to 50 per cent, a trend similar to that of Colombia and Bolivia.

Venezuela witnessed a structural change different from other sample countries. Agriculture sector recorded a decline of −0.13 per cent annually, with a marginal decrease from 4.21 to 3.99 per cent. As far as the manufacturing sector is concerned, its share has been fluctuating over the sample period with an overall declining rate of −1.32 per cent, with its share of 20.34 per cent in 1991 and 15.11 per cent in 2013. On the other hand, the trend followed by the Venezuelan services sector is very similar to other sample countries. It experienced a positive change from 34.24 in 1991 to 42.90 per cent in 2013, with annual growth rate of 1.53 per cent. Apparently, Venezuela concentrated more on services rather than agriculture and manufacturing sectors.

Table 2.3 presents analysis of other sectors, namely, mining, utilities and construction. These sectors have been analysed separately as their share magnitude is very small. It can be seen from the figure that in Argentina, the share of these sectors almost remained unchanged. Although the share of construction sector has marginally improved compared to the other two sectors. The trend of the Bolivian economy is different from that of Argentina, as the mining sector has much greater share than utilities and construction. The Brazilian economy had experienced negligible change as far as the shares of mining, utilities and construction are concerned. Colombia experienced increasing trend in mining sector and stagnant in construction, but decline in utility shares.

Mexico shows a declining trend in mining, while stagnant in utilities and construction. The slight decrease in the mining sector in Venezuela is highly

Table 2.3 Change in value-added share in mining, utilities and construction (1991–2013)

Country	MIN_91	MIN_13	UTI_91	UTI_13	CON_91	CON_13
Argentina	5.54	4.26	1.27	1.76	4.74	5.58
Bolivia	11.28	13.86	2.66	3.33	3.13	3.50
Brazil	2.20	2.84	3.66	4.37	6.12	5.79
Colombia	8.22	9.70	5.25	4.31	7.63	7.45
Mexico	8.78	6.64	1.31	1.88	7.84	7.34
Venezuela	29.94	26.41	1.16	1.46	10.11	10.28

Source: Based on GGDC Structural Transformation Data

noticeable as it changed from 29.94 per cent in 1991 to 26.41 per cent in 2013. Although mining share has declined, it is still very high as compared to other sample economies. Mining sector in Venezuela is largely represented by oil exploration activities. The construction and utilities sectors indicate a stagnant trend.

2.7.2 Employment

Figure 2.11 depicts the shift of employment share in various sectors of sample LA economies. It can be seen from the figure that in most of the economies, the share of employment in agriculture was high in 1991, but declined sharply afterwards.

The employment share of agriculture in Argentina declined sharply (−2.99 per cent) from 11.15 to 6.03 per cent in 2013, and manufacturing sector share declined at the rate of −1.94 per cent resulting in its share of 11.47 in 2013. At the same time, services sector share witnessed a positive growth of 0.54 per cent. Consequently, services sector had a share of 48.94 per cent in 2013. It appears that Argentina has paid more attention to services sector resulting in nearly half of the employment from it.

Bolivia has experienced the largest change in employment shares. For instance, share of agriculture declined from 44.27 to 15.90 per cent in 2013 with annual declining rate of −4.34 per cent. On the other hand, services sector experienced a positive growth (2.25 per cent) from 37.78 to 61.76 per cent in 2013. It is evident that the services sector emerged as the highest employer in 2013, contradicting the notion that agriculture sector provides maximum employment in developing countries. Among the services sector, "trade, restaurants and hotels,"

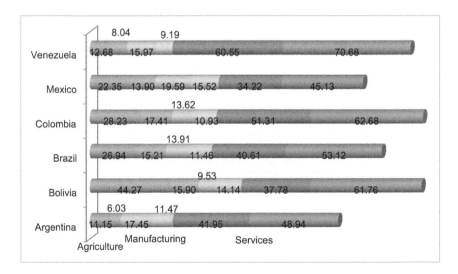

Figure 2.11 Shift of employment share in main sectors (1991 to 2013)

Source: Figure is based on GGDC Structural Transformation Data.

and "finance, insurance, real estate and business services" recorded the growth of employment at the rate of 6.97 and 6.15 per cent respectively.

Similarly, services sector employment in Brazil grew from 40.61 in base year to 53.12 per cent in 2013 with annual growth rate of 1.13 per cent. The positive growth of employment in services sector has been at the cost of employment in agriculture and manufacturing sectors. Employment share in both the sectors declined at the rate of –2.63 and –0.38 per cent, respectively. It is clear from the analysis that Brazil also focussed its policies more towards services sector. Labour productivity might have also played a role in this type of structural shift, which will be discussed in the following chapter.

The structural transformation of Colombia with respect to employment has been similar to that of Bolivia. The share of employment in agriculture declined from 28.23 per cent to 17.41 per cent in 2013, while services sector share increased from 51.31 per cent to 62.68 per cent with an annual growth rate of 1.06 per cent. The share of manufacturing declined slightly from 13.62 per cent to 10.93 per cent. Noteworthy fact from the analysis is that more than 50 per cent was coming from services sector in 1991, which increased to 62.68 per cent, suggesting that services sector provided plenty of opportunities for youth in Colombia. The results show that with proper policy regime and appropriate training and skill development, the services sector has the potential to provide large-scale employment.

Although share of services sector employment in Mexico grew during the study period, the pace (1.26 per cent) was lower than that of Bolivia. It increased from 34.22 per cent in 1991 to 45.13 per cent in 2013. On the other hand, share of employment in the other two sectors declined. The agriculture sector experienced the sharpest decline (–2.34 per cent), while the manufacturing sector's declining rate was –1.18 per cent.

The share of employment in Venezuela followed the similar trend as that of Bolivia in the services sector. The agriculture and manufacturing sectors experienced negative trends, –2.13 and –2.22 per cent, respectively. It may be worth mentioning that employment share of manufacturing in 1991 was 15.97, but sharply declined to 9.19 in 2013. The employment structural transformation in services increased from 60.55 in 1991 to 70.68 in 2013. Noticeable fact is that almost two-thirds of the total employment came from the services sector alone. Within the services sector, "transport, storage and communication," and "trade, restaurants and hotels" recorded an impressive growth rate of 5.93 and 3.67 per cent respectively. The services sector employment in Venezuela is a case in point to visualise the potential of employment in the sector.

Table 2.4 presents the employment structural transformation in mining, utilities and construction sectors of these economies. It is presented and discussed separately due to the same reasons mentioned earlier.

From Table 2.4, it can be seen that the construction sector experienced major employment change in Bolivia and Mexico, but remained almost static in other countries. In fact, in Bolivia, employment share in construction changed from 5.35 to 10.39 per cent in 2013, while in Colombia, the rate of change has been

Table 2.4 Change in employment share in mining, utilities and construction (1991–2013)

Country	MIN_91	MIN_13	UTI_91	UTI_13	CON_91	CON_13
Argentina	0.39	0.73	0.85	0.82	6.83	8.01
Bolivia	2.81	0.73	0.26	0.26	5.35	10.39
Brazil	0.44	0.30	0.61	0.36	6.58	8.07
Colombia	1.56	2.58	0.34	0.27	4.95	6.81
Mexico	0.85	0.42	0.65	0.34	7.14	9.64
Venezuela	1.47	3.45	1.02	0.55	8.31	8.47

Source: Based on GGDC Structural Transformation Data

slower. The share of employment in mining and utilities is very small compared to other sectors. The employment share (3.45 per cent) of mining in Venezuela in 2013 is not in proportion with that of value added (26.41 per cent), suggesting that oil exploration did not contribute much to employment.

2.7.3   *Comparative analysis of LA economies*

Comparative analysis of value added share in LA suggests that contribution of agriculture is very small and has a declining trend, except in Brazil, where it marginally increased at the annual growth rate of 1.05 per cent. Bolivia had the largest share (12.04 per cent) in agriculture in 2013. It can be inferred from the findings that LA economies have moved away from agriculture. As far as manufacturing value-added share is concerned, it has decreased in Argentina, Colombia, Mexico and Venezuela, while it remained stagnant in Bolivia and Brazil. In Argentina, the sector's share is almost one-fourth, while in other economies, it ranges from 14.26 per cent in Bolivia to 18.97 per cent in Mexico.

The growth of the services sector share is not uniform across all countries, although it has witnessed a positive growth in all the countries except Brazil, while stagnant in Bolivia. Venezuela recorded the highest annual growth rate of 1.53 per cent. The growth rate was 0.74 in Argentina, 1.06 in Colombia and 1.26 per cent in Mexico. It is worth mentioning that value-added share of services sector in Bolivia and Colombia is more than fifty per cent, that is 53.05 and 55.33 per cent respectively in 2013. In Mexico also, it has increased to 49.98 per cent in the same year. The share of mining sector in Venezuela was highest (29.94 per cent in 1991) among sample countries and retained its position in 2013 at 26.41 per cent. In the construction sector also, it retained its highest share.

The employment share in agriculture saw a decline in all the sample countries of LA. The highest decline was experienced in Bolivia (–4.43 per cent) and lowest in Venezuela (–0.13 per cent). The declining rate in other countries are Argentina (–2.99), Brazil (–2.63), Colombia (–2.22) and Mexico (–2.34). The decline in employment share is in proportion to that of value added, except in Brazil, where despite the decline in employment, value-added share has increased suggesting that the productivity in the sector has gone up.

The share of employment in manufacturing sector witnessed a negative trend in all the sample countries except Bolivia, where it grew at the rate of 1.81 per cent. It appears that the loss of employment in agriculture in Bolivia has been compensated with the increase in employment in manufacturing. It can therefore be inferred that Bolivia paid more attention to manufacturing compared to agriculture. The declining rate in other countries are Argentina (–1.94), Brazil (–0.38), Colombia (–0.96), Mexico (–1.18) and Venezuela (–1.32).

All the countries in LA witnessed an increase in employment share in the services sector. The rate of increase is highest in Bolivia (2.25 per cent) and lowest in Argentina (0.54 per cent). The annual growth rates in other countries are Brazil (1.13), Colombia (1.06), Mexico (1.26) and Venezuela (1.53). It can be inferred that the services sector has the potential to provide employment to youth in developing economies. To create employment in the sector, the governments need to provide training and develop appropriate skills to enable them to utilize the opportunities created by the sector. For creation of employment in the sector, the role of new technologies must be kept in mind because services are catered predominantly in online mode. Therefore, while providing training, focus has to be on new technologies.

2.8   Summary and conclusion

The structural change measured on a 100-point scale in African economies are Botswana (12.40), Ghana (8.44), Kenya (6.41), Nigeria (25.11), South Africa (12.45), Tanzania (1.88) and Uganda (33.32); whereas, CAGR of GDP per capita were 2.98, 2.88, 0.76, 3.65, 1.38, 2.74 and 3.57 per cent, respectively. On the other hand, compound annual growths of employment were Botswana (2.18), Ghana (2.61), Kenya (3.50), Nigeria (2.58), South Africa (1.33) and Tanzania (3.01). It is clear that structural change is directly proportional to growth of wealth. For instance, the structural change (6.41) is second lowest in Kenya, and the GDP growth is also lowest (0.76 per cent), while Uganda experienced highest structural change (33.32) and highest GDP growth rate (3.57 per cent). Therefore, it can be inferred that structural change has contributed to wealth creation significantly, and relationship between the two is linearly positive. As far as employment is concerned, the association with structural change is not straight forward. For instance, structural change (1.88) in Tanzania was lowest, while employment has recorded second highest growth rate (3.01) per cent. On the other hand, Kenya witnessed highest employment growth (3.50 per cent), but experienced second lowest structural change. In other economies, the employment growth was around 2.5 per cent, except in South Africa, which experienced lowest employment growth of 1.33 per cent. From the results, we find that while structural change contributes to wealth creation, it does not necessarily guarantee employment creation.

The pattern of structural change in Asian economies were China (17.19), India (17.48), Indonesia (8.86), Malaysia (14.05), Philippines (9.76), Sri Lanka

(16.85) and Thailand (15.82), and GDP per capita grew at the rate of 9.24, 5.19, 2.68, 2.99, 2.55, 4.39 and 2.84, respectively. The growth of employment was the following: China (0.80), India (1.65), Indonesia (1.40), Malaysia (2.48), Philippines (2.47) and Thailand (1.20). It can be noticed that variability of structural change in Asian economies is not very high. Most of the economies witnessed the change around 16 point on a 100-point scale, although GDP per capita grew from 2.25 per cent in Philippines to 9.24 per cent in China. The variability in wealth creation is much higher compared to structural change. Hence it can be argued that the contribution of structural change to wealth creation has not been uniform in Asian economies. As far as the employment scenario is concerned, the data show that it has been a jobless growth in China as it recorded very impressive GDP growth, but employment has been almost stagnant. On the other hand, Malaysia and Philippines succeeded in creating employment and GDP growth despite the lower structural change compared to other economies.

Latin American countries experienced structural change with Argentina (14.22), Bolivia (13.11), Brazil (9.72), Colombia (13.83), Mexico (14.22), and Venezuela (34.92). The GDP per capita grew at the following rates: Argentina (2.20), Bolivia (1.80), Brazil (1.89), Colombia (1.79), Mexico (1.15) and Venezuela (0.58), CAGR of employment rates were the following: Argentina (2.25), Bolivia (2.94), Brazil (2.03), Colombia (2.75), Mexico (2.68) and Venezuela (2.80). The structural change in Latin American economies was around 13 in most of the countries, except Venezuela, where it was 34.92. Venezuela recorded such a large change in structural change due to substantial decline of mining and manufacturing sectors. Consequently, growth of GDP was very low (0.58 per cent). It can be seen from the data that the association between structural change and employment creation is positive. For instance, Brazil experienced lowest structural change (9.72), and growth rate of employment was also lowest (2.03 per cent) while in Venezuela, it was second highest (2.80 per cent) with highest structural change (34.92). The relationship between structural change and wealth creation is not straight forward. It appears that structural change in Latin American economies led to greater employment creation rather than growth of wealth.

Bibliography

Ackah-Baidoo, Patricia (2016). "Youth unemployment in resource-rich Sub-Saharan Africa: A critical review." *The Extractive Industries and Society*, vol. 3(1): 249–261.

African Economic Outlook (AEO) (2012). "Promoting Youth Employment," online, available at http://www.africaneconomicoutlook.org/en/theme/youth_employ ment/education-skills-mismatch/ (accessed on March 12, 2016).

Anyawu, J. C. and Augustine, D. (2012). "Towards Inclusive African Labor Market: Empirical Analysis of Gender Equality in Employment and Its Implications for Policy," online, available at afdb.org/fileadmin/uploads/afdb/Documents/Knowledge/ (accessed on March 31, 2016).

Asia Development Bank (ADB) (2012). "Youth Employment in Asia: 12 Things to Know," online, available at http://www.adb.org/features/12-things-know-2012-youth-employment (accessed on March 14, 2016).

Asia Development Bank (ADB) (2013). "Youth Employment and Skills Development in Asia and the Pacific: By the Numbers," online, available at http://www.adb.org/features/youth-employment-and-skills-development-asia-and-pacific-numbers (accessed on March 13, 2016).

Barsoum, Ghada (2015). "Striving for job security: The lived experience of employment informality among educated youth in Egypt." *International Journal of Sociology and Social Policy*, vol. 35(5/6): 340–358.

Barton, D., Farrell, D. and Mourshed, M. (2013). "Education to Employment: Designing a System That Works," McKinsey Center for Government.

Brixiová, Zuzana, Ncube, Mthuli and Bicaba, Zorobabel (2015). "Skills and youth entrepreneurship in Africa: Analysis with evidence from Swaziland." *World Development*, vol. 67: 11–26.

Calvès, Anne-Emmanuèle and Schoumaker, Bruno (2004). "Deteriorating economic context and changing patterns of youth employment in urban Burkina Faso: 1980–2000." *World Development*, vol. 32(8): 1341–1354.

Cooke, Fang Lee (2001). "Equal opportunity? The role of legislation and public policies in women's employment in China." *Women in Management Review*, vol. 16(7): 334–348.

Economist, The (2012). "Education in South Africa still dysfunctional: Standards still leave a lot to be desired." January 21st 2012.

International Labour Office (ILO) (2008). "Employment for Social Justice and A Fair Globalization: Overview of ILO programmes," online, available at http://www.ilo.org/wcmsp5/groups/public/@ed_emp/documents/publication/wcms_140957.pdf (accessed on March 15, 2016).

International Labour Organization (ILO) (2011). *Key Indicators of the Labour Market (KILM)*. Geneva: ILO.

International Labour Organization (ILO) (2014). "100 Million Women in Latin America's Labour Force," online, available at http://www.ilo.org/global/about-the-ilo/newsroom/comment-analysis/WCMS_237488/lang—en/index.htm (accessed on March 10, 2016).

International Labour Organization (ILO) (2015). *Global Employment Trends for Youth 2015*. Geneva: ILO.

International Labour Organization (ILO) (2016). *World Employment and Outlook: Trends 2016*. Geneva: ILO.

International Monetary Fund (IMF) (2015). *World Economic Outlook: A Survey by the Staff of the International Monetary Fund*. Washington, DC: IMF.

Mitra, Arup (2011). "Trade in services: Impact on employment in India." *The Social Science Journal*, vol. 48(1): 72–93.

Oseifuah, Emmanuel Kojo (2010). "Financial literacy and youth entrepreneurship in South Africa." *African Journal of Economic and Management Studies*, vol. 1(2): 164–182.

Pio, Edwina and Syed, Jawad (2013). "Our bodies, our minds, our men: Working South Asian women." *Gender in Management: An International Journal*, vol. 28(3): 140–150.

Reardon, Thomas, Berdegué, Julio and Escobar, Germán (2001) "Rural nonfarm employment and incomes in Latin America: Overview and policy implications." *World Development*, vol. 29(3): 395–409.

United Nations (2016). "Sustainable Development Goals: 17 Goals to Transform Our World," online, available at http://www.un.org/sustainabledevelopment/economic-growth/ (accessed on March 11, 2016).

United Nations Development Programme (UNDP) (2015). "Human Development Report 2015: Work for Human Development," online, available at http://hdr.undp.org/sites/default/files/2015_human_development_report_1.pdf (accessed on March 10, 2016).

United Nations Economic Commission for Africa (UNECA) (2015). *Economic Report on Africa: Industrialization through Trade*. UNECA, Addis Ababa.

Weller, J. (2011). "Instituciones laborales y formación profesional: dos aspectos claves para la productividad y la calidad del empleo", in Weller, J. (ed.), *Fortalecer la productividad y la calidad del empleo: Colección Documentos de proyectos* (pp. 11–36). Santiago de Chile: CEPAL.

World Bank (2012). "Gender Differences in World Employment and Why They Matter," online, available at http://siteresources.worldbank.org (accessed on March 20, 2016).

3   Productivity growth

3.1   Introduction

The classical economy tradition (dual economy) draws a sharp distinction between the traditional and modern sectors of the economy, typically characterized as agriculture and industry, respectively.[1] On the contrary, the neoclassical model argues the view that different types of economic activity are structurally similar enough to be aggregated into a single representative sector. However, in reality and as the dual economy model suggests, considerable structural heterogeneity characterizes the economies of developing countries. Different drivers are at play, and dissimilar economic logics are at work in traditional and modern parts of the economy, so these two cannot be lumped together. Accumulation, innovation and productivity growth all take place in the modern sector – often in unexplained ways – while the traditional sector remains technologically backward and stagnant. Economy-wide growth therefore depends in large part on the rate at which resources – principally labour – can migrate from the traditional to the modern sectors.

Developing African countries for example have recorded impressive economic growth but have had far less success in managing the high-productivity industrialization process that has historically propelled several countries on the catch-up path. Evidently, the relationship between industrialization and urbanization rates with productivity vary considerably over time, not only by income groups, but also across and within regions, reflecting the multiplicity of factors affecting urbanization and urban productivity.

Despite differences in the pace of productivity growth relative to the pace of urbanization, the urban dominance in economic productivity is evident in all regions of the world. For high-income economies, the average urban contribution to the national income is 85 per cent, yet urban proportion of the national population is about 79 per cent. In the case of the middle-income group, an urban share of the population of about 50 per cent contributes about 73 per cent of the national output. In the low-income countries where the urban population accounts for about 32 per cent of the total population, the proportional contribution to the national income is about 55 per cent. This clearly shows that urbanization is a significant factor in the explanation of relative trend in prosperity of nations.

All through history, cities have been intimately linked with economic and social progress. The creation of geographical space called "city" is perhaps humanity's most important innovation today. No country has ever achieved significant economic growth in the modern age by retaining its population in rural areas (Martine *et al.* 2008). Since the beginning of the industrial revolution, cities have been essential for the realization of productivity gains in the process of production of goods (Polèse 2000). Economic advancement has both depended on more people living in cities, and it has generated the resources to support continued urbanization through essential infrastructure and services. More people living in cities have expanded the supply of labour and entrepreneurs, and stimulated mutual learning and creativity. The outcome of this virtuous circle has been raising national productivity, higher average incomes and greater all-round prosperity.

Cities provide productive space for excess labour from the rural sector to earn higher value for their efforts that were hitherto cheap in the rural areas (Lewis 1954). The opportunity for the same unit of labour from rural sector to earn better income in the city suggests that productivity of labour is higher in cities and urban areas in general. This translates to higher contributions to national products, increased capacity to provide more employment, and greater overall welfare and prosperity of not the city alone but the national economy in general.

Cities are logically more productive than rural areas, as they benefit from larger pools of labour and talent, concentration efficiencies for both producers and consumers, and a more fluid exchange of ideas and innovations (UN-Habitat 2010). Evidence abound across all regions in the developed, developing and least developed countries that ability of nations to be internationally competitive, innovative and productive increasingly depends on the success of their cities. The increasing trend in city productivity is a major explanation for increasing economic growth in many countries. For example, the predominantly urban regions in OECD countries had on average a GDP per capita 64 per cent higher than that of predominantly rural ones. Likewise, European cities with more than one million inhabitants have, on average, a GDP per capita that is 25 per cent higher than that of the EU as a whole, and 40 per cent higher than that of their home nations (European Commission 2009).

This chapter will examine productivity growth across selected African, Asian and Latin American countries and the part played by structural transformation in long-term development.

3.2 Literature review

Both academic and policy literatures recognize the impact of production efficiency on city prosperity, which in turn fosters employment generation, productivity, equity and quality of life. The traditional economic rationale for urbanization is underpinned by two basic concepts – the *division of labour* and *economies of scale*. The former was introduced by Adam Smith and explains the benefits of productivity arising from specialization among producers. It accounted for the change from simple craft processes to factory production that led to the industrial revolution. *Internal economies of scale* are the efficiencies arising from larger units of organized production. Larger firms can spread their fixed costs (rent, rates, R&D etc.) over a larger volume of output and buy their inputs at lower prices. Higher efficiencies are also obtained by workers becoming more specialized and adept in particular tasks. *External economies of scale* (or *agglomeration economies*) on the other hand, are the benefits firms get from locating near their customers and suppliers in order to reduce transport and communication costs. They also include proximity to a large labour pool, competitors within the same industry and firms in other industries.

The measure of input use reflects the time, effort and skills of the workforce. The denominator of the ratio of labour productivity, the input measure is the most important factor that influences the measure of labour productivity. Labour input is measured either by the total number of hours worked of all persons employed or total employment (head count) (Freeman 2008).

There are both advantages and disadvantages associated with the different input measures that are used in the calculation of labour productivity. It is generally accepted that the total number of hours worked is the most appropriate measure of labour input because a simple head count of employed persons can hide changes in average hours worked, caused by the evolution of part-time work or the effect of variations in overtime, absence from work, or shifts in normal hours. However, the quality of hours-worked estimates is not always clear. In particular, statistical establishment and household surveys are difficult to use because of their varying quality or hours-worked estimates and their varying degree or international comparability (Freeman 2008: 5).

In contrast, total employment is easier to measure than the total number of hours worked. However, total employment is less recommended as a measure of labour productivity, because it neither reflects changes in the average work time per employee nor changes in multiple job holdings and the role of self-employed persons (nor in the quality of labour) (Freeman 2008: 5).

3.3   Rising urbanization, increasing productivity and economic power of cities

As a rule of thumb, as countries urbanize and rural residents move to urban areas, their productivity increases, and consequently, the productivity of the country as a whole. As shown in Figure 3.1, rising per capita income has been consistent with the rising trend in urbanization in the last five decades or so. While urbanization worldwide increased from 33 to 51 per cent between 1960 and 2010, per capita income increased by 250 per cent – from USD 2,376 to USD 6,000 over the same period (World Bank 2011).

Urban regions are vital competitive geographic spaces that serve as a major contributor to generating and sustaining growth and rising quality of life for communities and nations. Other than the nation itself, cities and the urban

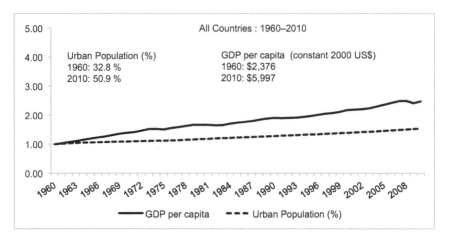

Figure 3.1 Urbanization and per capita GDP across countries as percentage of base
year (1960–2010)

Source: World Bank (2011)

regions in general are the most important geographic units of economic activities in the world today. The state of cities provides the necessary conditions for
the rate and direction of economic development. Thus, the evidence on the
positive links between cities, enhanced opportunities, higher productivity and
higher incomes is considerable (Polèse 2000). Studies have confirmed the positive links between per capita income and levels of urbanization (Jones and Koné
1996). Similarly, there are also demonstrated positive links between productivity
and agglomeration of people and economic activity in cities as more than half of
the national income across the world and in every country is generated in urban
areas (Henderson 1988; Krugman 1991; Ciccone and Hall 1996; Glaeser 1998;
Weiss 2005).

Cities all over the world, rich or poor, in developing or developed countries,
and on every continent followed such comparative advantage in terms of higher
productivity than the rest of the economy. Data for 151 cities in 61 countries,
comprising of least developed, developing, emerging and developed economies
shows that, overall, cities' population is only about 9 per cent of the 61 countries,
but those cities contribute 14 per cent of the national GDP on the average, ranging from 0.33 per cent in Changchun in China to 63.4 per cent in Buenos Aires
in Argentina. The average GDP per capita for the 151 cities in 61 countries shows
that the city income per capita is multiple of the national average for all countries.
Calculations based on 2008 data of 151 cities in 61 countries indicate that average
GDP per capita for the cities is USD 34,516 compared to the national average
figure of USD 24,454, suggesting that the value of the marginal product of labour
in the city outweighs the national average.[2]

3.4 Productivity analysis

3.4.1 *Methodology*

Structural changes occur as a result of productivity increase and efficient allocation of human and other resources. On the other hand, productivity is a measure of the efficiency of production expressed as the ratio of production output to what is required to produce it (inputs). The measure of productivity is therefore defined as a total output per unit of a total input. The benefits of high productivity are manifold; at the national level, productivity growth raises living standards because more real income improves people's ability to purchase goods and services, enjoy leisure, improve housing and education and contribute to social and environmental programmes. Productivity growth is important to the firm because it means that the firm can meet its (perhaps growing) obligations to customers, suppliers, workers, shareholders and governments (taxes and regulation), and still remain competitive or even improve its competitiveness in the market place.

Productivity is considered a key source of economic growth and competitiveness and, as such, is basic statistical information for many international comparisons and country performance assessments. There are different measures of productivity, and the choice between them depends either on the purpose of the productivity measurement and/or data availability. One of the most widely used measures of productivity is gross domestic product (GDP) per hour worked (OECD 2008: 11).

Another productivity measure is the multi-factor productivity (MFP) also known as total factor productivity (TFP). It measures the residual growth that cannot be explained by the rate of change in the services of labour, capital and intermediate outputs, and is often interpreted as the contribution to economic growth made by factors such as technical and organizational innovation (OECD 2008: 11).

Labour productivity is a revealing indicator of several economic indicators as it offers a dynamic measure of economic growth, competitiveness and living standards within an economy. It is the measure of labour productivity (and all that this measure takes into account) which helps explain the principal economic foundations that are necessary for both economic growth and social development.

Although the ratio used to calculate labour productivity provides a measure of the efficiency with which inputs are used in an economy to produce goods and services, it can be measured in various ways. Labour productivity is equal to the ratio between a volume measure of output (gross domestic product [GDP] or gross value added [GVA]) and a measure or input use (the total number of hours worked or total employment) (Freeman 2008: 5).

Labour productivity = volume measure of output / measure of input use

The volume measure of output reflects the goods and services produced by the workforce. Numerator of the ratio of labour productivity, the volume measure of output is measured either by GDP or GVA. Although these two different measures can both be used as output measures, there is normally a strong correlation between the two (Freeman 2008: 5).

The discussion in the chapter will be limited to labour productivity; TFP is not included in the analysis due to lack of data. There are two major sources of change in productivity namely technological progress within the sector and productivity gains due to structural change. Also, growth of productivity has been decomposed into two components using shift-share analysis, namely, intra-sector changes and changes due to structural change. The theoretical concept applied for the decomposition analysis is adopted from van Ark and Timmer (2003) who posit that growth of productivity could be defined as:

$$\Delta P = \sum_{i=1}^{n} (Pi^{T} - Pi^{o})Si^{m} + \sum_{i=1}^{n} (Si^{T} - Si^{o})Pi^{m}$$

Where i is number of sectors could vary from 1 to n

Pi^{T} is productivity in sector i in year T
Si^{T} is share of employment in sector i in year T
Pi^{m} is average of productivity in sector i
Si^{m} is average of employment share in sector i

The first part of the decomposition equation is known as "intra-sector productivity changes," and the second part is called "reallocation-effect" also known as "shift-effect" or "structural change effect." Shift-share analysis would reveal the effect of structural change on productivity in each sector. The economy has been reduced to three sectors, namely, agriculture, industry/manufacturing and services. Sectors such as "mining, utilities and constructions" have been included in industry, while services such as "trade, restaurants and hotels," "transport, storage and communication," "finance, insurance, real estate and business services" and "community, social and personal services" have been merged into the service sector. The analysis of each country is presented in following sub-sections.

3.4.2   Data analysis

The two components of productivity growth, that is, intra-sectoral and structural change, could take negative or positive value. A negative value of contribution of intra-sectoral changes suggests that productivity of several sectors have declined and a negative value of contribution of structural change could mean that the employment share of high value-added sectors have declined.

3.5   Comparative analysis

3.5.1   Africa

The overall productivity growth in African economies was positive during the period under consideration in Botswana, Ethiopia and Ghana, although it was negative in the initial period in other countries. Productivity growth has however followed an increasing trend during the concluding period. Productivity growth in Ethiopia was highest, followed by Nigeria. The highest productivity growth (5.72 per cent) in Ethiopia was recorded during 2007–2011, while it was 3.75 per cent during 2003–2007 in Nigeria. As far as the contribution of structural change in productivity growth is concerned, it was always positive in Ghana, Nigeria and Tanzania. Increase in productivity in sectors other than agriculture could be attributed to this phenomenon, but Nigeria remains the only country where the productivity and employment share have increased during the study period.

3.5.2   *Asia*

The pattern of productivity growth and the contribution of structural change are very similar in all the countries, but the magnitude of productivity growth in Asia was much higher than that of Africa. Second, as distinct from African economies, productivity growth has never been negative in the sample Asian countries. Thirdly, the contribution of structural change to productivity growth was rarely negative; for example, it was negative in China during 1999–2003, which may be attributed to varying levels of productivity growth in various sectors. A distinguishing characteristic of the Asian countries is that explicit economic and industrial policies have been deployed to ensure the absorption of labour surplus from agriculture into other sectors leading to high value-added jobs. Consequently, the productivity growth in other sectors has been positive.

3.5.3   *Latin America*

Contrary to expectations, the productivity growth in Latin American economies has been worse than in the other two continents. Argentina is the only exception where productivity has been positive except in 1999–2003. The magnitude of productivity in the country has been much higher than in other Latin American countries. It varied from 5.54 per cent during 1991–1995 to 0.85 per cent during 1995–1999. The contribution of structural change was also negative in all other countries, except in Argentina and Venezuela during 1999–2003. Another noticeable fact is that the employment share in agriculture declined in the sample economies and it increased in all other sectors. However, there have been some exceptions; for instance, the share of employment in manufacturing in Brazil also declined along with agriculture. Similarly, employment share in manufacturing in Colombia experienced a declining trend.

3.6   Shift-share analysis of African economies

The contribution of structural change to labour productivity growth has been negative. Negative contribution of structural shift during 1991–1995 could be attributed to the decline in employment share in the mining sector. The displaced labour from the mining sector was partly absorbed in agriculture and has resulted

Table 3.1 Decomposition of labour productivity growth in Botswana

	Period	1991– 1995	1995– 1999	1999– 2003	2003– 2007	2007– 2011	2011– 2013
Average annual productivity growth	Agriculture	1.72	-0.69	1.00	7.24	5.67	3.39
	Industry	8.00	1.33	7.76	11.89	1.34	2.93
	Manufacturing	3.72	5.73	-6.16	4.46	3.48	2.32
	Services	8.14	8.55	-2.47	3.46	3.66	3.32
	Total	2.76	2.37	2.49	3.76	0.65	0.94
Decomposition of productivity growth	Intra-sector productivity growth (%)	182.98	156.19	128.20	196.45	729.29	119.65
	Productivity growth due to structural change (%)	-82.98	-56.19	-28.20	-96.45	-629.29	-19.65

in wider unemployment. Therefore, structural change due to change in employment resulted in negative contribution. Similar arguments are valid for other time period (refer to Table 3.1).

A very high value (positive for one component and negative for the other) means that the contributions of both components are similar, but in the opposite direction. For instance, during 1991–1995, the contribution of intra-sectoral changes was 182.98 per cent and that of structural change was –82.98 per cent. Such a high differential percentage of contribution is due to intra-sectoral change that contributed to the increase in productivity of all the sectors. At the same time, –82.98 per cent contribution of structural change was due to a drastic reduction of employment share in industry and manufacturing. In industry, employment share declined from 17.29 per cent in 1991 to 12.58 per cent in 1995, while in manufacturing, it declined from 6.12 per cent to 5.55 per cent during the same period. In 2007–2011, the employment share in industry declined from 7.27 per cent to 4.98 per cent, but average labour productivity during the same period was very high (416937.59) in the sector. This resulted in negative contribution of structural change to productivity growth. The productivity in other sectors was much lower than the industry sector.

3.6.1   *Botswana*

Figure 3.2 presents the annual growth of productivity of major sectors of Botswana.

From the figure, there is a clear pattern of productivity change. In agriculture, it fluctuated from –21.35 per cent in 2002 to 18.90 per cent in 2003. On the other hand, productivity in industry was highest (26.57 per cent) in 2005 and lowest (–27.99 per cent) in 2009. Similarly, it also fluctuated widely in manufacturing

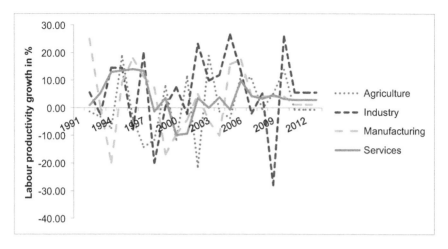

Figure 3.2 Labour productivity growth by main sectors in Botswana

(–19.94 per cent in 1994 to 24.98 per cent in 1992) and services (–9.39 per cent in 2009 to 8.83 per cent in 2002).The analysis presented suggests that variation in labour productivity growth was lowest in services (standard deviation: 6.34) amongst all the sectors analysed. It can be inferred therefore, that policies towards the service sector have been more consistent that in other sectors.

3.6.2 *Ghana*

The analysis of labour productivity of the Ghanaian economy is presented in Table 3.2.

This shows that the contribution of structural change to productivity growth during 1995–1999 was lowest (8.64 per cent) amongst all the sample period. This was due to highest decline in employment in the manufacturing sector, which dropped from 12.24 per cent to 11.20 per cent during the period, while changes in employment in other sectors were marginal. On the other hand, the contribution of structural change to productivity growth was highest (49.26 per cent) in 2007–2011. This may be attributed to the marginal increase in employment share from 11.108 per cent to 11.114 per cent, while augmenting the productivity substantially from 1218.10 during 1991–1995 to 1590.36 during 2011–2013.

Although the average annual productivity during 1999–2003 was positive in all sectors, employment share in agriculture and industry declined. In the agricultural sector, it declined from 54.10 per cent in 1999 to 50.81 per cent in 2003, while it declined from 4.77 per cent to 4.37 per cent in industry during the same period, resulting in lower contributions to productivity due to structural change. Also, the intra-sector productivity gains have been much higher than changes in productivity growth due to structural change.

Table 3.2 Decomposition of labour productivity growth in Ghana

	Period	1991– 1995	1995– 1999	1999– 2003	2003– 2007	2007– 2011	2011– 2013
Average annual productivity growth	Agriculture	2.00	2.88	3.46	3.36	2.53	1.67
	Industry	-2.67	-2.98	3.15	6.81	5.61	2.66
	Manufacturing	3.80	3.80	1.57	0.08	0.08	1.21
	Services	3.46	3.00	1.17	-0.60	-0.58	-0.16
	Total	2.70	2.98	2.70	2.33	2.89	2.92
Decomposition of productivity growth	Intra-sector productivity growth (%)	91.36	76.76	83.19	69.96	50.74	69.15
	Productivity growth due to structural change (%)	8.64	23.24	16.81	30.04	49.26	30.85

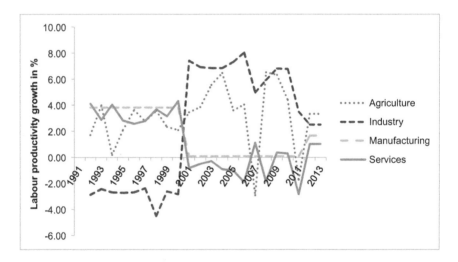

Figure 3.3 Labour productivity growth by main sectors in Ghana

Figure 3.3 depicts the fluctuations in productivity growth of the Ghanaian economy.

The industrial sector experienced fluctuations from –4.50 per cent in 1998 to 8.04 per cent in 2006. On the other hand, growth of labour productivity in manufacturing was positive ranging from 0.08 in 2001 to 3.80 in 1992, with the productivity growth in manufacturing experiencing the least variance (standard deviation:1.81), and industry experiencing the highest volatility (standard deviation: 4.64).

3.6.3 *Kenya*

The decomposition of productivity growth in Kenya is presented in Table 3.3 below.

Table 3.3 Decomposition of labour productivity growth in Kenya

	Period	*1991– 1995*	*1995– 1999*	*1999– 2003*	*2003– 2007*	*2007– 2011*	*2011– 2013*
Average annual productivity growth	Agriculture	−1.70	2.63	1.32	1.99	−0.30	0.96
	Industry	−9.68	−9.23	−2.24	1.27	−0.36	−3.45
	Manufacturing	−10.40	−9.77	−5.69	−0.71	1.11	−2.95
	Services	−4.92	−4.71	−2.62	2.04	1.41	−0.81
	Total	−2.49	−1.53	−0.87	1.81	1.32	0.27
Decomposition of productivity growth	Intra-sector productivity growth (%)	340.22	272.02	202.32	70.64	3.64	−1197.02
	Productivity growth due to structural change (%)	−240.22	−172.02	−102.32	29.36	96.36	1297.02

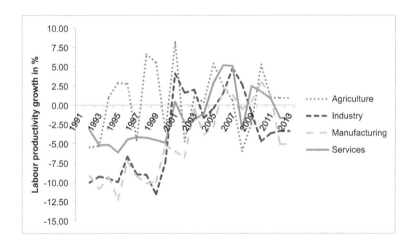

Figure 3.4 Labour productivity growth by main sectors in Kenya

It shows that until 1999–2003, the contribution of structural change has been negative, suggesting that employment share in some sectors reduced drastically. In fact, the agricultural sector provided employment for 70.35 per cent of the labour force in 1991, but its share of employment reduced to 45.68 per cent in 2013. On the other hand, the share of employment in other sectors experienced positive growth rate.

In addition, almost all sectors – except agriculture – experienced a decline in productivity during 1991–2003, which marginally increased subsequently. However, the employment share in sectors other than agriculture increased. It may however be inferred that the loss of employment has been partly compensated in other sectors at the cost of productivity.

The annual change in productivity of the Kenyan economy is depicted in Figure 3.4.

The industrial sector experienced the wildest fluctuations in productivity growth ranging from –11.29 per cent in 1999 to 4.81 per cent in 2007. The trend is followed by manufacturing sector which varied from –12.29 per cent in 1995 to 3.02 per cent in 2010. The variability of productivity growth in the service sector has been the lowest (standard deviation: 3.39), suggesting that policies towards the service sector were more consistent and robust.

3.6.4 Nigeria

The growth in productivity analysis of the Nigerian economy is presented in Table 3.4.

It can be observed that the contribution of intra-sector and structural transformation to productivity growth during 1991–1995 was –633.81 per cent and 733.81 per cent respectively.

A share of –633.81 of contribution in productivity suggests a decline in the agricultural sector (average annual productivity growth –2.58 per cent). At the same time, a very high contribution of structural change (733.81 per cent) is due to the substantial productivity gains in the industrial sector in which the average annual productivity growth in industry was 4.83 per cent during the period. Similar arguments hold true for 1995–1999, where productivity gains due to intra-sectoral changes and structural changes went in opposite direction with almost similar magnitude.

The situation changed since then, and both components contributed positively, but within 2003–2007, the contribution of intra-sectoral changes became negative. This was due to a decline in productivity in the largest employment sector, that is, agriculture. The employment share in agriculture during the period was 62.82 per cent. In the subsequent five years, the contribution of intra-sectoral

Table 3.4 Decomposition of labour productivity growth in Nigeria

	Period	1991–1995	1995–1999	1999–2003	2003–2007	2007–2011	2011–2013
Average annual productivity growth	Agriculture	–2.58	–0.96	11.80	4.66	3.70	4.12
	Industry	4.83	5.92	–0.90	–4.65	–11.45	–5.74
	Manufacturing	0.37	0.37	2.24	2.71	2.15	1.19
	Services	2.37	1.04	6.65	9.81	11.12	10.51
	Total	–1.13	–1.04	6.12	3.75	2.82	3.42
Decomposition of productivity growth	Intra-sector productivity growth (%)	–633.81	–173.19	56.13	–3.81	2.09	88.38
	Productivity growth due to structural change (%)	733.81	273.19	43.87	103.81	97.91	11.62

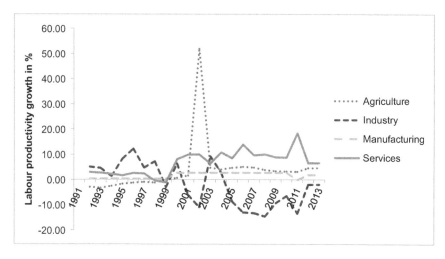

Figure 3.5 Labour productivity growth by main sectors in Nigeria

change was positive, but marginal (2.09 per cent). However, during 2011–2013, the contribution of intra-sectoral productivity gains reached 88.38 per cent due to productivity gains in agriculture and industry.

The annual growth of productivity in the different sectors of the Nigerian economy is presented in Figure 3.5.

There was a sudden change in the labour productivity in agriculture. It was difficult to determine if it was a data-related problem because the output in agriculture almost increased by 50 per cent, while keeping the similar employment levels leading to a high productivity in 2002.

The industrial sector however witnessed variations in productivity growth from –14.67 per cent in 2008 to 12.29 per cent in 1996. On the other hand, productivity growth in manufacturing sector varied from –0.10 in 2011 to 2.71 in 2000, leading to the lowest volatility in productivity growth (standard deviation: 1.17)

3.6.5   South Africa

The decomposition of productivity growth of the South African economy is presented in Table 3.5 below.

The table shows that the contribution of structural transformation in productivity growth was positive during 1991–1995, 2003–2007 and 2011–2013. On the other hand, contribution of intra-sectoral changes during 1995–1999 was –99.89 per cent. This contributed to a decline in productivity in the agricultural and service sectors and a decline in agricultural employment. The share of employment in agriculture declined from 20.23 per cent in 1995 to 19.02 per cent in 1999, while it declined from 13.94 per cent to 9.50 per cent in industry during same period. Hence the contribution of intra-sectoral changes in productivity growth was negative.

Table 3.5 Decomposition of labour productivity growth in South Africa

	Period	1991–1995	1995–1999	1999–2003	2003–2007	2007–2011	2011–2013
Average annual productivity growth	Agriculture	−4.61	1.05	5.40	8.23	2.07	−2.92
	Industry	0.26	6.49	5.42	−2.05	1.26	1.83
	Manufacturing	1.78	1.17	1.17	3.51	2.80	1.48
	Services	−0.51	1.94	5.42	2.45	3.40	2.66
	Total	−0.26	1.10	3.22	3.36	2.42	1.15
Decomposition of productivity growth	Intra-sector productivity growth (%)	−99.89	168.29	103.13	58.48	219.68	94.07
	Productivity growth due to structural change (%)	199.89	−68.29	−3.13	41.52	−119.68	5.93

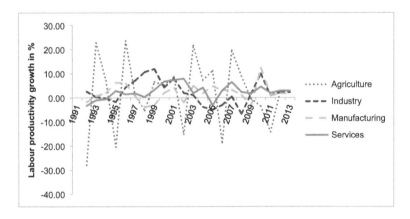

Figure 3.6 Labour productivity growth by main sectors in South Africa

In the subsequent five years, productivity rebounded in agriculture, which resulted in reversing the contribution of both factors to productivity growth. In fact, the intra-sectoral contribution became positive, while at the same time, the contribution of the structural change became negative. This negative contribution could be attributed to decline in productivity in the manufacturing sector. The scenario remained similar in the succeeding five years, but during 2003–2007, the contribution due to structural change became positive. This may be attributed to an increase in productivity during the period when annual average productivity growth in agriculture became 8.23 per cent. During the ensuing five years, labour productivity in the sector declined resulting in negative contributions (−119.68 per cent) of structural change.

Figure 3.6 depicts the annual growth of labour productivity in various sectors.

The figure shows that the agricultural sector experienced the wildest fluctuations in productivity growth ranging from –27.91 per cent in 1992 to 23.58 per cent in 1996 following a cyclical pattern. The variability of productivity growth, measured in the form of standard variation was 14.34.

Variability in other sectors has been comparatively low. In industry for instance, the annual growth of productivity varied from –6.72 per cent in 2008 to 11.94 per cent in 1999. At the same time, the growth of productivity in the services sector varied from –3.28 per cent in 1992 to 7.36 per cent in 2002. It may be inferred that policies towards services sector have been more robust.

3.6.6 *Tanzania*

The productivity analysis of the Tanzanian economy is presented in Table 3.6 below.

The total productivity growth from 1991 to 1995 was negative. Looking at the sectoral productivity growth, the industrial and services sectors growth was negative, both components contributing to the downfall in productivity. The contribution of intra-sectoral changes was almost double to that of structural change (35.06 per cent). The contribution of the first component was higher because, although employment in industry was smaller (1.27 per cent) compared to services (8.17 per cent), the average labour productivity however, was much higher in industry compared to services.

In the succeeding five years, productivity in industry as well as services improved reversing the contribution of intra-sector and structural changes. The contribution of the latter component became 93.32 per cent and continued to contribute substantially to productivity growth.

Table 3.6 Decomposition of labour productivity growth in Tanzania

	Period	1991– 1995	1995– 1999	1999– 2003	2003– 2007	2007– 2011	2011– 2013
Average annual productivity growth	Agriculture	1.34	1.87	2.79	2.00	1.32	1.66
	Industry	–3.07	–0.59	–0.03	–0.35	2.46	0.01
	Manufacturing	0.01	0.01	–1.07	–4.30	0.01	–0.94
	Services	–2.69	–1.63	–0.56	–0.06	0.33	–0.43
	Total	–1.29	1.51	3.29	3.01	2.65	2.24
Decomposition of productivity growth	Intra-sector productivity growth (%)	64.96	6.68	30.35	8.76	38.24	8.19
	Productivity growth due to structural change (%)	35.06	93.32	69.65	91.24	61.76	91.81

It is worth noting that overall productivity of the Tanzanian economy has been declining since the 1999–2003 period. The employment share in agriculture declined from 80.39 per cent in 2003 to 74.65 per cent in 2007 and average annual productivity growth in other sectors were-0.35, –4.30 and –0.06 per cent, respectively. This kind of structural change was very detrimental to the Tanzanian economy as it created unemployment in the agricultural sector and was unable to provide displaced labour in high value-added activities in other sectors. Surplus labour from agriculture was absorbed in low value-added activities of other sectors resulting in low productivity of the sectors. It also appears that this form of structural change created unemployment at the national level. To overcome this problem, the Tanzanian government needs to put in place skills development programmes for youths to enable their absorption in other sectors than agriculture and in high value-added activities.

Figure 3.7 depicts the trend in productivity growth in various sectors in Tanzania.

Barring 1994, the growth of productivity recorded a positive trend in agriculture. The positive growth rate and declining employment share in agriculture may be attributed to the fact that the agricultural sector became more capital intensive so that production levels can be maintained or increased with a smaller number of workers. Given this situation, the Tanzanian government needed to create more employment opportunities by providing appropriate training to the youths.

Moreover, productivity growth in all other sectors was almost negative except for few years (2007 to 2011). The Tanzanian government therefore needs to embark on policies to augment labour productivity in various sectors. One of the possible ways to ensure higher productivity is to focus on proper human development policies for youth so that they can be absorbed in high value-added jobs.

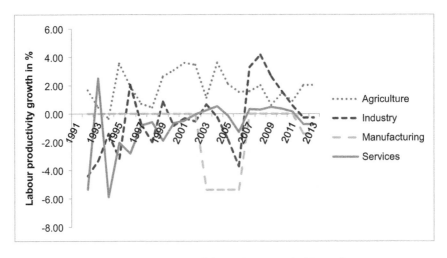

Figure 3.7 Labour productivity growth by main sectors in Tanzania

3.6.7 Ethiopia

Table 3.7 presents the productivity analysis of the Ethiopian economy. The table shows that except during 1995–1999, the contribution of structural change to productivity growth was positive.

The situation in Ethiopia is very different from that of Tanzania; the total productivity in the economy was not only positive, but it also followed an increasing trend. The reason for overall positive growth rate during 1991–1995, despite the negative average annual productivity growth of all sectors, was that the decline of productivity in base year (1991) was very high, but improved subsequently in all the sectors except manufacturing. The contribution of structural change to productivity growth was not only positive, but it was also more than 100 per cent suggesting that structural change led to positive contribution and helped in controlling the decline of productivity due to intra-sectoral changes.

In the succeeding five years, the contribution of structural transformation became negative, with almost similar magnitude to that of intra-sectoral change, but with opposite signs. This was due to the drastic decline in productivity of industrial and agriculture sectors which contributed to more than 90 per cent of employment share. During the ensuing five years, the scenario was reverse due to containment of the decline in productivity in agriculture and industry, while achieving 2.00 per cent growth rate in services sector. Consequently, the contribution of structural transformation and intra-sectoral changes almost became similar with opposite signs. The structural change contributed positively to this productivity growth, and in the subsequent period, both components contributed positively to productivity growth.

Table 3.7 Decomposition of labour productivity growth in Ethiopia

	Period	*1991– 1995*	*1995– 1999*	*1999– 2003*	*2003– 2007*	*2007– 2011*	*2011– 2013*
Average annual productivity growth	Agriculture	−0.61	−1.61	−1.57	5.94	5.44	3.67
	Industry	−0.91	−4.02	−3.85	−3.50	−5.95	−3.57
	Manufacturing	−3.10	−3.10	−3.10	−3.10	−3.10	−1.06
	Services	−0.66	0.68	2.00	1.51	0.81	3.13
	Total	1.57	0.68	0.72	5.65	5.72	5.00
Decomposition of productivity growth	Intra-sector productivity growth (%)	−81.14	238.61	−1152.27	61.31	38.00	46.81
	Productivity growth due to structural change (%)	181.14	−138.61	1252.27	38.69	62.00	53.19

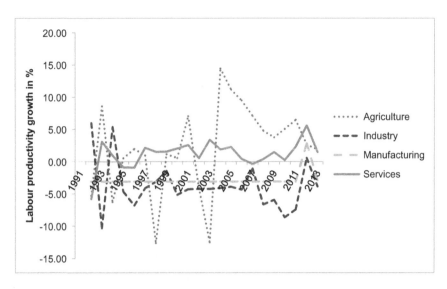

Figure 3.8 Labour productivity growth by main sectors in Ethiopia

The growth of labour productivity in various sectors of the Ethiopian economy is depicted in Figure 3.8.

It is shown that productivity growth in agriculture was highly volatile ranging from –12.91 per cent in 1998 to 14.42 per cent in 2004. The productivity growth in industry was however negative except for few years (1992, 1994 and 2012), which is not a very healthy situation for any economy. Similarly, annual productivity growth in manufacturing was positive only in 2012 based on estimated data. The situation could be that the industrial sector in Ethiopia is on a dying path, which could be economically unsustainable. The services sector recorded positive productivity growth with very small magnitude, signaling some hope for development. The Ethiopian government therefore needs to reorient its economic policies towards appropriate human development policies for youth so that their employment could lead to higher productivity of the Ethiopian economy.

3.7   Shift-share analysis of Asian economies

The economic conditions of Asian countries are slightly different from the economies in Africa. Asian economies attempted to have a balanced approach of economic development. Due attention has been paid to modern sectors while retaining focus on traditional sectors such as agriculture. Consequently, the structural transformation of Asian economies had a greater contribution than in other countries. The sub-section presents and analyses the productivity growth in the sample Asian economies.

3.7.1 China

Table 3.8 presents the decomposition of labour productivity growth in China.

In China, the productivity growth was substantially higher than in the African economies. During 1991–1995, the overall annual productivity growth was 13.19 per cent. The decomposition analysis suggests that the contribution of structural change was less compared to intra-sectoral changes. This may have contributed to the decline of employment share in agriculture during this period, from 59.70 per cent in 1991 to 52.20 per cent in 1995. Hence, the structural changes contributed to productivity growth by 20.34 per cent.

During the succeeding five years, not only employment share in agriculture declined, but also did labour productivity growth. For instance, the annual labour productivity growth in 1995 was 8.25 per cent, and it declined to 1.10 per cent in 1999, resulting in the reduction of overall productivity growth. This was substantiated by the fact that average annual productivity during 1991–1995 was 13.19 per cent, and during 1995–1999, it reduced to 8.80 per cent. Hence, there was an overall productivity growth reduction. In this productivity growth, the contribution of intra-sectoral changes was 94.98 per cent, while structural transformation also contributed at the rate of 5.02 per cent.

The annual productivity declined from 8.80 per cent during 1995–1999 to 7.74 per cent during 1999–2003. The decline was as a result of negative growth rate of productivity in the industrial and manufacturing sectors. However, labour productivity in agriculture recorded a positive growth from 1.10 per cent in 1999 to 3.73 in 2003, while the employment share in agriculture remained stagnant during this period. On the other hand, employment in industry and manufacturing declined resulting in a negative contribution to productivity growth as a result of structural change.

Table 3.8 Decomposition of labour productivity growth in China

	Period	1991–1995	1995–1999	1999–2003	2003–2007	2007–2011	2011–2013
Average annual productivity growth	Agriculture	7.14	4.51	2.09	8.31	8.01	6.70
	Industry	10.16	8.58	9.55	12.31	5.13	5.58
	Manufacturing	23.85	12.81	11.14	5.19	9.72	11.78
	Services	1.65	4.80	6.46	9.50	9.44	6.30
	Total	13.19	8.80	7.74	11.10	10.56	9.58
Decomposition of productivity growth	Intra-sector productivity growth (%)	79.66	94.98	101.53	70.18	82.52	82.97
	Productivity growth due to structural change (%)	20.34	5.02	−1.53	29.82	17.48	17.03

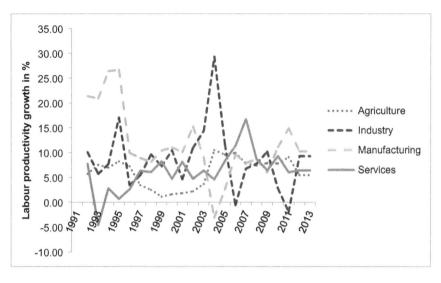

Figure 3.9 Labour productivity growth by main sectors in China

The productivity growth was positive during 2003–2007, higher than the earlier periods and the contribution of structural change to productivity growth was positive due to the increase of productivity in industry. The positive contribution of intra-sector changes originated from increased productivity growth in services sectors from 6.41 per cent in 2003 to 16.75 per cent in 2007. Subsequently, overall labour productivity declined and the contribution of structural change was lesser compared to intra-sectoral changes.

The change in annual productivity growth is presented in Figure 3.9. The figure suggests that labour productivity growth was very volatile in the industrial as well as manufacturing sectors.

The annual productivity growth in the industrial sector varied from –1.91 per cent in 2011 to 29.34 per cent in 2004, while in manufacturing sector, it ranged from 26.69 per cent in 1995 to –3.12 per cent in 2004. The services sector also experienced volatility in productivity growth, which varied from –4.59 per cent in 1993 to 16.75 per cent in 2007.

3.7.2 *India*

The decomposition analysis of India, the third largest economy of the world, is presented in Table 3.9.

India witnessed positive contribution of both factors to labour productivity growth. This could be attributed to robust economic policies and slow pace of structural transformation. India's economic policies have never allowed sudden and drastic changes in any sector, thus leading to an overall productivity growth

Table 3.9 Decomposition of labour productivity growth in India

	Period	1991–1995	1995–1999	1999–2003	2003–2007	2007–2011	2011–2013
Average annual productivity growth	Agriculture	2.40	3.05	1.49	3.51	4.55	2.33
	Industry	–10.57	0.29	–0.28	5.08	2.94	0.17
	Manufacturing	4.26	4.00	0.36	8.37	6.95	3.78
	Services	0.98	5.29	3.76	7.88	6.24	5.21
	Total	3.29	5.58	3.49	6.82	7.11	4.96
Decomposition of productivity growth	Intra-sector productivity growth (%)	4.55	77.00	39.35	91.95	80.27	66.83
	Productivity growth due to structural change (%)	95.45	23.00	60.65	8.05	19.73	33.17

which varied from 3.29 during 1991–1995 to 7.11 per cent in 2007–2011, indicating an increasing trend, except a decline in productivity growth which occurred during 1999–2003.

In addition, the average productivity growth in the industrial sector from 1991–1995 was –10.57. This is because the base year productivity growth (1991) started at –14.32 per cent. For the overall productivity growth between 1991 and 1995, the contribution of structural change was 95.45 per cent. This considerable positive contribution could be attributed to the positive productivity growth of the manufacturing sector during the period. Within the same period, employment declined marginally in agriculture, but the labour productivity growth was positive.

In the succeeding five years, the average annual productivity growth reached 5.58 per cent. The contribution of structural change to this productivity growth was positive at the rate of 23.00 per cent, while the remaining change in productivity emanated from intra-sector changes. Average annual productivity growth was also positive in all sectors. The employment share decreased marginally in agriculture and increased in all other sectors. However, it may be inferred that the surplus of labour was not only absorbed in other sectors, but also provided high value-added jobs that contributed to overall productivity growth.

From 1999 to 2003, the industrial sector witnessed a downturn in average annual productivity growth resulting in a reduced contribution (39.35 per cent) of intra-sectoral change to productivity growth. Productivity growth declined in manufacturing during this period also. Only agriculture and services recorded positive productivity growth.

In subsequent years, productivity growth followed a positive trend. The contribution of structural change to overall productivity growth was 8.05 per

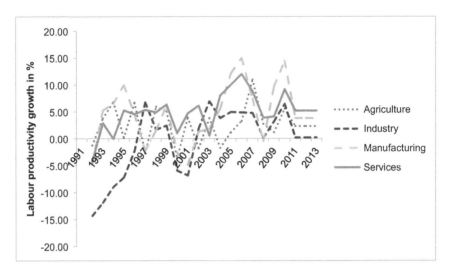

Figure 3.10 Labour productivity growth by main sectors in India

cent during 2003–2007 and 19.73 per cent during 2007–2011. The positive contribution during 2003–2007 was as a result of an increase in productivity in all sectors, while the contribution during 2007–2011 resulted from an increase in productivity in agriculture, which is still the largest employer of labour force.

The annual growth of productivity in the main sectors of the Indian economy is presented in Figure 3.10. From the figure, the volatility in productivity growth was highest in industrial sector ranging from –14.32 per cent in 1992 to 6.94 per cent in 2003.

The manufacturing sector also experienced volatility to a similar extent, as the annual labour productivity growth significantly increased from –4.89 per cent in 2001 to 15.00 per cent in 2006. However, the volatility of productivity growth was lower in India compared to other countries; this might be due to robust and consistent economic and industrial policies.

3.7.3 *Indonesia*

Table 3.10 presents the productivity analysis of the Indonesian economy. The table shows that annual average productivity growth was highest (7.32 per cent) during 1991–1995.

The Indonesian economy never rebounded to such a high level of productivity with the contribution of structural transformation to the productivity growth being 63.88 per cent during this period. This was due to the increase in productivity in agriculture, manufacturing and services sectors.

In the succeeding five years, overall productivity growth was very low (0.35 per cent). In the decline of productivity growth, the structural change contributed negatively (–5.59 per cent), while intra-sectoral change contributed more than

Table 3.10 Decomposition of labour productivity growth in Indonesia

	Period	1991–1995	1995–1999	1999–2003	2003–2007	2007–2011	2011–2013
Average annual productivity growth	Agriculture	7.37	4.52	0.97	2.57	3.74	5.22
	Industry	−0.27	0.93	0.21	1.19	−2.09	−4.89
	Manufacturing	4.32	1.22	2.34	2.16	2.70	1.19
	Services	2.43	−3.63	3.51	2.85	2.71	3.89
	Total	7.32	0.35	2.56	2.22	3.04	3.34
Decomposition of productivity growth	Intra-sector productivity growth (%)	36.12	105.59	95.64	46.45	64.12	53.20
	Productivity growth due to structural change (%)	63.88	−5.59	4.36	53.55	35.88	46.80

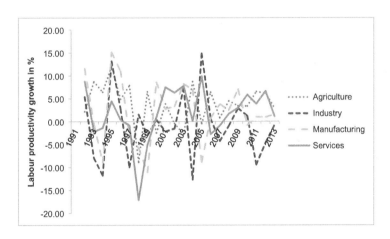

Figure 3.11 Labour productivity growth by main sectors in Indonesia

100 per cent. The major reason for the low negative productivity growth was the negative average annual productivity growth (−3.63) in the services sector.

The labour productivity growth increased from 1999 to 2003, but not in 2003–2007. The contribution of structural change followed an increasing trend, it contributed 4.36 per cent from 1999–2003 and 46.80 per cent from 2011–2013. The increased contribution in 1999–2003 may be explained by drastic changes in productivity growth in the services sector. This trend continued in the subsequent period. However, productivity in the industrial sector has been declining since 2003–2007.

The annual fluctuations in productivity growth of the various sectors of the Indonesian economy are presented in Figure 3.11. From the figure, the volatility of productivity growth is very high in Indonesia compared to other countries.

Amongst all the sectors, productivity growth in the industrial sector experienced the largest variations, ranging from −12.64 per cent in 2004 to 14.92 per cent in 2005. Such a drastic change in productivity growth in consecutive years could be related to data issues as well. In the manufacturing sector, changes in annual productivity ranged from −11.09 per cent in 1999 to 15.14 per cent in 1995. The larger variability of productivity growth questions the economic and industrial policies. This volatility in productivity growth could also be due to frequent changes in policy regime.

3.7.4 Malaysia

The productivity analysis of the Malaysian economy is presented in Table 3.11. The table shows that overall productivity experienced declining trend until 1999–2003, and have fluctuated afterwards.

The larger share of intra-sectoral change during 1991–1995 to productivity contribution may be attributed to the productivity of the industrial sector. The productivity growth in agriculture declined in the subsequent period to 0.29 per cent. This decline in productivity growth resulted in a negative contribution to structural change (−0.55 per cent) in productivity growth. In the following period, changes in productivity in agriculture resulted in a positive contribution of structural change.

The productivity growth increased from 1.15 per cent in 2007–2011 to 2.41 per cent in 2011–2013. It could be attributed to the achievement of productivity growth in the agricultural sector, which changed from 3.81 per cent in

Table 3.11 Decomposition of labour productivity growth in Malaysia

	Period	1991–1995	1995–1999	1999–2003	2003–2007	2007–2011	2011–2013
Average annual productivity growth	Agriculture	4.03	0.29	4.57	2.16	3.81	8.70
	Industry	0.49	3.31	−0.97	1.65	−3.76	−2.73
	Manufacturing	2.26	2.99	5.17	7.75	2.18	2.67
	Services	8.27	3.64	1.51	3.65	2.47	2.15
	Total	5.66	3.20	2.18	3.81	1.15	2.41
Decomposition of productivity growth	Intra-sector productivity growth (%)	66.66	100.55	93.50	120.52	43.50	93.51
	Productivity growth due to structural change (%)	33.34	−0.55	6.50	−20.52	56.50	6.49

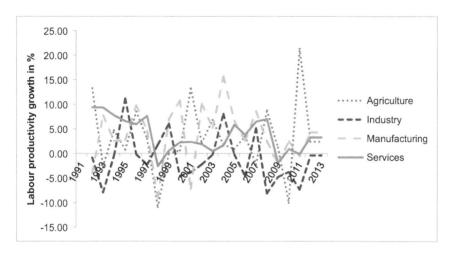

Figure 3.12 Labour productivity growth by main sectors in Malaysia

2007–2011 to 8.70 per cent during 2011–2013, while remaining almost stagnant in other sectors. The change in employment share in the services sector during 2011–2013 might have also contributed to the phenomenon, increasing from 43.99 per cent to 45.05 per cent during the period. Structural change contributed positively to productivity growth due to agriculture.

The annual productivity growth in the main sectors in Malaysia is shown in Figure 3.12. The volatility of productivity growth in agriculture was highest (standard deviation: 7.17) amongst all sectors. The change varied from –10.90 per cent in 1998 to 20.31 per cent in 2011.

On the other hand, the services sector recorded the lowest fluctuations (standard deviation: 3.51) ranging from –2.58 per cent in 1998 to 9.39 per cent in 1992. Productivity in the services sector declined, while its employment share increased, thus indicating a possibility that the Malaysian government might have initially focused on high valued-added services and percolated down to activities in services sector that are low value-added resulting in declining productivity in this sector.

3.7.5 Philippines

Table 3.12 presents the decomposition analysis of productivity growth in the Philippines.

Labour productivity growth in the country recorded an increasing trend, except for a minor decline in 2007–2011.

The table shows that the contribution of structural change was negative during the last two periods. This may be due to a decline in productivity in agriculture and industry. The positive contribution of structural change during 1991–2007

Table 3.12 Decomposition of labour productivity growth in Philippines

	Period	1991–1995	1995–1999	1999–2003	2003–2007	2007–2011	2011–2013
Average annual productivity growth	Agriculture	−0.60	2.03	3.83	2.58	1.59	1.83
	Industry	2.94	−1.73	0.40	3.51	2.27	2.52
	Manufacturing	0.98	1.95	1.69	2.95	3.87	4.57
	Services	−0.49	0.91	1.45	3.41	0.89	2.49
	Total	0.42	1.52	2.10	3.37	2.16	3.36
Decomposition of productivity growth	Intra-sector productivity growth (%)	77.28	36.56	92.33	99.25	119.49	100.77
	Productivity growth due to structural change (%)	22.72	63.44	7.67	0.75	−19.49	−0.77

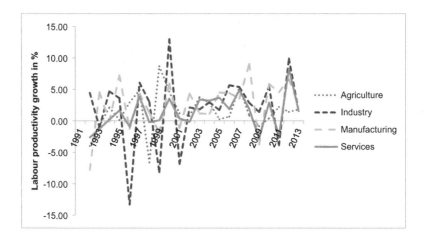

Figure 3.13 Labour productivity growth by main sectors in Philippines

fluctuated. For instance, during 1991–1995, it was 22.72 per cent and changed to 63.44 per cent during 1995–1999. On the other hand, the contribution of intra-sectoral change declined to 36.56 per cent in 1995–1999 from the earlier period. This may be attributed to a decline in the productivity of the industrial sector. In the subsequent period, industrial productivity registered a positive growth and the contribution of intra-sectoral change also increased.

The annual labour productivity growth in various sectors of the Filipino economy is presented in Figure 3.13.

As mentioned earlier, the fluctuations in productivity growth in Philippines was lesser. Amongst the various sectors in the country, the industrial sector witnessed the largest changes (standard deviation: 5.83), ranging from −13.27 per cent in 1996 to 13.01 per cent in 2000.

On the other hand, the services sector recorded the least variability (standard deviation: 2.72). The annual productivity growth varied from −2.80 per cent in 2009 to 8.32 per cent in 2012. The figure also shows that, except for industry, the productivity growth was rarely negative in most of the sectors in the Philippines.

3.7.6 Sri Lanka

The labour productivity analysis of the Sri Lankan economy is presented in Table 3.13.

Data for Sri Lanka were derived from the World Development Indicator online rather than GGDC; hence, the analysis is limited to three sectors only, namely, agriculture, industry and services.

During 1991–1995, the contribution of intra-structural change to productivity growth was positive (97.18 per cent). This could be due to the two-digit positive productivity growth in all sectors and the shift of employment from agriculture and industry to the services sector. During the succeeding five years, the contribution of structural change was negative. This may be due to the decline of average annual productivity growth in the agriculture and services sector.

During the following five years, industry and services experienced a positive trend in productivity growth and the contribution of structural change was positive (39.83 per cent). During 2003–2007, almost the entire productivity could be attributed to intra-sectoral change. Productivity growth rebounded in this period resulting in further positive trend. The Sri Lankan economy could not sustain this pace of productivity growth in the succeeding five years and productivity growth drastically declined in agriculture sector. It declined from 3.12 per cent to −5.18

Table 3.13 Decomposition of labour productivity growth in Sri Lanka

	Period	*1991–1995*	*1995–1999*	*1999–2003*	*2003–2007*	*2007–2011*	*2011–2013*
Average annual productivity growth	Agriculture	2.98	1.12	−2.25	3.18	3.12	−5.18
	Industry	8.50	0.93	3.11	2.97	16.60	23.81
	Services	2.08	4.60	3.11	5.01	4.81	5.88
	Total	4.31	2.73	3.50	4.77	5.68	6.50
Decomposition of productivity growth	Intra-sector productivity growth (%)	97.18	122.65	60.17	84.76	130.94	81.90
	Productivity growth due to structural change (%)	2.82	−22.65	39.83	15.24	−30.94	18.10

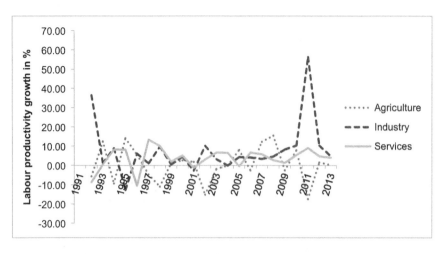

Figure 3.14 Labour productivity growth by main sectors in Sri Lanka

per cent in agriculture sector. The contribution of structural change to the decline of productivity growth was moderate (18.10 per cent).

As depicted in Figure 3.14, labour productivity growth in Sri Lanka suggests that industrial sector was very volatile.

The annual productivity change ranges from −4.59 per cent in 1995 (the only year when it was negative) to 68.68 per cent in 2011. Therefore, it may be inferred that policies towards industry have not been consistent.

The figure also shows that unlike many countries, productivity growth was positive except for a few years. Annual growth in agriculture was negative most of the time, while the variability for the services sector was comparatively low with positive growth.

3.7.7 *Thailand*

Table 3.14 presents the decomposition of productivity growth in the main sectors of the Thailand economy.

The average annual growth of productivity fluctuated, taking the shape of a sinusoidal wave but was much lower quantitatively compared to China, India and Sri Lanka. The table shows that overall productivity declined in the periods including 1995–1999, 2003–2007 and 2007–2011. Although overall productivity growth during 1991–1995 was positive, the productivity growth in the industrial sector declined at the rate of −2.79 per cent annually. This was compensated by the augmentation of productivity in other sectors. For instance, average annual productivity grew at the rate of 5.10 per cent in agriculture. Consequently, the contribution of structural change to productivity growth was 55.57 per cent.

Table 3.14 Decomposition of labour productivity growth in Thailand

	Period	1991–1995	1995–1999	1999–2003	2003–2007	2007–2011	2011–2013
Average annual productivity growth	Agriculture	5.10	4.62	6.22	3.39	2.34	2.93
	Industry	-2.79	1.11	-0.18	1.66	-1.18	-2.10
	Manufacturing	4.92	1.44	1.90	5.04	2.63	0.11
	Services	3.20	-5.08	-2.06	1.54	0.31	0.60
	Total	6.75	0.96	2.78	3.78	1.36	1.05
Decomposition of productivity growth	Intra-sector productivity growth (%)	44.43	221.22	16.92	81.73	80.86	33.83
	Productivity growth due to structural change (%)	55.57	-121.22	83.08	18.27	19.14	66.17

In the subsequent five years, the services sector witnessed a major decline in productivity resulting in –5.08 per cent rate of decline. Both intra-sectoral and structural changes contributed to productivity growth, but with reverse signs, with the contribution of intra-sectoral changes being higher than 100 per cent. During 1999–2003, productivity growth in services improved, but at the same time, the industrial sector registered a decline in productivity. However, the overall productivity growth remained positive due to high-productivity growth in agriculture. The contribution of structural change to the productivity growth was positive (83.08 per cent) and may be attributed to the increasing productivity growth in agriculture and services sectors.

Although average annual productivity growth was positive during 2003–2007, productivity in manufacturing experienced a declining trend varying from 9.69 per cent in 2003 to 0.65 per cent in 2007. Moreover, average annual productivity growth in agriculture declined from the preceding five years. Consequently, the contribution of structural change declined from earlier periods with a continued trend in the ensuing five years. The table shows that overall productivity growth declined from 3.39 per cent during 2003–2007 to 2.34 per cent during 2007–2011. The contribution of structural change in declining productivity growth was slightly higher (19.14 per cent) than the preceding period. During 2011–2013, the increase in productivity growth of services sector led to a positive contribution of structural change in productivity growth, but the contribution of structural change improved substantially (66.17 per cent) due to productivity improvements in the agriculture sector.

The labour productivity growth in the Thai economy is depicted in Figure 3.15. From the figure, all sectors experienced high level of volatility in productivity growth; the largest being in manufacturing (standard deviation: 6.43).

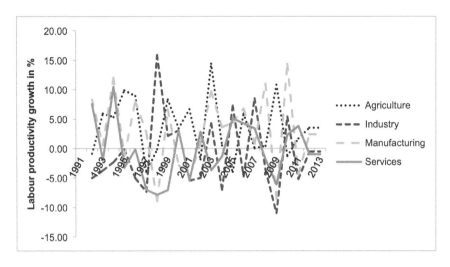

Figure 3.15 Labour productivity growth by main sectors in Thailand

The productivity growth in this sector changed from –8.98 per cent in 1998 to 14.39 per cent in 2010.

The volatility of the industrial sector is almost similar to manufacturing (standard deviation: 6.30), but the lowest fluctuations were witnessed by the agricultural sector (standard deviation: 4.98). Such a high volatility in productivity growth could be a result of frequent changes in economic and industrial policies which may not lead to sustainable economic development. The Thai government therefore needs to focus on policies that are more sustainable.

3.8   Shift-share analysis of Latin American economies

Latin American countries are likely to follow a path of economic development similar to that of Asian countries. However, access to the North American market might enhance varying degree of productivity gains. The sub-section presents the productivity analysis of sample Latin American countries using same analytical techniques.

3.8.1   *Argentina*

The decomposition of productivity growth at various time periods in the main sectors of the Argentinean economy is presented in Table 3.15.

From the table, productivity growth declined continuously until 1999–2003; it improved subsequently, and again declined in the 2011–2013 period. The decline in productivity growth during 1991–1995 may be attributed to declining productivity growth in the manufacturing and services sectors. The annual productivity growth in manufacturing declined from 9.72 per cent to 5.98 per cent during the period, while in services, it changed from 6.77 per cent to 1.86 per cent. The

Table 3.15 Decomposition of labour productivity growth in Argentina

	Period	1991–1995	1995–1999	1999–2003	2003–2007	2007–2011	2011–2013
Average annual productivity growth	Agriculture	5.75	4.95	3.65	5.67	2.92	1.72
	Industry	11.88	0.35	–1.99	–3.49	–2.15	–1.61
	Manufacturing	8.33	3.69	–1.52	2.97	4.39	4.03
	Services	4.17	0.88	–4.39	4.31	6.43	4.16
	Total	5.54	0.85	–3.17	3.47	3.80	2.57
Decomposition of productivity growth	Intra-sector productivity growth (%)	114.00	343.43	60.44	68.14	107.78	146.22
	Productivity growth due to structural change (%)	–14.00	–243.43	39.56	31.86	–7.78	–46.22

contribution of structural change to the productivity growth was –14.00 per cent. The negative contribution of structural change is however primarily due to declining productivity trends in various sectors.

The trend continued in the succeeding five years as the industrial sector witnessed the sharpest fall in productivity growth. In fact, productivity had a declining trend in all the sectors of the economy with productivity growth declining from 5.54 per cent to 0.85 per cent. Consequently, the contribution of structural change to declining productivity further declined with the contribution of both components exhibiting similar magnitude, but with opposite signs.

Although the average productivity growth in almost all sectors was negative during 1999–2003, there was a positive trend in productivity growth. However, the productivity growth in agriculture changed from 4.21 per cent in 1999 to 11.79 per cent in 2003. Consequently, there was a positive productivity growth, and the intra-sectoral and structural changes contributed to this positive growth by 60.44 per cent and 39.56 per cent, respectively. The trend continued in the following five years when the average annual productivity reached 3.47 per cent in 2003–2007, leaving the contributions of both components as almost similar to that of preceding period.

In the succeeding five years, the average annual productivity in agriculture declined from the preceding period to 2.92 per cent, and at the same time productivity in industrial sector improved resulting in a higher contribution to productivity growth by intra-sectoral changes (107.78 per cent) and a negative contribution (–7.78 per cent) by structural transformation. The Argentinean economy could not sustain the trend in productivity growth in the subsequent period, and this resulted in further decline in the contributions of structural change.

The annual labour productivity growth of Argentinean economy is depicted in Figure 3.16 below.

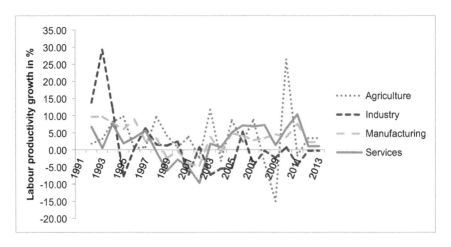

Figure 3.16 Labour productivity growth by main sectors in Argentina

From the figure, the productivity growth of the industrial sector was negative, except for few years in the beginning, and it was also the most volatile (standard deviation: 8.48) with the growth rate ranging from –7.75 per cent in 1995 to 29.34 per cent in 1993.

Productivity growth in the agricultural sector followed the reverse trend. It was initially stable, but became volatile in the latter period. Overall variability (standard deviation: 7.78) was close to that of industry. It is clear from the graph that there were no major change in productivity growth on annual basis suggesting that there was a relative stability in economic and industrial policies.

3.8.2　*Bolivia*

The productivity analysis of the Bolivian economy is presented in Table 3.16. It can be deduced from the table that productivity growth in the Bolivian economy was lower than that of Argentina, but also followed the shape of sinusoidal wave.

During 1991–1995, the average annual productivity growth was negative in manufacturing and services sectors leading to a positive contribution (319.39 per cent) of structural change to productivity growth. During the subsequent five years, the productivity in all other sectors improved except industry resulting in overall productivity growth. Consequently, the contribution of intra-sectoral changes to productivity growth became positive. Structural transformation contributed 72.62 per cent, while the remaining 27.38 per cent was due to intra-sectoral changes.

The table also shows that during 1999–2003, productivity declined in all the sectors except agriculture, where it increased to 9.97 from 3.96 per cent recorded in the previous period. Consequently, the contribution to productivity growth by both components was almost identical, but with opposite signs. The contribution

Table 3.16 Decomposition of labour productivity growth in Bolivia

	Period	1991– 1995	1995– 1999	1999– 2003	2003– 2007	2007– 2011	2011– 2013
Average annual productivity growth	Agriculture	1.21	3.96	9.97	5.24	7.34	4.46
	Industry	1.93	0.98	−3.86	−0.26	−0.20	0.58
	Manufacturing	−2.83	−1.44	−1.77	3.10	−0.10	−1.04
	Services	−1.40	0.09	−3.48	−1.61	−1.23	−0.96
	Total	0.37	1.90	−0.50	0.66	1.44	1.15
Decomposition of productivity growth	Intra-sector productivity growth (%)	−219.39	27.38	994.19	125.96	42.41	−41.65
	Productivity growth due to structural change (%)	319.39	72.62	−894.19	−25.96	57.59	141.65

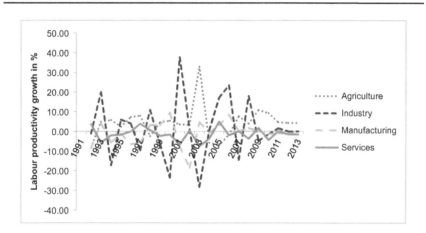

Figure 3.17 Labour productivity growth by main sectors in Bolivia

due to structural change was −894.19 per cent, which may be due to negative declining trend in productivity growth in industry, manufacturing, and services; while the positive contribution of intra-sectoral changes could be due to increasing trend of productivity growth in agriculture.

In subsequent periods also, except in the last phase analysed, the contribution of intra-sectoral changes was positive. During 2011–2013, the contribution of intra-sectoral change was negative (−41.65 per cent). This could be due to a decline in the productivity of the sector that has an important employment share. In the case of services, the average employment was 69.70 per cent and the average annual productivity growth was −0.96 per cent during the period.

The pattern of annual change in productivity of the different sectors is depicted in Figure 3.17.

Similar to Argentina, the industrial sector was the most volatile (standard deviation: 15.63) in terms of productivity growth. It varied from −28.18 per cent in 2003 to 37.75 per cent in 2001. Agriculture followed similar trends with the second highest volatility (standard deviation: 8.15).

The productivity in the services sector was not subjected to much volatility, but fluctuated between −7.54 per cent to 5.00 per cent. Therefore, large volatility in productivity growth needs to be an utmost concern of the Bolivian government.

3.8.3 Brazil

The productivity analysis of the Brazilian economy is presented in Table 3.17. The table shows that the scenario of productivity growth in Brazil is similar to that of Bolivia.

During 1991–1995, the average annual productivity growth was marginally positive (0.36 per cent) resulting in 1.77 per cent contribution to overall growth to productivity coming from structural change. All sectors, with the exception of services, recorded a positive productivity growth. However, in the subsequent five years, the agriculture sector experienced an increase in productivity growth. At the same time, it declined substantially in industry, while slight improvement in productivity growth was realized in the services sector. Consequently, the Brazilian economy witnessed an overall positive change in productivity growth, which may be attributed to structural change. This contribution drastically improved to 57.40 per cent.

From 1999 to 2003, the productivity growth further declined in all sectors except agriculture. It improved from 4.72 per cent to 5.16 per cent. This positive

Table 3.17 Decomposition of labour productivity growth in Brazil

	Period	1991– 1995	1995– 1999	1999– 2003	2003– 2007	2007– 2011	2011– 2013
Average annual productivity growth	Agriculture	2.97	4.72	5.16	3.42	6.01	4.99
	Industry	4.18	0.57	−0.69	1.84	−1.22	−0.84
	Manufacturing	3.76	3.93	−0.30	−0.66	1.49	1.84
	Services	−2.38	−1.07	−2.68	0.59	1.56	−0.85
	Total	0.36	0.83	−0.79	0.91	1.84	0.57
Decomposition of productivity growth	Intra-sector productivity growth (%)	98.23	42.60	864.51	67.84	62.99	46.06
	Productivity growth due to structural change (%)	1.77	57.40	−764.51	32.16	37.01	53.94

change in productivity growth and declining share of employment resulted in a positive contribution (864.51 per cent) to overall productivity by intra-sectoral changes. In the succeeding five years, the economy improved, and all sectors except agriculture recorded positive productivity growth resulting in a positive contribution to structural change by 32.16 per cent.

In the subsequent five years, productivity in all other sectors improved except industry in which drastic change was realized. It declined from 1.84 per cent in the previous period to –1.22 per cent. Moreover, productivity growth and shift in employment were incommensurable. Consequently, the contribution of structural change further improved from the previous period. In the final period, that is 2011–2013, the economy further deteriorated and productivity growth declined in all sectors except in the industrial sector where it marginally improved. This resulted in reduced contribution of intra-sectoral changes to productivity growth from the previous period.

Figure 3.18 depicts the annual growth of productivity in the various sectors of Brazilian economy.

The productivity growth experienced fluctuations in all sectors. However, there was a drastic change in the pattern of several sectors. For instance, productivity growth was positive in agriculture and below zero in the services sector although employment share increased during the entire period of analysis.

On the other hand, employment share declined in the agriculture sector. It may be inferred that labour displaced from agriculture was absorbed in low value-added jobs in services. This might be due to the lack of appropriate training of youth that consequently cannot be absorbed in high value-added jobs. The government can change this situation by implementing appropriate human resource development programmes.

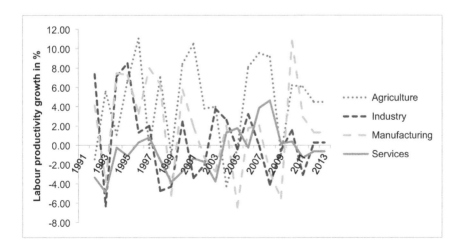

Figure 3.18 Labour productivity growth by main sectors in Brazil

3.8.4   Colombia

The productivity analysis of the Colombian economy is presented in Table 3.18.

The productivity growth scenario in Colombia is similar to other Latin American countries. The economy was marked by either marginal or negative productivity growth. During the first period of the analysis, there was an improvement in productivity growth in agriculture and industry; it significantly increased from –4.40 per cent in 1992 to 18.76 per cent in 1995 in agriculture, while the change in industry was from –13.30 per cent to –9.86 during the same period. However, the productivity in other sectors had a declining trend. Due to large share of employment in services and declining productivity growth, the contribution of intra-sectoral change to productivity growth was negative (–47.23 per cent), while the contribution of structural change was positive.

In the succeeding five years, the productivity in all the sectors except services improved, although the services sector experienced a decline from 1.55 per cent in the previous period to –1.51 per cent. Since the services sector was the largest employer, the overall productivity declined in this period. Consequently, the contribution of both factors are of the similar magnitude, but with opposite signs. Intra-sectoral changes contributed –823.16 per cent to this decline and structural change contributed 923.16 per cent. The reverse was the case in the subsequent period, leading to positive contribution of intra-sectoral changes in productivity growth (154.43 per cent). This may be attributed to an increasing trend in productivity growth in agriculture sector. The average annual productivity changed from 0.08 per cent in 1999 to 10.54 per cent in 2002. The scenario in the subsequent two periods, that is 2003–2007 and 2007–2011 also changed

Table 3.18 Decomposition of labour productivity growth in Colombia

	Period	1991–1995	1995–1999	1999–2003	2003–2007	2007–2011	2011–2013
Average annual productivity growth	Agriculture	1.16	3.49	2.09	0.69	2.39	1.47
	Industry	–5.29	4.76	–0.85	0.06	4.92	1.11
	Manufacturing	0.35	1.32	0.47	1.95	0.16	1.45
	Services	1.55	–1.51	–2.71	1.75	0.48	0.24
	Total	1.11	0.32	–1.53	1.52	1.59	1.11
Decomposition of productivity growth	Intra-sector productivity growth (%)	–47.23	–823.16	154.43	56.30	49.53	–2.12
	Productivity growth due to structural change (%)	147.23	923.16	–54.43	43.70	50.47	102.12

from the previous period with a positive contribution of structural transformation to productivity growth. In 2003–2007, the average annual productivity growth was positive, and it increased from the previous period in all sectors, with the exception of agriculture where productivity growth declined due to comparatively less employment share; however, the overall productivity growth in this period was positive. This was the first period where the contributions of both factors were positive although the contribution of structural change was smaller (43.70 per cent). In the concluding period of the study (2011–2013) the economic performance deteriorated, and productivity growth declined in most of the sectors resulting in a negative contribution of intra-sectoral changes to productivity growth.

The annual productivity growth in the main sectors of the Colombian economy is depicted in Figure 3.19 below.

The volatility in productivity growth in agriculture (standard deviation: 8.79) and industry (standard deviation: 11.40) was very high. Growth rates have been fluctuating on yearly basis, which gives reason to worry. It varied from –15.90 per cent in 1996 to 18.76 per cent in 1995 in agriculture. Such a drastic change in one year indicates data-related problems. In industry, it changed from –17.11 per cent in 2002 to 21.10 per cent in 1996. Therefore, the drastic change in labour productivity in 1996 makes the output of these sectors questionable.

In addition, productivity growth fluctuated on a yearly basis, thus questioning the consistency of economic and industrial policies in the country. The situation in Colombia is similar to that of Brazil where employment share in agriculture consistently declined, while it increased in the services sector. The same argument could be extended to the Colombian case where displaced labour in agriculture was absorbed in low value-added activities in the services sector resulting in fluctuating productivity growth.

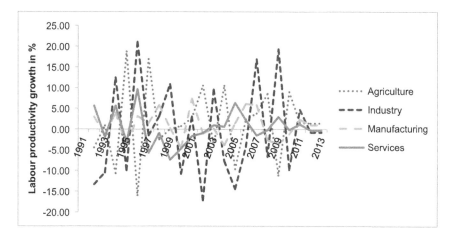

Figure 3.19 Labour productivity growth by main sectors in Colombia

3.8.5 Mexico

Table 3.19 presents the productivity analysis of the Mexican economy.

Despite its proximity to North America, the productivity growth scenario is very dismal in Mexico. During 1991–1995, all the sectors except agriculture and manufacturing recorded negative productivity growth resulting in overall negative productivity growth. Consequently, structural change contributed negatively to the decline of productivity. The contribution of structural change was –19.32 per cent. Subsequently, the productivity growth improved in 1995–1999, and the contribution of structural change to productivity was positive (109.48 per cent).

The negative contribution of intra-sectoral changes could be attributed to a change in employment share and productivity growth which were not commensurate. For instance, the average productivity growth in agriculture sector changed to 0.57 per cent in 1999–2003 from 2.76 per cent in previous period, but the employment in the sector was much smaller compared to services sector, where productivity growth increased from –3.23 per cent in 1995–1999 to –1.77 in 1995–2003. Consequently, the contribution of structural change (–4.87 per cent) to productivity growth was negative.

Productivity gains in various sectors in the succeeding two periods led to positive contributions of structural change. It was 54.11 per cent and 43.61 per cent in 2003–2007 and 2007–2011 respectively. In the last period under consideration, the scenario changed again resulting in negative contribution of structural change. This was primarily due to a decline in the productivity of the services sector, which holds the highest employment share in the Mexican economy with the average employment share during 2011–2013 accounting for 44.68 per cent.

The variation in productivity growth of the various sectors is depicted in Figure 3.20.

Table 3.19 Decomposition of labour productivity growth in Mexico

	Period	1991–1995	1995–1999	1999–2003	2003–2007	2007–2011	2011–2013
Average annual productivity growth	Agriculture	0.38	2.76	0.57	4.22	–0.43	–1.13
	Industry	–0.20	–2.15	–0.72	–3.63	–1.43	–0.05
	Manufacturing	0.96	1.30	–0.11	0.66	–0.35	0.96
	Services	–3.64	–3.23	–1.77	1.84	0.22	0.19
	Total	–1.42	–0.78	–1.08	0.88	–0.59	0.17
Decomposition of productivity growth	Intra-sector productivity growth (%)	119.32	–9.48	104.87	45.89	56.39	199.03
	Productivity growth due to structural change (%)	–19.32	109.48	–4.87	54.11	43.61	–99.03

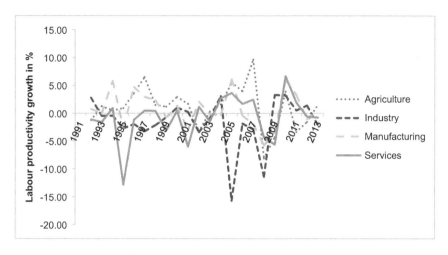

Figure 3.20 Labour productivity growth by main sectors in Mexico

The productivity growth not only witnessed fluctuations (standard deviation: 4.48), but it was also negative during most of the years. Labour productivity growth in the industry sector varied from –15.70 per cent in 2005 to 3.30 per cent in 2009. However, when comparing the variability with other economies in the region, it is found that the variability in productivity of all sectors was comparatively low. It may be inferred that the proximity of the country to the North American market plays a role in pursuing more consistent economic policies.

3.8.6 *Venezuela*

The labour productivity analysis of the Venezuelan economy is presented in Table 3.20.

The table shows that the overall productivity growth in the country was negative except in 2003–2007 and 2011–2013. It can also be deduced that during 1991–1995, the overall productivity growth was negative (–0.004 per cent). The manufacturing and industrial sectors had a positive productivity growth, while productivity growth was negative in the other two sectors. The contribution of the two factors to the almost zero growth was very high. Both contributions were almost equal but with opposite signs. In the two subsequent periods, the overall productivity growth was negative. In 1995–1999, the contribution of structural change to the decline in productivity was 91.16 per cent, while in 1999–2003, it reduced to 33.29 per cent. In 2003–2007, productivity in all the sectors (except industry) improved, consequently leading to a positive growth in labour productivity. The contribution of structural change in the productivity growth was 86.17 per cent, suggesting that change of employment share and productivity moved in the opposite direction. The similar scenario persisted in subsequent periods with a declining contribution of structural change.

Table 3.20 Decomposition of labour productivity growth in Venezuela

	Period	1991– 1995	1995– 1999	1999– 2003	2003– 2007	2007– 2011	2011– 2013
Average annual productivity growth	Agriculture	–3.60	4.77	–1.39	1.56	2.28	5.29
	Industry	1.56	3.46	–1.37	-6.55	–3.21	0.61
	Manufacturing	6.66	–0.48	–2.25	0.88	–1.41	2.80
	Services	–2.60	–2.73	–3.87	6.82	0.43	0.61
	Total	–0.004	–0.16	–4.72	1.65	–1.18	1.02
Decomposition of productivity growth	Intra-sector productivity growth (%)	1415.30	8.84	66.71	13.83	84.33	97.10
	Productivity growth due to structural change (%)	–1315.30	91.16	33.29	86.17	15.67	2.90

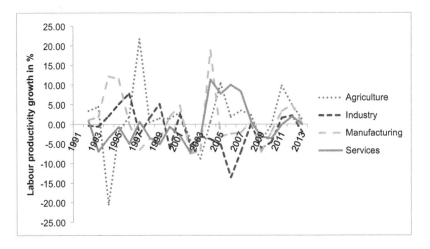

Figure 3.21 Labour productivity growth by main sectors in Venezuela

During 2011–2013, although average annual productivity growth was positive, it had a declining trend over the period. In the agriculture sector for example, it was 9.79 per cent in 2011, but it declined to 1.17 per cent in 2013. Similarly, it decreased in the manufacturing sector from 3.34 per cent to 0.6 per cent during the same period. Consequently, the contribution of structural change was positive but marginal in the overall productivity growth.

The annual productivity growth is depicted in Figure 3.21. The figure shows that fluctuations in productivity growth are enormous.

Fluctuations in agriculture were highest (standard deviation: 7.73) in terms of labour productivity growth with a drastic increase from –20.44 per cent in 1994 to 21.70 per cent in 1997. Similar fluctuations (standard deviation: 6.69) were also observed in manufacturing as well. Productivity growth in the services sector had lesser fluctuation but remained negative, except from 2004 to 2008. Fluctuation in industry that encompasses oil exploration, which largely contributed to the Venezuelan economy, can be related to market demand of oil with the output being controlled by the government accordingly.

The negative productivity growth in the services sector could be attributed to the absorption of displaced workers from the agricultural sector. The employment share in the agriculture and services sectors was consistently moving in the opposite direction. One option for Venezuelan government to augment productivity in these sectors is to provide high value-added jobs to workers moving away from the agriculture sector. The necessary condition to achieve this is to provide appropriate skills development policies for youths so that they become employable in high-productivity jobs.

3.9   Conclusion

The labour productivity analysis presented in the chapter suggests that in many countries, it increased due to structural transformation, while in others, it was due to intra-sectoral changes. For instance, in Botswana, the productivity growth was due to intra-sectoral changes rather than structural transformation in all periods. In fact, the structural change contributed negatively to productivity growth. In Ghana, the growth in productivity was due to structural transformation as well as intra-sectoral change. In all periods, the contribution of structural transformation in productivity growth was higher than intra-sectoral change. This may be treated as the best example of structural transformation going in the right direction. On the other hand, in Kenya, the contribution of structural transformation was 29.36 per cent in 2003–2007, while it was 96.36 per cent in 2007–2011. The structural transformation contributed very highly in 2011–2013. It may be noted that structural transformation contributed negatively in other years.

In Nigeria, the contribution of structural transformation towards productivity growth was positive for all the years and was higher than intra-sectoral change. However, in South Africa, structural transformation contributed positively in 1991–1995, 2003–2007 and 2011–2013 but the contribution was smaller than intra-sectoral change most of the time. Tanzania moved in the right direction of structural transformation, resulting in its positive contribution to productivity growth. It may also be noted that the contribution of structural transformation was higher in the entire period, except 1991–1995 (35.06 per cent). In Ethiopia, the contribution of structural transformation to productivity growth was positive, except in 1995–1999, and in most of the years, it was higher than the contribution of intra-sectoral change.

China and India are the two Asian economies where structural transformation contributed positively to productivity growth in most of the years. However, the contribution of structural transformation was less than intra-sectoral change in China, while it was greater in 1991–1995, and 1999–2003 in India. In Indonesia, the structural transformation witnessed a similar pattern to that of China and India, but the contribution of structural transformation to productivity growth was higher than that of intra-sectoral changes in several years. In other economies such as Malaysia, Philippines, Sri Lanka and Thailand, the pattern has been similar with a contribution of structural transformation to productivity growth being positive in most of the years. However, the magnitude of this contribution varied from one economy to another. For instance, in Malaysia and the Philippines, it was less than that of intra-sectoral change in all the years except 2007–2011 and 1995–1999, respectively. In the case of Sri Lanka, the contribution of structural transformation was always smaller, while in Thailand, it was smaller only in the later part of the study period.

In Latin American sample countries, the contribution of structural transformation to productivity growth was mixed. For instance, in Argentina and Bolivia, it was positive only in 1999–2003 and 2003–2007. However, the magnitude of the contribution of structural transformation in Argentina was less than that of intra-sectoral change, although in Bolivia, it was the opposite. On the other hand, in Brazil and Colombia, structural transformation contributed positively except during 1999–2003, but the magnitude of contribution followed the opposite trend: in Brazil, the contribution of structural transformation was smaller in most of the time periods, and it was the opposite in the case of Colombia. In Mexico, the contribution of structural transformation was positive in 1995–1999, 2003–2007 and 2007–2011. Like many other countries, the magnitude of contribution was also higher than that of intra-sectoral change. The structural transformation experienced in Venezuela was similar to that of Brazil and Colombia. The contribution of intra-sectoral change to productivity growth was positive only in 1991–1995. Like Mexico, the magnitude of the contribution of structural transformation was higher in most of the years in Venezuela.

Notes

1 According to Rodrik (2013), there are two traditions that exist side-by-side within growth economics. The first has its origin in development economics, and it is based on the dual economy approach which was initially developed by Lewis (1954) and Ranis and Fei (1961). The second tradition has its origin in macroeconomics and stems from the neoclassical growth model of Solow (1956).
2 GDP per capita is the income per head and a measure of productivity per unit of labour.

Bibliography

Ciccone, A. and Hall, R. E. (1996). "Productivity and density of economic activity." *The American Economic Review,* 86(1), 54–70.

European Commission. (2009). *Promoting Sustainable Urban Development in Europe – Achievements and Opportunities,* Brussels: European Union.

Freeman, R. (2008). "Labour Productivity Indicators: Comparison of Two OECD Databases, Productivity Differentials and the Balassa-Samuelson Effect," online, available at http://www. oecd. org/dataoecd/57/15/41354425.pdf (accessed on April 15, 2016).

Glaeser, E. L. (1998). "Are cities dying?" *The Journal of Economic Perspectives*, 12(2), 139–160.

Henderson, J. V. (1988). *Urban Development: Theory, Fact and Illusion*, Oxford: Oxford University Press.

Jones, B. G. and Koné, S. (1996). "An exploration of relationships between urbanization and per capita income: United States and countries of the world," *Papers in Regional Science*, 75(2), 135–153.

Krugman, P. R. (1991). *Geography and Trade*, Cambridge, MA: MIT Press.

Lewis, W. A. (1954). "Economic development with unlimited supplies of labour," *The Manchester School*, 22(2), 139–191.

Martine, G., McGranahan, G., Montgomery, M. and Fernandez-Castilla, R. (eds.). (2008). *The New Global Frontier: Urbanization. Poverty and Environment in the 21st Century*, London: Earthscan.

OECD. (2008). *OECD Compendium of Productivity Indicators 2008*, Paris: OECD.

Organization for Economic Cooperation and Development (OECD). (2008). OECD Compendium of Productivity Indicators. OECD Statistics Directorate. OECD Directorate for Science, Technology and Industry, online, available at http://www. oecd.org/std/productivity-stats/40605524.pdf.

Ranis, G. and Fei, J (1961, September). "A theory of economic development," *The American Economic Review*, 51(4), 533–565.

Rodrik, D. (2013). "Structural Change, Fundamentals, and Growth: An Overview Institute for Advanced Study," online, available at http://drodrik.scholar.harvard. edu/files/dani-rodrik/files/structural-change-fundamentals-and-growth-an-over view_revised.pdf?m=1435004204 (accessed on August 20, 2015).

UN Habitat. (2010). *State of the World's Cities 2010/2011 — Cities for All: Bridging the Urban Divide*, Nairobi: UN-HABITAT.

van Ark, B. and Timmer, M. P. (2003). "Asia's Productivity Performance and Potential: The Contribution of Sectors and Structural Change," University of Groningen and Conference Board, online, available at http://www.researchgate.net/publication/ 245504593 (accessed on August 11, 2015).

Weiss, A. M. (2005). "Teamwork: Why metropolitan economic strategy is the key to generating sustainable prosperity and quality of life for the world," *Global Urban Development*, 1(1), 1–11.

World Bank. (2011). *World Development Indicators 2011*. Washington: World Bank.

4 Urbanization

4.1 Introduction

Urbanization and structural transformation are two processes going hand in hand and mutually reinforcing each other. Urbanization is a powerful force for transformation as it enables agglomeration that facilitates industrial productions and economies of scale. Hence, urbanization is a significant force for accelerating economic growth and development.

Urbanization is one of the most significant global trends in the 21st century. More than 50 per cent of the world population now lives in urban areas, while about 5 billion people or 60 per cent of the world population will live in urban areas by 2030. Approximately 90 per cent of the world urban population growth will take place in developing countries by 2030. Hence, cities are the locus of significant global challenges.

Sustainable urbanization is known to be a vehicle for national economic and social transformation. Sustainable urbanization refers to the transition of rural-urban landscape that structures both rural and urban economy, ecology and society in ways that reward the present generation with higher quality of life without endangering and diminishing the living standards of future generations. This structural shift is underpinned by proper planning, supported by enforce-able legal mechanisms and, in turn, brings about rapid economic progress and equitable development of citizens. When rural-urban shift is properly managed alongside industrialization, and planned urban space, it tends to lead to higher productivity and eventually, rising living standards and better quality of life. Sustainable urbanization spawns cities that evolve into centres of change and innovation, mainly because the concentration of people, resources and activities supports human creativity.

However, research has shown that there are a number of countries that are highly urbanized without having seen a large shift of economic activity towards manufacturing and services in most developing countries. This phenomenon is discussed in this study, particularly in the case of Africa.

In large part, successful countries that have been able to sustain a rapid transition out of poverty, due to rapid rise of productivity in the agricultural sector in ways that transformed the rural-urban economies, achieved sustained urbanization. Conventional wisdom interprets this process as a successful structural transformation, where agriculture through higher productivity provides food, surplus of labour with skills, and even savings to the process of urbanization and industrialization. Clearly, a vibrant agriculture raises labour productivity in the rural economy, pulls up wages, and gradually eliminates the worst dimensions of absolute poverty. Concomitantly, the process also leads to a gradual decline in the relative importance of agriculture to the overall economy, as the industrial and service sectors grow even more rapidly, partly through stimulus from a modernizing agriculture and migration of rural workers to urban jobs (Timmer 2007; Timmer and Akkus 2008).

This chapter sheds light on the linkages between urbanization, structural transformation and development. First, a literature review presents the different mechanisms at stake. The next section provides comparative empirical evidences bridging urbanization and economic development through structural transformation in Africa, Asia and Latin America. The last section presents the summary of empirical findings and concludes on the links between urbanization and structural transformation.

4.2 Literature review

Urbanization, structural transformation and development

Urban areas are crucial for national development. According to conventional wisdom, no developed country has achieved its level of development or prosperity without urbanizing, but this statement must be qualified: not all types of urbanization are beneficial, but only *sustainable urbanization* has to be enhanced for the purpose of development. Most of a country's wealth is created in its cities; hence it is said that *cities are the engines of economic growth and development*. However, it is not the case for all cities, but specifically for productive cities, that is cities where less productive agriculture has been replaced by more productive sectors such as industry and manufacturing.

Cities account for about 70 per cent of global GDP (World Bank 2009a). Economic activities in urban areas account for as much as 55 per cent of the GDP in low-income countries, 73 per cent in middle-income countries and 85 per cent in high-income economies (UN-HABITAT and DFID 2002). Moreover, it is anticipated that 80 per cent of future economic growth will be in cities (Swedish International Development Agency [SIDA] 2006). In some countries, a single city could account for a significant share of the national wealth. For example, Seoul, Budapest and Brussels respectively account for over 45 per cent of the GDP of South Korea, Hungary and Belgium (UN-HABITAT 2010). In other countries, it is a group of cities that contributes a significant share of GDP. For example, in South Africa, six major cities collectively account for 55 per cent of the GDP. The case of China is quite remarkable, with 50 per cent of the GDP generated in the coastal areas that constitute 20 per cent of the territory (World Bank 2009b). For all cities, their contribution to GDP is greater than their contribution to the national population. However, the disproportionate economic contribution of urban areas is often ignored in development policy or not duly integrated in development strategies and plans.

Besides the positive contribution of cities to growth, urban areas are associated with higher levels of income. Indeed, the relationship between the level of urbanization and per capita income across countries is positive. Figure 4.1 suggests that few countries have reached income levels of USD 10,000 per capita before becoming 70 per cent urbanized. Among developing regions, few countries attain income levels of USD 5,000 before becoming 60 per cent urbanized. Corresponding figures for Africa, Asia and Latin America and Caribbean can be gleaned from the empirical analysis. This shows that as countries urbanize, they get richer, and they accumulate skills and infrastructural assets to modernize.

From the figure below, urbanization correlates strongly with wealth generation at the early stages of development, but this relationship weakens as countries get richer. The positive relationship between urbanization and income also applies at the regional level. The regions that have the highest levels of urbanization are the ones with the highest levels of GDP per capita. Among developing regions, Latin America and Caribbean, with 78 per cent of its population residing in urban areas, have a GDP per capita of USD 4,580, as against USD 601 and USD 647 for sub-Saharan Africa and South Asia, which are 36 per cent and 29 per cent urbanized, respectively (UN-HABITAT 2010).

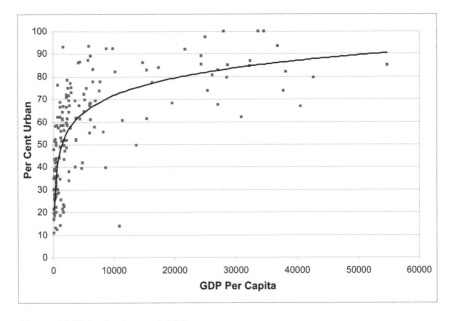

Figure 4.1 Urbanization and GDP

There are however few exceptions, Figure 4.1 also shows that there are several countries with relatively high levels of urbanization, but with low levels of income. This implies that high levels of urbanization alone are not sufficient to generate high levels of prosperity. Such countries might not be drawing on the full benefits of agglomerations (Polèse and Stren 2000; Polèse 2005), or urbanization might occur in the absence of long-term economic growth or in a situation where growth has been too low. The latter is common in sub-Saharan Africa and has been characterized by rapid urban growth occurring within the context of low economic growth[1] (Fay and Opal 2000), poor agricultural performance, climate change, rising unemployment, financially weak municipal authorities incapable of providing basic services, poor governance, and the absence of coherent urban planning policy that integrates economic, social and physical planning among many others issues (Cheru 2005; Barrios *et al.* 2006; Annez *et al.* 2010). Under such conditions, "rapid urban growth . . . has been an inevitable recipe for the mass production of slums" (Davis 2004: 10–11).

Figure 4.1 further indicates that when countries reach urbanization levels of over 70 per cent, the link between urbanization and income weakens. Beyond this point, increasing levels of urbanization contribute little to income. This suggests that there are other key factors besides the level of urbanization that contribute to the prosperity of cities. Some of these factors relate to appropriate urban policy, planning, design, management, and governance, as well as the existence of institutions capable of responding to the problems, consequences and challenges associated with rapid urbanization.

Given the size of the contribution of cities to the national economy, the future of African countries will be determined by the productivity of urban areas and the extent to which urban growth and the accompanying challenges are managed. Developing countries that want to grow must engineer sustainable urbanization. There at least three ways by which this can be achieved (Spence 2008; Oyelaran-Oyeyinka and Gehl-Sampath 2010). The first is to nurture the growth of high-productivity activities – particularly manufacturing followed by services, both of which benefit from agglomeration economies. The sectoral composition of countries that have experienced long-term growth shows that urban sectors in the form of manufacturing and services led the growth process. In developing countries, 86 per cent of growth in value-added activities between 1980 and 1998 came from the urban sectors – manufacturing and services (Montgomery *et al.* 2003).

The convergence of urbanization and structural change

Structural transformation is defined as the development of an economy's structure from low productivity, and labour-intensive activities to higher-productivity, and capital and skill-intensive activities. It involves a long-term shift in the fundamental institutions of an economy and helps to explain the pathways of economic growth and development (Etchemendy 2009; McMillan *et al.* 2013). In technical terms, four essential and interrelated processes define structural transformation in any economy:

1   a declining share of agriculture in GDP and employment;
2   a rural-to-urban migration underpinned by rural and urban development;
3   the rise of a modern industrial and service economy; and
4   a demographic transition from high rates of births and deaths (common in underdeveloped and rural areas) to low rates of births and deaths – associated with better health standards in developed and urban areas.

In sum, the process leads to the reallocation of economic activities across three broad sectors (agriculture, manufacturing and services) that accompanies the process of modern economic growth, and the changes to the structures of the economy and society.

Structural change is strongly linked to urbanization as both phenomena are characterized by the movement of the workforce from labour-intensive activities to skill-intensive based in urban areas. The key constraint to the movement of labour from rural to urban space is the lack of opportunities in skill-intensive sectors such as manufacturing. When labour migrates to cities with little or no opportunities, available labour is underemployed or employed inefficiently. Clearly, the analysis of productivity change is utmost important to our understanding of the causes of urbanization and structural transformation. Productivity growth, the main characteristic of economic transformation, results from sustainable urbanization. The study uses the ratio of value-added to total employment in a particular sector as a measure of labour productivity. Labour productivity is decomposed into two components, namely, (1) change in productivity due to structural change and (2) intra-sectoral productivity growth. The analysis helps in quantifying the association between labour productivity and structural transformation (see Chapter 3).

Urbanization without change in labour productivity: the case of Africa

Recent empirical evidence suggests that structural change could take place without much change in labour productivity; this is the case of many African countries. Most natural resource exporters in Africa and elsewhere do not conform to the standard model of urbanization (Jedwab *et al*. 2013). For example, in 2010, Asia and sub-Saharan Africa were both at the same level of urbanization; while the former recorded the fastest-growing nations (which are South Korea and China), the latter has equally rising wealth but has seen very little growth in income per capita over the years.

One of the reasons for this phenomenon is that in Africa, the peculiar urban dynamics occurs with little change in deep-going type of economic structure that accompanies transitions observed in industrial settings, but is caused largely by the export of natural resource-based products, which Africa tends to specialize in. A recent study that focused on structural transformation in 11 sub-Saharan African countries examined its implications for productivity growth during the past fifty years (McMillan *et al.* 2013). They found that the expansion of manufacturing activities during the early post-independence period led to growth enhancing the reallocation of resources, but the process of structural change was stalled in the mid-1970s and 1980s. Growth then rebounded in the 1990s, but workers mainly relocated to the services industries rather than manufacturing and industrial activities (de Vries *et al.* 2013). The present study analyses the reasons for stagnant or declining productivity in modern sectors in the African continent.

Structural transformation and urban challenges

Employment creation and structural economic transformation are amongst the two major challenges at the forefront of current African growth and development strategies. At the micro level, employment creation provides opportunities for earnings and underpins increases in household expenditures and secure livelihoods. At the macro level, development occurs through the reallocation of labour across sectors toward those with the greatest growth potential and the highest productivity. Jobs also facilitate social (e.g. female wage employment) and political (seeking identity) transformations. However, it is not easy to achieve sustained employment generation (World Bank 2013).

African countries will achieve high and sustained economic growth rates, alongside improved levels of social development, only if productivity changes based on widespread economic diversification (UNECA 2011). The achievement of development goals and higher living standards will therefore depend on the ability of countries to foster entrepreneurship and promote innovation, including the spread, adaptation and adoption of pre-existing know-how and techniques, services, processes and ways of working. Unfortunately, much of the growth in low-income countries over the last decade has not led to structural changes.

Urbanization is a major instrumental mechanism in the process of structural transformation; however, this phenomenon also brings about a number of challenges. About 70 per cent of the total population in large metropolis lives in slum communities. Research revealed that there is a negative correlation between informal employment and GDP per capita; hence, the growth in the informal sector tends to reduce economic growth in developing countries. Thus, informal workers tend to be worse-off compared to those working and living in more formal settings. The formation of cities in mostly poor developing countries takes the shape of informality, illegality and slums, especially where urbanization is unregulated and unplanned. As well, urban inequality has grown due to differentiated wealth concentration in cities. For example, in Africa, statistics show that about 81.7 per cent of Africans live on less than USD 4 per day, with 60.8 per cent falling below the USD 2 per day mark; associated with this also is the problem of high costs of informal services provision and the absence of social safety net.

In order to become a force for structural transformation and, in turn, for development, urbanization has to be mainstreamed through proper policies adopted and implemented by national and local governments. Urbanization and structural transformation will enhance development only if the needed infrastructure and services are delivered, the appropriate institutions are established and development planning is defined.

4.3   Empirical analysis

To our knowledge, little or no systematic empirical work has been done to identify the relationship between structural transformation and urbanization in ways that foster economic development. It is argued in the study that the association is mutually reinforcing. In order to establish a correlation, measurable indicators are needed. From the perspective of industrialization, labour productivity is considered an appropriate proxy. The sources of productivity growth are numerous. For instance, optimum allocation of resources and technological advancement are expected to lead to higher productivity. Industrial policies coupled with human resource development initiatives could also lead to higher productivity. The changes in productivity within various sectors result is structural change with respect to employment and contributions of sectors to total value-added or GDP growth.

This study proposes to quantify associations between urbanization[2] and quality of life, which is measured by human development index (HDI[3]). The HDI is a geometric mean of three indices, that is, life expectancy, education and income per capita. Life expectancy is measured as the life expectancy at birth, whereas education index is based on mean years of schooling and expected years of schooling. The income index is based on Gross National Income (Purchasing Power Parity [PPP] USD). HDI is considered as a better measure of prosperity than simply income. The non-availability of HDI data before 2005 has limited us to use the data of other indicators for 2005–2013. Section 4.3.1 presents the analysis of sample economies of the African continent, while that of Asian and Latin American countries are presented in Sections 4.3.2 and 4.3.3 respectively.

4.3.1   Africa

Before going into the analysis of each country separately, it is crucial to present the overall picture of quality of life and urbanization in the African continent. The relationship between HDI and degree of urbanization has been quantified using TOBIT analysis, and results are presented in Table 4.1.

TOBIT is preferred over Ordinary Least Square (OLS) estimates as the dependent variable, that is, HDI is a truncated non-negative variable with 1 as upper limit. One of the differences between TOBIT and OLS estimates is the iterative procedure followed in TOBIT resulting in more robust and precise estimates, while base results of TOBIT are similar to that of OLS. It is seen from the table that the coefficient of the degree of urbanization is statistically significant at the 1 per cent level (highest level) for all the countries except South Africa, where the level of significance is 5 per cent, suggesting that the relationship between the two is very strong in all countries.

Table 4.1 Economic development and urbanization in Africa

Country	Constant Term	Degree of Urbanization			Log Likelihood	Significance level
		Coeff.	t-value	P > |t|		
Botswana	−1.364	0.036	17.26	0.00	35.879	0.00
Ethiopia	−0.256	0.038	10.15	0.00	28.801	0.00
Ghana	0.013	0.011	21.68	0.00	41.389	0.00
Kenya	0.114	0.017	18.59	0.00	40.965	0.00
Nigeria	0.277	0.005	11.89	0.00	40.054	0.00
South Africa	0.270	0.006	3.01	0.015	30.015	0.011
Tanzania	0.074	0.014	32.72	0.00	43.802	0.00
Uganda	0.080	0.027	10.53	0.00	34.280	0.00

Note: Dependent variable is HDI.

From the table, the coefficients of degree of urbanization are positive for all sample countries, suggesting that there is a positive association between HDI and the degree of urbanization. The magnitude of the coefficients represents the slope of the line of the association. The results show that the slopes of the line are different for all countries. The slope is highest in the case of Ethiopia suggesting that Ethiopia witnessed the highest change in HDI controlling for urbanization. On the other hand, the slope (0.036) of the line for Botswana is second smallest. Although Ethiopia and Botswana witnessed almost similar urbanization growth, the degree of urbanization at base year (2000) is very different. It was 14.74 per cent and 53.22 per cent respectively. These findings show that despite such a high level of urbanization in Botswana, HDI and urbanization are going hand in hand. This is not the case for South Africa, which is at the comparable level with Botswana.

The slope of the line for Nigeria is smallest (0.005). The association between HDI and urbanization in Nigeria is similar to that of South Africa. The degree of urbanization changed from 39.07 per cent in 2005 to 46.09 per cent in 2013, while HDI changed from 0.47 to 0.50. In Nigeria, urbanization is increasing rapidly, but its contribution to the national income is not commensurable. As it is clear from structural change in Nigeria, the focus was on agriculture sector, where the productivity and the contribution to the national income are low, but the sector provides employment opportunity to a large population.

The remainder of the section presents analysis of each country separately.

Botswana

The relationship between economic development and the degree of urbanization in Botswana is depicted in Figure 4.2. Other forms of associations such as linear, log-linear, power functions were tried. The functional form that gave the

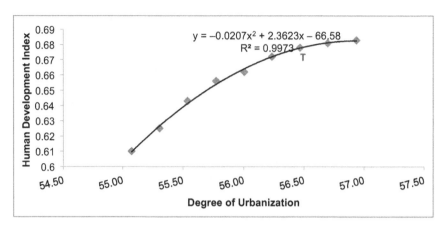

Figure 4.2 Urbanization and living standard in Botswana

highest R-square has been considered the best fit. This shows that the association between the two is quadratic in nature with a very high R-square. The quadratic form of the association suggests that the rate of change of HDI becomes inelastic to the change in the degree of urbanization at a certain level of HDI. That level is defined as the threshold level of HDI. It is marked by "T" in the figure. It can be seen from the figure that it reached a threshold level of HDI at 0.678 in 2011 when the degree of urbanization was 56.47 per cent. Since 2011, there has been very little change in HDI although urbanization increased to 56.94 per cent in 2013. This means that the contribution to economic development by new migrants is comparatively low.

Figure 4.3 presents the linkages between structural transformation measured by growth in value added per worker, and employment with the degree of urbanization.

The figure shows that productivity of the industrial sector was the highest among all sectors. On the other hand, agriculture was least productive. In addition, almost all sectors witnessed moderate productivity growth from 2005 to 2013.

Looking at employment across sectors, it remained the highest in agriculture in the same period. Despite being the least productive sector, agriculture is very important for employment generation. However, the services sector that had the second position in providing employment in 2005 almost employed as many persons as agriculture did in 2013. Hence services may be considered as the best sector in terms of employment. In terms of productivity, it is the second least after the industrial sector. Although productivity of the industrial sector is highest, employment in the sector declined rapidly resulting in the lowest share of employment in 2013. This needs to be a concern for policymakers in Botswana. Moreover, the manufacturing sector that had similar productivity levels to that

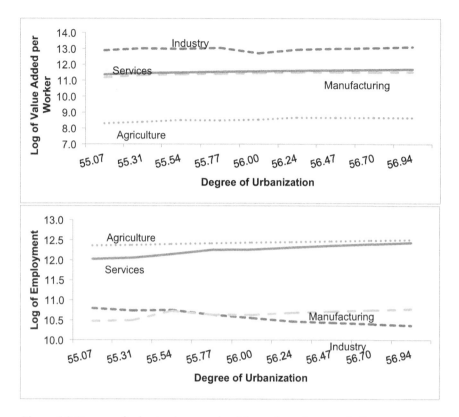

Figure 4.3 Degree of urbanization, productivity and employment in Botswana

of services provided the lowest number of jobs in 2005 and has maintained its employment level in 2013. The analysis shows that the services sector mainly contributed to urbanization in Botswana. The situation in Botswana after 2011 may be termed as a situation of jobless growth.

Ethiopia

The association in the case of Ethiopia is presented in Figure 4.4. The figure shows that the rate of change of HDI after 2011 is marginal. It reached a HDI threshold level of 0.42 in 2011, while the degree of urbanization (DU) was 17.74 per cent. Since then the DU increased to 18.59 per cent, while HDI changed to 0.44 in 2013.

The associations between DU and productivity as well as employment are depicted in Figure 4.5. The association between productivity in industrial sector is negative suggesting that high-productivity jobs reduced over time, although the degree of urbanization increased. Figures suggest that employment in the

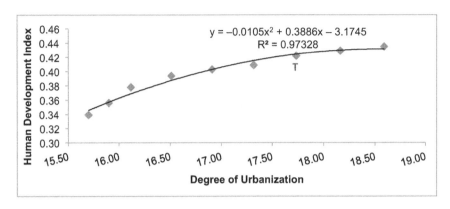

Figure 4.4 Urbanization and living standard in Ethiopia

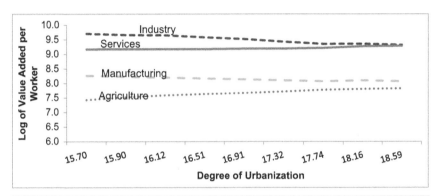

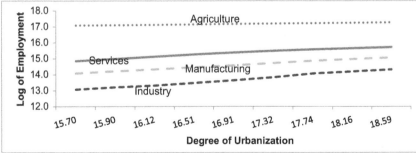

Figure 4.5 Degree of urbanization, productivity and employment in Ethiopia

industrial sector also increased. This implies that high value-added jobs are being replaced by low value-added ones, resulting in both productivity reduction and employment increase.

The productivity in the services sector almost remained static from 2005 to 2013 but employment in the sector experienced positive growth. With growing urbanization and employment, the services sector was able to maintain its pro-ductivity levels. This could have been achieved by providing appropriate skills to the youth that could be absorbed in this sector.

On the other hand, productivity in the manufacturing sector declined in spite of maintaining its third position during 2005–2013. Employment in the sector experienced a positive growth rate suggesting that high value-added activities decreased. The trend is similar to that of the industrial sector.

All sectors experienced a positive trend in employment with increasing urban-ization, but employment growth in agriculture was less important compared to other sectors. The analysis suggests that the migration of workers from agriculture to other sectors took place, resulting in the increase of urbanization. Migrant workers were absorbed in industry and manufacturing sectors for low value-added activities, which is against the true spirit of structural transformation. The decline in productivity in the industry and manufacturing sectors resulted in less contribu-tion to the national income, thereby making HDI inelastic to urbanization. This situation may be regarded as jobless growth.

Ghana

Figure 4.6 presents the relationship between development and urbanization in Ghana. Empirical evidences indicate that urbanization and HDI are going hand in hand despite the fact that Ghana attained an urbanization level of 52.74 per cent and a HDI value of 0.573 in 2013. Findings suggest that additional degrees of urbanization commensurately contribute to the national economy.

Figure 4.7 presents the association between urbanization, value-added activities and employment. Data analysis established that value-added activities and employ-ment in industrial sector increased along with urbanization. Therefore, it may be inferred that the sector is not only contributing to employment, but particularly

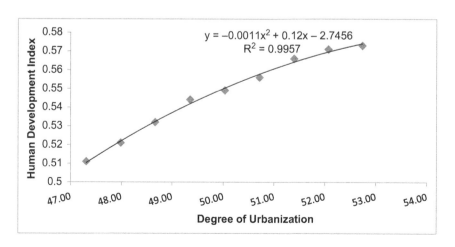

Figure 4.6 Urbanization and living standard in Ghana

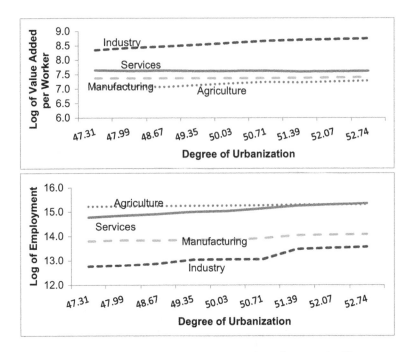

Figure 4.7 Degree of urbanization, productivity and employment in Ghana

to employment in high value-added activities. One way to generate employment in high value-added activities is to provide skill upgrading opportunities to all, including youths, to ensure their employability in highly productive economic activities.

Although employment in services recorded a positive growth, productivity in the sector witnessed a negative trend with the increase in DU. The decline in productivity suggests that the additional workforce absorbed in the sector is engaged in less productive activities. This is to some extent surprising as workers in industrial sector are absorbed in highly productive jobs on the contrary. One reason could be the size of employment in both sectors. The level of employment in services was much higher than that of industry. The services sector encompasses telecommunications which is expanding very fast, and the sector might have generated a lot of low-skilled jobs. Consequently, the productivity of services declined but generated a lot of employment.

Manufacturing holds the third position in terms of value-added activities, as well as employment. Both employment and productivity increased in this sector with the increase of DU. Increasing productivity of industrial and manufacturing sectors might have resulted in higher per capita income, which is captured in Figure 4.7. Agriculture on the other hand is least productive but has the highest levels of employment, although employment in services has surpassed agriculture with higher DU. In addition, productivity in the agriculture sector has increased as urbanization grew. Results presented in Figures 4.6 and 4.7 suggest that increasing productivity in all sectors accompanied by higher DU resulted in better national income and improved HDI. The type of structural change taking place in Ghana contributes to urbanization and the improvement of the quality of life.

Kenya

Figure 4.8 shows the linkage between economic development and DU in Kenya. Evidences suggest that urbanization and HDI increased proportionately. The pattern of growth of urbanization and HDI in Kenya is similar to that of Ghana. In both countries, HDI did not reach the threshold level at which it becomes inelastic to urbanization.

The association between productivity and employment with DU in Kenya is presented in Figure 4.9.

It is seen from the figure that as urbanization occurred, productivity increased – or remained static – in all sectors except industry. Productivity in the manufacturing sector did not change with increased urbanization. These findings suggest that urbanization in Kenya did not increase at the cost of productivity but equally contributed to the national income by raising productivity. The phenomenon is rightly captured by data presented in Figure 4.8, where DU and HDI go hand in hand.

Concerning employment in various sectors, the industrial sector which is highly productive has the lowest levels of employment. On the other hand, agriculture which is least productive provides employment to a larger population. Like productivity, employment in these sectors also registered positive growth with respect to urbanization.

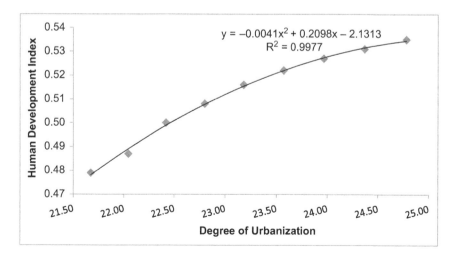

The equation shown on the chart:

$$y = -0.0041x^2 + 0.2098x - 2.1313$$
$$R^2 = 0.9977$$

Figure 4.8 Urbanization and living standard in Kenya

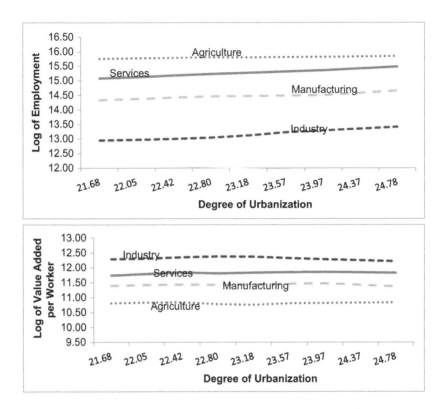

Figure 4.9 Degree of urbanization, productivity and employment in Kenya

Findings reveal that structural change in Kenya contributes to higher productivity and also provides more employment in major sectors of the economy. Therefore, it is argued that structural transformation has a positive impact on the Kenyan economy, thereby increasing the quality of life of its citizens.

Nigeria

The association between urbanization and HDI in Nigeria is depicted in Figure 4.10. The graph shows a strong quadratic association between DU and prosperity, which is the result of structural change. The nature of the quadratic association is that DU and HDI go hand in hand up to a certain level of urbanization beyond which HDI becomes almost inelastic to DU. However, in the case of Nigeria, it did not reach the HDI threshold level.

Figure 4.11 shows the association between value-added per capita and employment with DU in the four major sectors of the Nigerian economy. The figure shows that the level of employment in all sectors and urbanization went in the same direction from 2005 to 2013. It may also be noticed that the relative

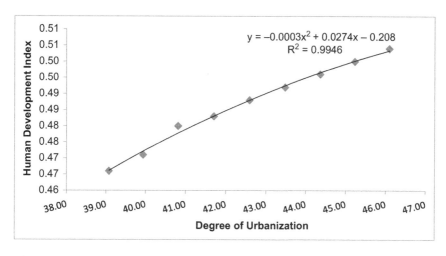

Figure 4.10 Urbanization and living standard in Nigeria

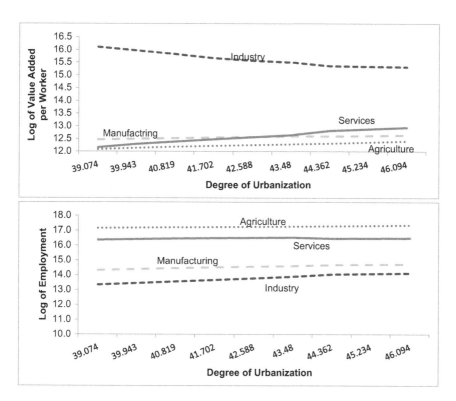

Figure 4.11 Degree of urbanization, productivity and employment in Nigeria

position of the different sectors in terms of employment remained unchanged suggesting that employment growth had similar trends in all sectors.

On the other hand, the association between urbanization and value-added activities is not uniform across all sectors. Value-added activities marginally increased in agriculture and manufacturing, but in services, they surpassed manufacturing in 2013. On the other hand, a high negative slope suggests that high value-added activities diminished. The decline in value-added activities in the industrial sector which has the lowest level of employment share should be a concern of the Nigerian government. The augmentation of productivity in all other sectors contributed to the national income resulting in higher HDI, which is very well-captured by Figure 4.9. Therefore, it is highlighted that the additional workforce in all sectors – except industry – is employed in high value-added activities. Consequently, this type of activities generates more income and lead to a better quality of life with higher degree of urbanization.

South Africa

South Africa has a very high level of urbanization and HDI indicating that the association between both factors is positive without reaching any threshold level of HDI. The high value of R-square of the association depicted in Figure 4.12 suggests that they are concomitant. This could be explained in terms of change in productivity levels in various sectors of the country.

The correlation between productivity, employment and DU is presented in Figure 4.13. It is worth noting that the productivity of agriculture fluctuated, while it has increased in all other sectors with a growing degree of urbanization. In terms of relative position, agriculture is the least productive sector. Therefore, it is argued that structural transformation witnessed by the South African economy is on the right track.

In terms of employment, manufacturing is the only sector where employment declined with respect to urbanization. This implies that new migrant workers were absorbed in sectors other than manufacturing. Changes in the manufacturing

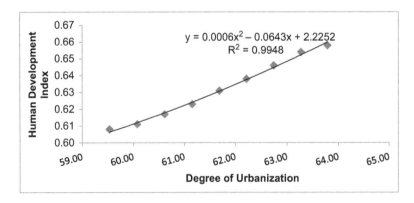

Figure 4.12 Urbanization and living standard in South Africa

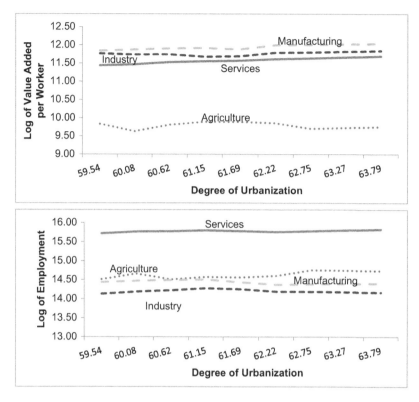

Figure 4.13 Degree of urbanization, productivity and employment in South Africa

sector, namely increasing productivity and decreasing employment, suggest that the sector consolidated in high-value activities. Comparatively, the productivity level in the sector is highest among all sectors. This is an appropriate step of the structural transformation process showing that South Africa is in the right direction.

The increase in employment and productivity in both industry and services with respect to DU suggests that the additional workforce was absorbed in highly productive activities resulting in better income. Therefore, the relationship between HDI and urbanization is still positive despite achieving such a high HDI because productivity in high value-added sectors continuously increased. This is captured in Figure 4.12. The other nations in the continent need to follow the structural transformation practiced by South Africa.

Tanzania

The relationship between economic development and urbanization in Tanzania is presented in Figure 4.14, showing that both factors proportionately increased. Although the best fit between the two is quadratic in nature, there is no sign of

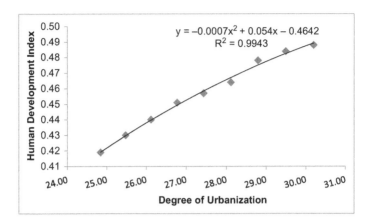

Figure 4.14 Urbanization and living standard in Tanzania

any threshold level of HDI being reached. It implies that the contribution of the newly urbanized population is similar to that of existing urbanized population. The phenomenon would be explained in terms of productivity growth of various sectors in Tanzania.

The linkages between productivity and employment with urbanization in the Tanzanian economy are presented in Figure 4.15. It shows that productivity in agriculture and industry increased with increasing degree of urbanization, while in manufacturing and services, it remained almost static.

In addition, employment recorded positive growth in all sectors. The industrial sector that had the highest level of productivity contributed the least in terms of employment. In a sense, productivity and employment are reversely positioned. For instance, agriculture which provides employment to a large segment of the population is the least productive sector. On the other hand, the services sector which is at the third position in terms of productivity is the second highest employer after agriculture.

It is clear from the analysis presented in Figure 4.15 that structural transformation in the Tanzanian economy led to higher degree of urbanization, which in turn contributed to both productivity and employment. The increasing levels of productivity suggest that the newly urbanized population is employed for highly productive activities resulting in higher national income. This is rightly captured in Figure 4.13 showing that the economic growth and urbanization increased proportionately.

Uganda

The association between economic development and urbanization in Uganda is presented in Figure 4.16.

It shows that economic development and urbanization increased commensurately, which indicates that the newly urbanized population equally contributes

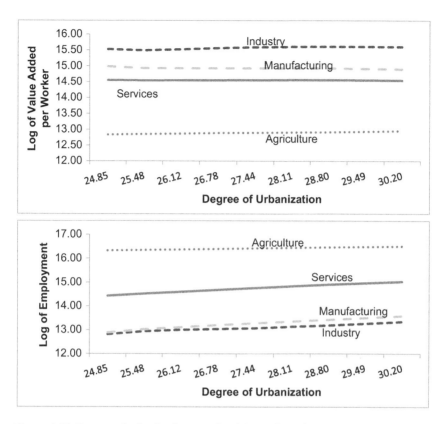

Figure 4.15 Degree of urbanization, productivity and employment in Tanzania

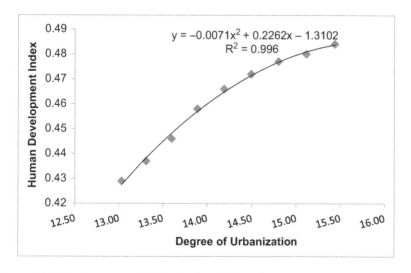

$$y = -0.0071x^2 + 0.2262x - 1.3102$$
$$R^2 = 0.996$$

Figure 4.16 Development and urbanization in Uganda

to the national economy by raising productivity levels. However, the argument cannot be substantiated by empirical evidence due to lack of data on productivity and employment for the Ugandan economy. Therefore, structural change in the country progressed in the right direction.

4.3.2   Asia

The TOBIT estimates of Asian sample countries are presented in Table 4.2. Similar to the African economies, the correlation between economic development and the degree of urbanization is positive in all countries – except Philippines and Sri Lanka.

The coefficients of the degree of urbanization in these two latter countries are negative, suggesting that economic development and urbanization do not grow in the same direction. This is captured in the graphs presented and discussed in detail in respective country analyses. Irrespective of the sign of the coefficient, the parameter estimates are highly significant (1 per cent level). Such a high level of significance indicates that urbanization significantly influenced economic development in Asian economies. The remainder of the section discusses the degree of urbanization and its linkages with productivity growth and employment in each country separately.

China

The correlation between HDI and urbanization is depicted in Figure 4.17. The R-square of the quadratic association between the two is almost close to 1, indicating that the regression almost fit the data perfectly. Therefore, it means that HDI and urbanization are highly associated. In addition, there is no sign of convergence of HDI.

This type of association could be explained in terms of productivity and employment growth presented in Figure 4.18.

Figure 4.18 show that productivity registered positive growth rates in all major sectors. Moreover, the manufacturing sector witnessed the highest growth,

Table 4.2 Economic development and urbanization in Asia

Country	Constant Term	Degree of Urbanization			Log Likelihood/F	Significance level
		Coeff.	t-value	P > |t|		
China	0.321	0.008	30.74	0.00	41.430	0.00
India	−0.194	0.025	20.52	0.00	39.581	0.00
Indonesia	0.307	0.007	15.25	0.00	40.216	0.00
Malaysia	0.449	0.004	11.45	0.00	41.241	0.00
Thailand	0.522	0.004	11.97	0.00	38.149	0.00

Note: Dependent variable is HDI.

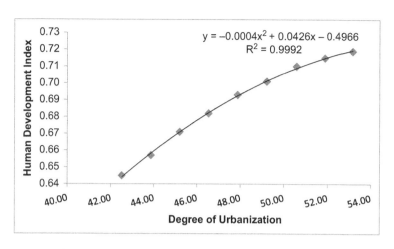

Figure 4.17 Urbanization and living standard in China

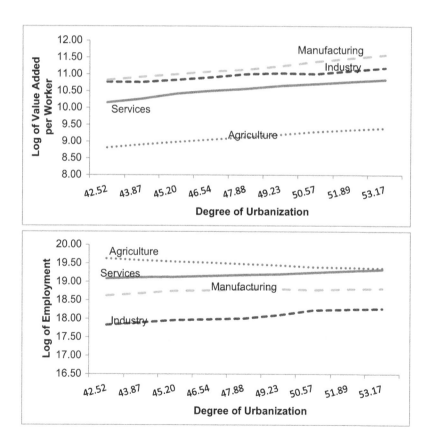

Figure 4.18 Degree of urbanization, productivity and employment in China

followed by industry, as the degree of urbanization increased. However, the relative position of these sectors in terms of productivity remained unchanged from 2005 to 2013.

Concerning employment, it has increased in all sectors except in agriculture. In fact, the levels of employment in the services and agriculture sectors almost became identical in 2013. This indicates that the workforce is moving away from low value-added sectors, namely agriculture, to high value-added sectors such as manufacturing and industry. Unlike several African economies, the surplus of labour coming from agriculture is not absorbed in low value-added activities but rather in highly productive sectors. This results in a higher degree of industrialization, which in turn generates higher national income and urbanization.

The type of structural transformation taking place in the Chinese economy is successful. As defined earlier, structural transformation should result in greater economic growth by replacing least-productive sectors with higher-productive ones. In the case of China, even the least-productive sector (agriculture) increased productivity, although employment declined in the sector, suggesting that agriculture became capital-intensive and involved technology transfer.

India

Figure 4.19 presents the correlation between economic development and the degree of urbanization in India. Empirical evidences suggest that the trend is similar to that of China, although the level of urbanization was much lower in India. In 2005, the urban population represented 29.24 per cent and 42.52 per cent in India and China respectively. However, it reached 31.99 per cent and 53.17 per cent respectively in 2013.

Productivity and employment growth could explain the association between the degree of urbanization and economic development as presented in Figure 4.20.

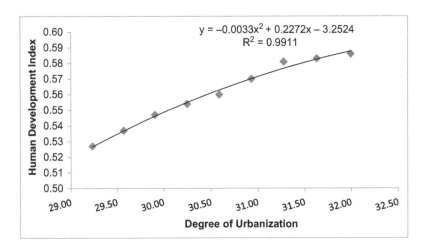

Figure 4.19 Urbanization and living standard in India

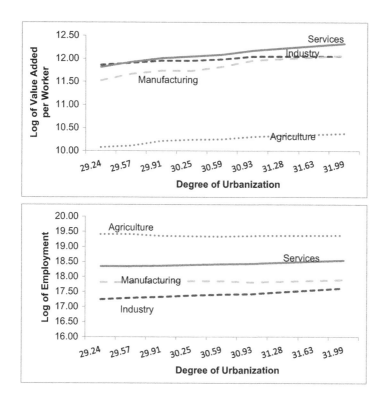

Figure 4.20 Degree of urbanization, productivity and employment in India

Like China, productivity registered a positive growth in all sectors as the degree of urbanization increased. In India, it is the services sector that has registered the highest productivity growth followed by manufacturing, while the change in productivity in industrial sector was the smallest. In terms of relative position, the services sector occupied the first position surpassing industry which was most productive in 2005. Furthermore, productivity levels in manufacturing and industry almost became similar in 2013.

In addition, employment increased in all sectors, except in agriculture, similar to the Chinese trend. It implies that the trend in structural change and the degree of urbanization in India is similar to that of China, although India is not as urbanized. However, the relative position of the sectors in terms of productivity in both countries is not identical. In China, services are at the third position in terms of productivity, while in India the same sector occupies the first position. It may be concluded that in India, services is given more importance than manufacturing and industry, while in China, there is a reverse preference. Another distinguishing aspect between the two countries is the change in the degree of urbanization from 2005 to 2013. It significantly increased from 42.52 per cent to 53.17 per cent in China, while in India, it merely increased from 29.24 to 31.99 per cent.

Indonesia

The linkage between economic development and DU in Indonesia is depicted in Figure 4.21. The situation is similar to that of China and India, not only in terms of trend, but also with respect to the inexistent threshold level. The curve does not show any sign of HDI being inelastic to the degree of urbanization.

The levels of productivity and employment presented in Figure 4.22 explain the links between economic development and urbanization.

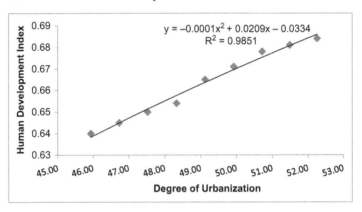

$$y = -0.0001x^2 + 0.0209x - 0.0334$$
$$R^2 = 0.9851$$

Figure 4.21 Urbanization and living standard in Indonesia

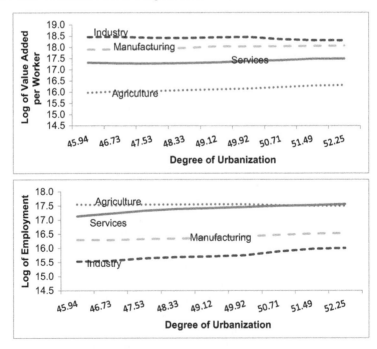

Figure 4.22 Degree of urbanization, productivity and employment in Indonesia

Although the relative position of productivity in the main sectors remained unchanged with an increasing degree of urbanization, the industrial sector slightly decreased from 2005 to 2013. The productivity in other sectors almost remained static over this period, while urbanization increased from 45.94 per cent to 52.25 per cent.

Looking at the levels of employment, it has declined in the case of agriculture, while in other sectors, it has marginally increased. These findings suggest that the workforce moving out of agriculture was absorbed in other sectors. On the other side, the increase in employment and the decrease in productivity in the industrial sector suggest that the labour surplus from agriculture was absorbed in industry with less productive activities resulting in a low national income. However, this is compensated by the increase in productivity and employment in the services sector.

Despite the slow growth in employment and productivity in the economy, the urban population increased from 45.94 per cent to 52.25 per cent from 2005 to 2013. This is different from the Indian situation. The change in urban population is much smaller in India, while it is very large in Indonesia during the same period. In Indonesia, the change in the degree of urbanization and HDI are not commensurate. This is because productivity increased in some sectors, while it decreased in others, resulting in very little contribution to national income. Consequently, the change in HDI is marginal (from 0.64 in 2005 to 0.68 in 2013), indicating that the additional workforce could not contribute proportionately to economic development. Therefore, the large change in the degree of urbanization contributed little to the change in HDI, which is captured in Figure 4.21.

Malaysia

Figure 4.23 presents the relationship between HDI and urbanization in Malaysia. Similarly to other Asian countries, the association is positive with a very high value of R-square. Although the levels of urban population and HDI are much higher

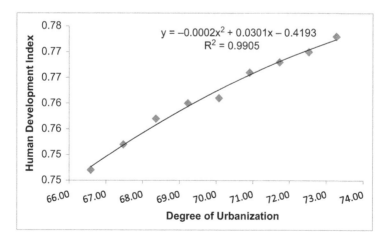

Figure 4.23 Urbanization and living standard in Malaysia

in Malaysia compared to China, there is no sign of HDI being inelastic to urban population beyond a threshold level.

The productivity and employment growth depicted in Figure 4.24 denote the reason behind this situation.

The scenario related to productivity growth is similar to that of Indonesia. Productivity increased in all sectors – except industry – with an increasing urban population. In industry however, it drastically declined, shifting from the first to the second position after manufacturing in 2013. The productivity in other sectors grew almost with similar rates.

On the other hand, the employment trends in Malaysia are different from most other countries. Levels of employment increased in all sectors except agriculture. The agriculture sector was found to be the largest employer in other countries, while in Malaysia it takes only the third position followed by services and manufacturing. The employment in the industrial sector that was lowest in 2005 reached similar levels to that of agriculture in 2013.

The figure shows that the workforce moved away from agriculture and was absorbed in all sectors, but most of all in services, which is the second least

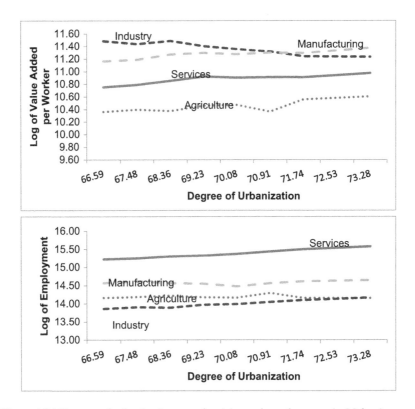

Figure 4.24 Degree of urbanization, productivity and employment in Malaysia

productive sector. Since the newly migrant workforce was absorbed in a comparatively more productive sector, it augmented overall productivity gains resulting in higher national income and consequently in higher HDI. It is therefore argued that in Malaysia, structural change led to a higher degree of urbanization and a better quality of life for its citizens.

Philippines

It may not be appropriate to relate the degree of urbanization to economic development in the Philippines as the definition of urbanization radically changed in 2003. Until 2003, the Philippines classified urban and rural areas using the physical and economic characteristics of barangays. The definition of urban areas, which has been in use since the 1970 census, considers population density, street pattern, and presence of establishments and facilities for basic services (National Statistical Coordination Board, Resolution no. 9, 2003). The new definition is based on 1) If a barangay has a population size of 5,000 or more, then a barangay is considered urban, or 2) if a barangay has at least one establishment with a minimum of 100 employees, a barangay is considered urban, or 3) if a barangay has five or more establishments with a minimum of 10 employees, and five or more facilities within the 2-kilometre radius from the barangay hall, then a barangay is considered urban.[4]

The new definition may lead to de-urbanization due to a movement of establishments to more than 2-kilometres away from barangay hall. Moreover, if the population of such barangay is less than 5,000, the barangay would become rural resulting in a virtual decline in the degree of urbanization. As a result, the urban population artificially declined from 46.60 per cent in 2005 to 44.63 per cent in 2013. However, the HDI level increased from 0.64 to 0.66 during the same period. On the other hand, productivity and employment levels in most sectors grew from 2005 to 2013, which is depicted in Figure 4.25.

The case of the Philippines is very unique. The productivity in all sectors registered a positive growth from 2005 to 2013, but the urban population percentage declined. This is due to the change of definition of urbanization as explained above. Employment also experienced a positive growth rate, except in the case of the manufacturing sector, where employment was almost stagnant. The services sector, the third most productive sector, not only experienced the highest employment growth, but was also the largest employer in the economy. An increased level of productivity is expected to lead to higher national income and this happened in the Philippines. Consequently, HDI increased over the period.

Sri Lanka

As for the Philippines, it might not be appropriate to link the degree of urbanization to economic development in Sri Lanka as the definition of urbanization is not stable. It is not based on any definite criterion such as the size of population, population density, proportion of the male population in non-agricultural

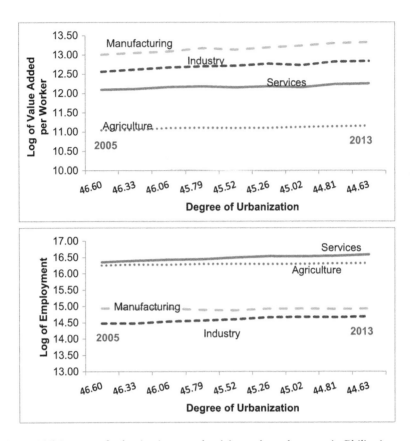

Figure 4.25 Degree of urbanization, productivity and employment in Philippines

occupations or status of civil administration (Panditharathne 1996). Conse-quently, the degree of urbanization virtually decreased from 18.38 per cent in 2005 to 18.30 per cent in 2013. The major reasons responsible for this decreasing trends are the absence of an acceptable definition of urban settlements and an island-wide census in 2001 (Uduporuwa 2010). In Sri Lanka, the urban status is conferred to areas by the minister in charge of local government purely for local administrative purposes (Uduporuwa 2010). However, the country experienced a positive economic growth, and that can be linked to productivity and employment growth presented in Figure 4.26.

Productivity increased in all sectors of the economy from 2005 to 2013. The highest growth was achieved by the industry sector, followed by services and agriculture. On the other hand, the employment scenario depicts a very grim situ-ation. Employment in services almost remained static, and it drastically declined in industry. It is only in the agriculture sector that employment increased. Need-less to mention that in Sri Lanka, agriculture was the least productive as in most

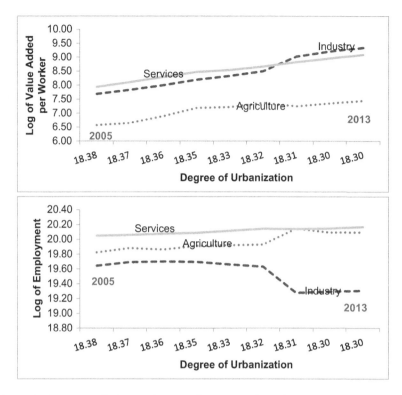

Figure 4.26 Degree of urbanization, productivity and employment in Sri Lanka

countries. The reason for productivity growth could be intra-sectoral changes such as technology transfer and optimum allocation of resources. It is worth mentioning that the manufacturing of garments in Sri Lanka has performed very well in national and international markets in recent years. From a productivity perspective, the structural change in Sri Lanka is in the right direction, but the phenomenon of de-urbanization cannot be explained with the help of data.

Thailand

Figure 4.27 presents the linkages between economic development and urbanization in Thailand. The nature of this association is similar to that of many sample economies, but the figure shows that the HDI became inelastic to urbanization after reaching a threshold level of 0.72. The HDI did not change after that, although urban population grew from 37.52 per cent to 47.94 per cent in 2013.

Productivity and employment growth presented in Figure 4.28 explain the nature of the association between HDI and degree of urbanization. It is shown that productivity growth in the industrial sector declined as urbanization increased. However, it increased in other sectors, although the change in the services sector

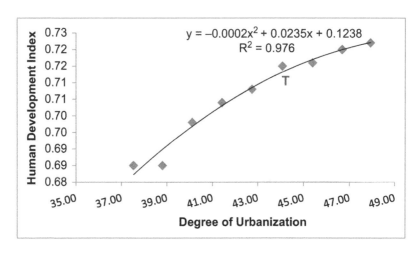

Figure 4.27 Urbanization and living standard in Thailand

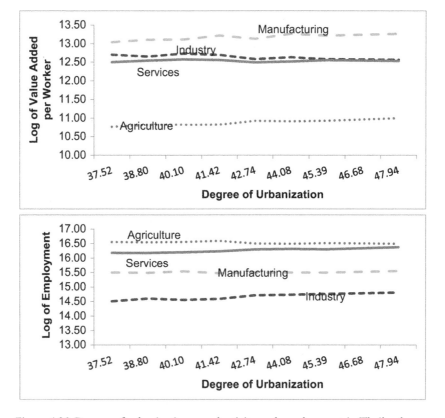

Figure 4.28 Degree of urbanization, productivity and employment in Thailand

was marginal. Consequently, the productivity levels of both the industry and services sectors almost became identical in 2013, while manufacturing maintained its top position. Like many other countries, the agriculture sector was least productive in Thailand.

On the other hand, the employment picture is somewhat different than that of productivity. Employment in agriculture declined with growing urbanization, whereas it has increased in other sectors. The relative position of sectors in terms of employment did not change with increasing degrees of urbanization. Productivity of the most productive sector, namely manufacturing, increased with the degree of urbanization. The figure also shows that productivity growth in agriculture, manufacturing and services is marginal. This might have resulted in a quasi-stagnation of the national income. Therefore, the stagnation of HDI may be attributed to the decline in productivity in the industrial sector and to the marginal increase in productivity in other sectors. Findings suggest that the contribution of urbanization to economic development is very marginal particularly after the threshold level of HDI was reached.

4.3.3 Latin America

TOBIT[5] estimates of the coefficient of the degree of urbanization in sample Latin American countries are presented in Table 4.3. The results are very similar to other countries. The table also shows that no country in Latin America has witnessed de-urbanization. The parameter estimates are significant at the highest level (1 per cent significance level). Such a high level of statistical significance suggests that the positive correlation between economic development and urbanization is very strong.

The rest of the section presents country-specific association and its interpretation in terms of productivity and employment growth.

Table 4.3 Urbanization and living standard in Latin America

Country	Constant Term	Degree of Urbanization			Log Likelihood/F	Significance level
		Coeff.	*t-value*	*P > |t|*		
Argentina*	−1.799	0.028	7.61	0.00	57.92	0.00
Bolivia	0.112	0.008	14.91	0.00	44.407	0.00
Brazil*	−0.673	0.017	15.78	0.00	248.90	0.00
Colombia	−0.448	0.015	14.89	0.00	42.450	0.00
Mexico*	−0.391	0.015	25.29	0.00	639.38	0.00
Venezuela*	−8.455	0.104	9.38	0.00	87.96	0.00

Note: Dependent variable is HDI.

*Base results rather than TOBIT results

Argentina

Figure 4.29 depicts the association between HDI and the degree of urbanization in Argentina. This association is similar to that of many other countries but differs in reaching the threshold level of HDI. The graph shows that the HDI reached a threshold level of 0.804 at 91.13 per cent degree of urbanization in 2011. Thereafter the rate of change of HDI with respect to the degree of urbanization was almost stagnant suggesting that urbanization beyond the threshold level is disproportionately contributing to national income.

The productivity and employment growth presented in Figure 4.30 is useful in establishing the linkages between urbanization and economic development.

Productivity in the industrial sector declined with an increase in the urban population, while the other sectors recorded an increase in productivity. The manufacturing sector maintained its first position from 2005 to 2013, while the agriculture sector moved to the second position by replacing industry. Surprisingly, the services sector in Argentina is least productive, a situation very different from most of the sample countries in Asia and Africa.

Regarding employment, the services sector occupies the top position providing jobs to the largest number of people, although it is the least productive. Usually, in other countries, this is applicable to the agriculture sector. The analysis of employment suggests that it was stagnant in agriculture as the urban population increased, while in industry and manufacturing, it marginally increased. Moreover, the services sector experienced a reasonable growth. The Argentinian economy may be regarded as a services sector–oriented economy. The sector being least productive did not contribute much to the national wealth resulting in almost stagnant HDI. On the other hand, the industrial sector whose productivity declined with increasing employment and urbanization suggests that the additional workforce from rural areas was absorbed in low value-added activities in this sector. Therefore the trends in this sector also explain the stagnation of HDI.

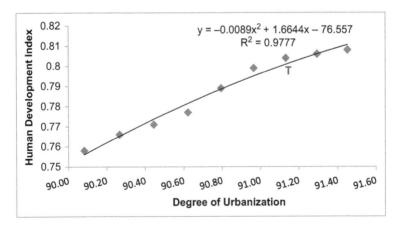

Figure 4.29 Urbanization and living standard in Argentina

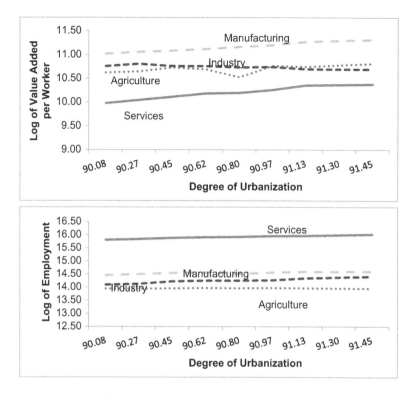

Figure 4.30 Degree of urbanization, productivity and employment in Argentina

Bolivia

Presented in Figure 4.31, the association between economic development and urbanization in Bolivia shows that the two are increasing proportionate.

Another noticeable fact is that the urban population has not reached any threshold level. This form of association is explained through productivity and employment growth depicted in Figure 4.32.

It is the services sector only that experienced a decline in productivity. In the industrial and manufacturing sectors, it has marginally increased. The highest productivity growth was achieved by the agriculture sector. The relative position of the sectors did not change with increasing urbanization from 2005 to 2013.

The analysis of employment level shows that it decreased in agriculture, sug-gesting that the workforce moved out from this sector. It was largely absorbed in services which registered the highest employment growth. Employment in the other two sectors, namely industry and manufacturing, marginally increased with urbanization. It implies that new migrants from rural areas were absorbed in highly productive activities within the industrial sector thereby contributing reasonably to the national income. Consequently, the HDI increased alongside

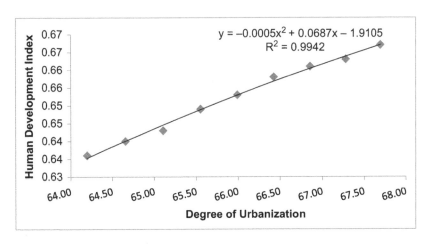

Figure 4.31 Urbanization and living standard in Bolivia

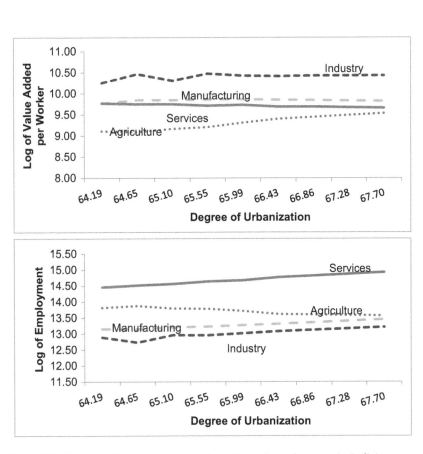

Figure 4.32 Degree of urbanization, productivity and employment in Bolivia

with urbanization. Therefore, the structural change witnessed in Bolivia is based on productivity gains in all sectors. This form of structural change contributes positively to urbanization and can offer a better quality of life to Bolivian citizens.

Brazil

The relationship between economic development and the degree of urbanization presented in Figure 4.33 in Brazil is somewhat different from that of Bolivia. The degree of urbanization reached a HDI threshold level of 0.739 with an urban population percentage of 84.34 per cent in 2011. Thereafter, the urban population increased to 85.17 per cent in 2013, with very little change in HDI. In general, the degree of urbanization is much higher in Brazil than in many other countries of the continent. This may be one reason explaining that HDI is inelastic to additional urban population.

An effort is made to explain this type of association with the analysis of productivity and employment growth presented in Figure 4.34.

The data analysis shows that productivity increased in all sectors, with the exception of industry. In fact, the manufacturing sector – the second most productive in 2005 – surpassed the industrial sector to become the most productive in 2013. During this period, the urban population grew from 82.83 per cent to 85.18. Although productivity was raised in services and agriculture, the relative position of each sector did not change with increasing urbanization. In addition, the agriculture sector remained least productive in 2013 as well.

The analysis of employment trends suggests that it decreased in the agriculture sector. However, the highest employment growth was achieved in the industrial sector. It is clear from the analysis that in case of the industrial sector, productivity decreased with a growing urban population, while employment increased. At the same time, employment in agriculture also declined. This means that the workforce migrated from rural to urban areas leading to a higher degree of

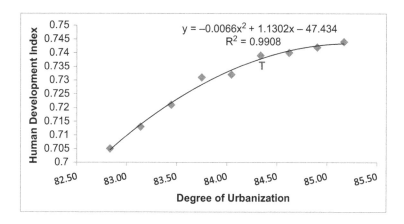

Figure 4.33 Urbanization and living standard in Brazil

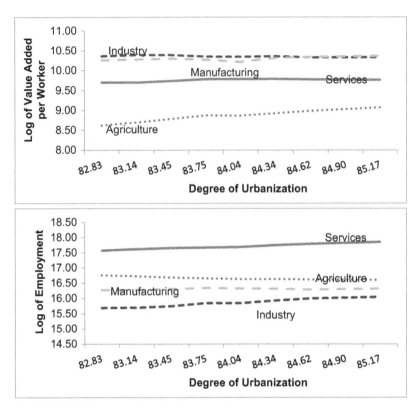

Figure 4.34 Degree of urbanization, productivity and employment in Brazil

urbanization. But these migrants were absorbed in low-value jobs in the industrial sector, thereby increasing employment. Consequently, the productivity of the sector declined as urban population increased. The net result is a very limited contribution to the national income with a newly urbanized population. This is captured by Figure 4.32 where HDI became stagnant with an increasing urban population. This kind of structural transformation may be regarded as jobless growth.

Colombia

Presented in Figure 4.35, the association between the economic development and the degree of urbanization in Colombia is similar to that of Brazil. The urban population reached a HDI threshold level of 0.710 with 75.32 per cent of urban population in 2011. Although the urban population slightly increased to 75.88 per cent in 2013, the HDI remained at the similar level of 0.711. In fact, in 2012, the HDI declined to 0.708, but recovered in the next year.

The Colombian economy might have gone through the same form of structural transformation as in Brazil (Figure 4.36).

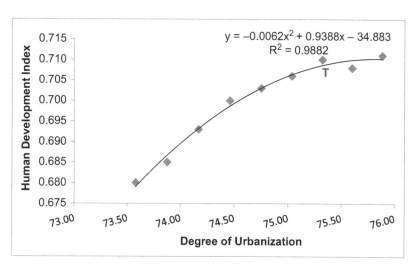

Figure 4.35 Urbanization and living standard in Colombia

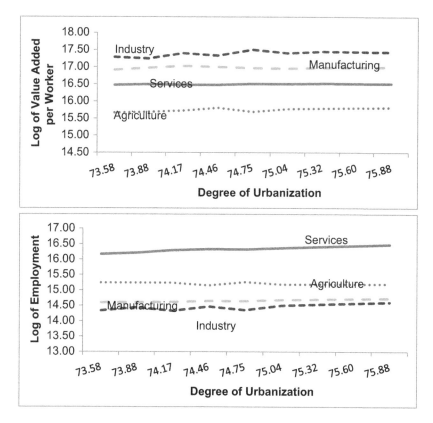

Figure 4.36 Degree of urbanization, productivity and employment in Colombia

Productivity levels in all sectors remained stagnant with an increasing number of urban residents from 73.58 per cent in 2005 to 75.88 per cent in 2013. However, productivity gains were almost negligible in all sectors. Consequently, the relative position of the sectors in terms of productivity did not change much.

Similarly, the relative position of the sectors related to employment did not change with increasing urbanization. However, employment growth varied among the different sectors. For instance, agricultural employment declined, while the services sector registered the highest employment growth followed by industry and manufacturing. In Colombia also, the workforce moved away from agriculture with relatively less productive activities to more productive activities in services. But the new migrants were also absorbed in other sectors with less value-added activities resulting in a stagnant overall productivity. Since the additional workforce moving away from agriculture was given less value-added jobs, its economic contribution was marginal leading to a stagnant HDI, which is rightly captured in Figure 4.35.

Like Brazil, this type of urbanization did not contribute to HDI. The newly urbanized population may not truly benefit from working in urban areas. Rather, this type of urbanization may contribute to slum formation. It is worth reminding that the migrant population moves from rural to urban areas due to the lack of employment opportunity in rural areas.

Mexico

Depicted in Figure 4.37, it is noticed that like many other countries in Latin America, the Mexican HDI reached a threshold level of 0.752 with an urbanization level of 78.12 per cent in 2011. Since then the rate of change of HDI declined as the urban population augmented. The urban population increased by 0.52 percentage points, while the HDI merely changed from 0.752 in 2011 to 0.756 in 2013.

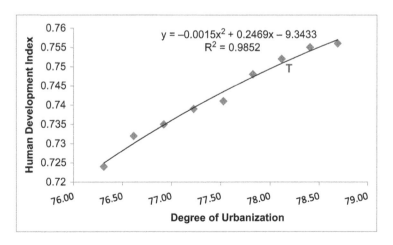

Figure 4.37 Urbanization and living standard in Mexico

The productivity and employment growth presented in Figure 4.38 explain the inelasticity of HDI to the degree of urbanization.

It is concluded from the graph that productivity in manufacturing and industrial sectors declined from 2005 to 2013, while urbanization increased. However, it almost remained stagnant in agriculture and services during the same period. Although the productivity of highly productive sectors (industry and manufacturing) declined, their relative position compared to other sectors remained unchanged. Agriculture remained the least productive sector.

The analysis of employment in various sectors suggests that a positive growth was registered in all of them. The services sector experienced the highest employment growth, while that of agriculture was the lowest. The trends suggest that there has been very little movement of workforce from agriculture to other sectors. The migrant population was absorbed in low value-added activities of manufacturing, and industrial sectors resulting in a decline in overall productivity. Although the services sector in Mexico provides employment to the largest percentage of workers, it only stands third in terms of productivity. Moreover, productivity in services stagnated with a growing urban population.

The analysis indicates that the migrant population was absorbed in least value-added economic activities in urban areas. Consequently, their contribution to the

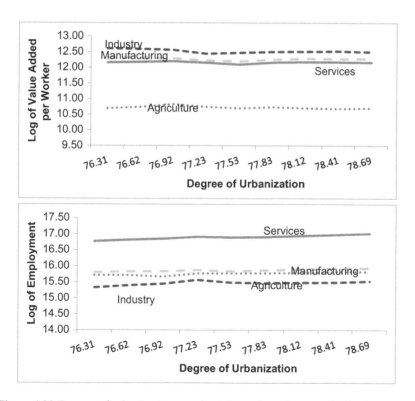

Figure 4.38 Degree of urbanization, productivity and employment in Mexico

national income was much smaller compared to that of the existing urban population, resulting in almost no change in HDI, which is captured in Figure 4.37. Findings also suggest that the degree of urbanization did not increase as opposed to the sample countries of Asia and Africa. This implies that Mexico reached a saturation level of urbanization, resulting in poor economic development.

Venezuela

Figure 4.39 depicts the relationship between economic development and urbanization in Venezuela. Trends are very different from other countries in the region and elsewhere. The HDI in Venezuela reached a threshold level of 0.758 in 2008, with 88.69 per cent of urbanization level. The country achieved a very high degree of urbanization and consequently the HDI was substantially high. However, since 2009 the HDI was almost stagnant.

The productivity and employment growth analysis are presented in Figure 4.40.

The empirical analysis shows that productivity in the industrial and manufacturing sectors declined with the intensified urbanization, while it recorded a positive growth in the two other sectors (agriculture and services). Despite these changes in productivity, the relative position of all sectors remained the same from 2005 to 2013. At the same time, the percentage of urban population marginally changed from 88.56 per cent to 88.89 per cent.

The analysis of sectoral employment growth suggests that it has increased in all sectors with the highest growth occurring in industry followed by services and manufacturing. The agriculture sector recorded the lowest employment growth. Findings also suggest that the industrial sector registered the highest employment growth, although its productivity declined with greater level of urbanization. A similar trend was experienced by the manufacturing sector.

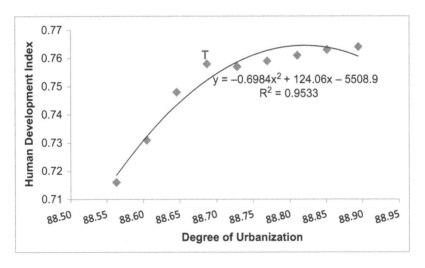

Figure 4.39 Urbanization and living standard in Venezuela

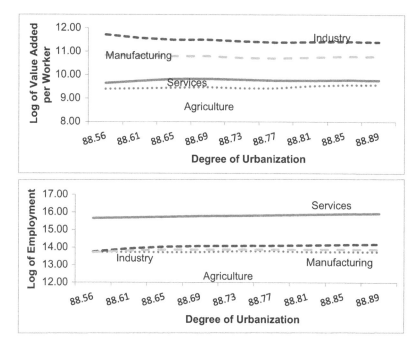

Figure 4.40 Degree of urbanization, productivity and employment in Venezuela

Declining productivity in addition to increasing employment suggest that additional workforce was absorbed in less value-added activities of the highly productive sectors resulting in a disproportionate contribution to the national income. Consequently, the HDI almost did not change from 2005 to 2013. It may also be noted that Venezuela achieved a very high degree of urbanization, while the urbanization rate used to be very low. It is emphasized that urbanization reached a saturation level and additional degree of urbanization did not generate further economic development.

4.4 Summary and conclusion

Sustainable and highly productive cities are key factors to enhance national development. Well-managed urbanization is fundamental in the process of structural transformation. The analysis of the linkages between urbanization and economic development presented in the chapter suggests that the association between both factors is positive in all countries (except the Philippines and Sri Lanka), although there are significant variations across and within continents. For instance, in Africa, in 2013, the degrees of urbanization vary from 18.59 per cent in Ethiopia to 63.79 per cent in South Africa, while in Asia they vary from 18.30 per cent in Sri Lanka to 73.28 per cent in Malaysia. The percentage of urban population is much higher in Latin America, ranging from 67.70 per cent in Bolivia to 91.45 per cent in Argentina in 2013.

In the African continent, Botswana and Ethiopia reached a threshold level of HDI. Beyond this point, the development index becomes inelastic to the growth of urban population. The stagnation of HDI with high degrees of urbanization is comprehensible, but it is unimaginable in countries like Ethiopia. For this country, the HDI became inelastic to urbanization at the level of 17.74 per cent of urban population. The decline in productivity in highly productive sectors such as industry and manufacturing constituted the major reasons for the slow urbanization process and the stagnation of economic development. In other African countries, the degree of urbanization and economic development increased proportionately as a result of structural transformation.

The analysis of Asian countries suggests that Thailand is the only exception where the HDI reached a threshold level of 0.72 and became inelastic to a degree of urbanization beyond 44.08 per cent of urban population. This phenomenon may be attributed to the decline in productivity of the industrial sector. Although the urban population grew from 44.08 per cent in 2008 to 17.91 per cent in 2013, the HDI remained stagnant at a level of 0.72. In other Asian countries, although the degree of urbanization varied drastically from one country to another, there was no sign of stagnation of HDI. For instance, the degree of urbanization in 2013 in China and India was 53.17 per cent and 31.99 per cent respectively, while it was 73.28 per cent in Malaysia. The Philippines and Sri Lanka experienced a decline in their urban population from 2005 to 2013. However, it is attributed to frequent changes in the definition of urbanization in both countries. In general, the association between economic development and urbanization was positive and significant.

The situation in Latin American countries is very different from the countries in the other two developing regions. Overall, all sample countries achieved a very high degree of urbanization. It varies from 67.70 per cent in Bolivia to 91.45 per cent in Argentina in 2013. Consequently, the HDI reached a threshold level at some point between 2005 and 2013 in all countries except in Bolivia. The proportionate increase in both HDI and urban population is understandable as urbanization started at a low level which left room for increasing urbanization. This is expected to result in better income and improved quality of life of the Bolivians. On the other hand, in the rest of Latin America, the HDI became inelastic to urban population as they reached a saturation level in terms of urban population. Additional urban population neither contributed to productivity nor cities were equipped to accommodate a population inflow.

Therefore, it implies that much of structural change took place in Asia and Africa resulting in higher income and better quality of life, but in Latin America, there is very little scope for further increase in urbanization. Cutting across region, the association between the degree of urbanization and economic development is found to be positive and significant.

Notes

1 Between 1970 and 1995, Africa's urban population grew at 5.2 per cent, while GDP per capita fell by an annual rate of 0.66 per cent.
2 Degree of urbanization data have been taken from World Development Indicator online.
3 HDI data is taken from UNDP. Website http://hdr.undp.org/en/content/human-development-index-hd is accessed on November 2, 2015.
4 From http://www.nscb.gov.ph/pressreleases/2004/30Jan04_urban.asp, accessed on December 10, 2015.
5 The regression model did not converge in TOBIT in many countries. Hence base results are presented in the table and such countries are marked with *.

Bibliography

Annez, P. C., Buckley, R. M. and Kalarickal, J. (2010) "African Urbanization as Flight? Some Policy Implications of Geography," *Urban Forum 08*, 21(3): 221–234.
Barrios, S., Bertinelli, L. and Strobl, E. (2006) "Climate Change and Rural–Urban Migration: The Case of Sub-Saharan Africa," *Journal Urban Economics*, 60(3): 357–371.
Cheru, F. (2005) *Globalization and Uneven Development in Africa: The Limits to Effective Urban Governance in the Provision of Basic Services*, online, available at www.globalizationafrica.org/papers/57.pdf (accessed March 25, 2016).
Davis, M. (2004) "Planet of Slums," *New Left Review*, 26: 1–23.
de Vries, G., Timmer, M. and de Vries, K. (2013) "Structural Transformation in Africa: Static Gains, Dynamic Losses," in *GGDC Research Memorandum 136*, University of Groningen, online, available at http://www.ggdc.net/publications/memorandum/gd136.pdf (accessed on March 16, 2016).
Etchemendy, S. (2009) *Models of Economic Liberalization: Regime, Power and Compensation in the Iberian-American Region*, online, available at http://papers.ssrn.com/abstract=1449085 (accessed on March 02, 2016).
Fay, M. and Opal, C. (2000) "Urbanization without Growth: A Not-So-Uncommon Phenomenon," *World Bank Policy Research Working Paper Series 2412*. Washington DC: World Bank.
Jedwab, R., Gollin, D. and Vollrath, D. (2013) *Urbanization with and without Industrialization*, online, available at www.gwu.edu/~iiep/assets/docs/papers/Jedwab_IIEPWP_2014–1 (accessed March 20, 2016).
McMillan, M., Rodrik, D. and Verduzco-Gallo, Í. (2013) *Globalization, Structural Change and Productivity Growth, With an Update on Africa*, online, available at http://margaretsmcmillan.com/wp-content/uploads/2013/12/McMillanRodrikVerduzco_Final_All.pdf (accessed February 20, 2016).
Montgomery, M. R., Stren, R., Cohen, B. and Reed, H. E. (eds.). (2003) *Cities Transformed: Demographic Change and Its Implications for the Developing World*. Washington, DC: National Academies Press.
Oyelaran-Oyeyinka, B. and Gehl-Sampath, P. (2010) *Latecomer Development: Innovation and Knowledge for Economic Growth*. Oxford, UK: Routledge.
Panditharathne, B. L. (1996) "The Development of the Sri Lankan Settlement System," in G. A. Paul (ed.) *Economic Development and Social Change in Sri Lanka: A Spatial and Policy Analysis* (pp. 3–40), New Delhi: Manohar Publishers.
Polèse, M. (2005) "Cities and National Economic Growth: A Reappraisal," *Urban Studies*, 42(8): 1429–1451.

Polèse, M. and Stren, R. E. (2000) *The Social Sustainability of Cities: Diversity and the Management of Change*. Toronto: University of Toronto Press.

SIDA. (2006) *Fighting Poverty in an Urban World – Support to Urban Development*, online, available at http://www.sida.se/contentassets/6107b402eb5444b0ba15 6af2741a815d/fighting-poverty-in-an-urban-world_1056.pdf (accessed January 6, 2016).

Spence, M. (2008) *The Growth Report: Principal Findings and Recommendations*, online, available at http://siteresources.worldbank.org/EXTPREMNET/ Resources/489960–1338997241035/Growth_Commission_Final_Report_ Launch_Presentation.pdf (accessed January 11, 2016).

Timmer, P. (2007) "Agricultural Growth," in D. Clark (ed.) *The Elgar Companion to Development Studies* (pp. 5–9), Cheltenham, UK: Edward Elgar Publishing.

Timmer, P. and Akkus, S. (2008, July) "The Structural Transformation as a Pathway Out of Poverty: Analytics, Empirics and Politics," *Working Papers 150, Center for Global Development*, online, available at http://www.cgdev.org/files/16421_file_ structural_transformation.pdf (accessed on March 18, 2016).

Uduporuwa, R. J. (2010) "An Analysis of Urban Growth and Urbanization in the Sabaragamuwa Province, Sri Lanka," *Sabaramuwa University Journal*, 9(1): 115–132.

UNECA. (2011) *Economic Report on Africa 2011: Governing Development in Africa – The Role of the State in Economic Transformation*. Addis Ababa, Ethiopia: United Nations Economic Commission for Africa (UNECA).

UN-Habitat. (2010) *State of the World's Cities 2010/2011: Bridging the Urban Divide*. Nairobi and London: UN-Habitat & Earthscan.

UN-Habitat and DFID. (2002) *Sustainable Urbanisation: Achieving Agenda 21*. Nairobi: UN-Habitat.

World Bank. (2009a) *Systems of Cities: Harnessing Urbanization for Growth and Poverty Alleviation–World Bank Urban and Local Government Strategy*. Washington, DC: World Bank.

World Bank. (2009b) *The World Bank Urban and Local Government Strategy: Concept and Issues Note, Finance Economics and Urban Department Sustainable Development Network*. Washington, DC: World Bank.

World Bank. (2013) *World Development Report 2013: Jobs*. Washington, DC: The World Bank.

5 Industrialization

5.1 Introduction

Throughout history, industrialization has shaped the economy of countries and regions most profoundly. It accounts in large part for the considerable divides between the rich and the poor countries and as well, for the significant differentials in wealth within countries. The mastery of industrialization tends to facilitate catch-up in technology and the growth convergence, South East Asian countries are evident examples (Amsden 1989; Amsden and Chu 2003). Clearly, the economic progress associated with emerging economies led by China is in large measure due to the maximization of relatively cheaper but skilled labour inputs in manufacturing processes.

Industrialization is commonly measured by manufacturing employment or output share in total employment or output, and it remains pivotal to trade and investment across countries of the world. It describes a process of resource real-location away from agriculture into manufacturing and is believed to be pivotal to the structural transformation of economies and the transition from stagnation to growth. Countries with a diversified manufacturing sector are more likely to exploit technological progress than those which specialize in primary products (Carmignani and Mandeville 2014). Moreover, manufacturing expansion triggers the rise of skilled workers with the attendant specialization for manufacturing complex and high-value products. However, with structural transformation comes the associated shift in the proportional contributions of the key sectors of agriculture, industry and services. Notably, countries tend to de-industrialize with employment and value added being largely reallocated to the services sector of the economy. Given that services tend to have lower productivity rates than manufacturing, rise in services could dampen growth prospects for countries so characterized when this phenomenon sets in prematurely.

De-industrialization describes a social, economic and structural change process caused by a reduction in industrial activity – particularly heavy manufacturing industry – in a particular country. It means that over the course of its development path, a country first industrializes, reflected in a rising share of resources, including labour, devoted to manufacturing. Thereafter, the services sector contribution to GDP becomes more important, and simultaneously, as de-industrialization sets in, this is reflected in a declining share of GDP and employment in industry. Increase in cost of labour and cost of raw materials processing and capital-intensive nature of manufacturing are among factors that trigger de-industrialization in developed countries (Subramanian 2014). This is the present reality for many advanced industrial economies across the world.

Therefore, positive de-industrialization features increased or constant manufacturing output, increased labour productivity, decrease in manufacturing employment share and an increase in service employment share. This is a common incident in advanced industrial societies whereby labour-saving technologies have triggered de-industrialization with no negative impact on output. Negative de-industrialization on the other hand is characterized by a decrease in output, lack of improvement in labour productivity, a decrease in manufacturing employment and an increase in services employment share. This is clearly the reality facing many low-income and middle-income African countries today – a phenomenon Rodrik describes as premature *de-industrialization* (Rodrik 2015). This reversed industrialization is reducing industrialization opportunities sooner than desired in national economies and at lower levels of national income than was the experience of the early industrializers.

Dasgupta and Singh (2006) in their reference to de-industrialization describes it as a situation where manufacturing begins to shrink or set off the path of being shrunk at income levels lower than that of those which the advanced industrial economies had when they began to de-industrialize. Since industrialization is the driving force behind globalization, urbanization and economic growth, the purveyor of the capitalist ideals, modernization of society and, to some extent, the development of a national middle class and as such the health of an economy; it is imperative to decipher what premature de-industrialization may portend for developing economies.

Since the 1960s, relationship between economic development and structural change has been topical in the analysis of development paths. As an important feature of economic growth, structural transformation connotes that some sectors of the economy experience faster long-term growth than other sectors, resulting to shifts in the share of the sectors in the total aggregate. Structural change (or transformation) undoubtedly plays a substantial role in the productivity catching up of developing countries.[1] More recent literature relates international income disparities with setbacks in the structural transformation processes. This chapter presents the link between structural transformation and industrialization trajectory across Africa, Asia and Latin America.

5.2   Literature review

Much of academic research on structural change, productivity and industrialization are done within the framing of the development of the three main sectors of the economy, multi-sector growth models, as well as evolutionary theories of structural change (Krüger 2008). Among the different strands of the literature on structural change and productivity are those which investigate the regular pattern of shifts among the primary, secondary and tertiary sectors. In addition to multi-sector growth models and evolutionary perspectives to structural transformation are empirical studies on resource reallocation and its relationship with different productivity growth alternatives. Overall, differences in income elasticity of demand and the varying impact of technological progress are factors believed to contribute immensely to structural change.

Studies which investigate the structural change process of developing countries vis-à-vis their productivity and industrialization trajectory, weigh their results against the conjectures of the three-sector hypothesis – which postulates the systematic succession of the three main sectors of the economy. According to the three-sector hypothesis, in the initial stage, the primary sector is dominant in the proportion of employment and fraction of total value added, whereas the secondary and tertiary sectors only account for a small share of employment and total value added. As industrialization sets in, the secondary sector begins to gain prominence, while primary sector shares decline, and tertiary sector is on standstill. However, later on the economic development path, labour and value added shifts from primary and secondary sectors to the tertiary sector of the economy. Ultimately, the tertiary sector will account for the largest percentage of employment as well as share of total value added. Data from developed economies such as the United States of America has been used to test the validity of the three-sector hypothesis.

In order to situate a theoretical explanation for the three-sector hypothesis, Fourastie (1949) used technological progress operationalized as growth rate of labour productivity, as the classification criteria for industries into the primary, secondary and tertiary sectors (Krüger 2008). Accordingly, he assigned industries with medium rates of technological progress to the primary sector and those with relatively high rate of technological progress to the secondary sector. The industries with relatively low rate of technological progress were considered part of the tertiary sector. Consistent with the literature survey carried out by Krüger (2008), both demand-side and supply-side factors contribute to structural change. On the demand side, relative prices, preference for higher quality, a craving for new goods and increasing saturation of existing goods impact on the quantity and composition of demand for the output of different industries. While on the supply-side, technological progress leads to improvements in production technologies or availability of new goods. Consequently, the interaction between demand-side and supply-side factors leads to structural change at the aggregate level, which in turn affects the growth of aggregate output, employment and productivity.

Attempts to examine the process of economic development as one which involves structural change and economic growth have shown that rates of productivity growth are significantly associated with changes in production structures across countries (Kuznets 1971). This makes it necessary to disaggregate components of growth within the countries before making useful comparisons across countries. Even so, more recent studies on economic growth drivers and catch up allude to the role transformation and upgrade of productive structures play in bringing about economic development (Lin 2011; McMillan and Rodrik 2011).

The upgrade in productive structures requires a shift from low-productivity activities to higher-productivity activities in the development process. Upon this foundation, development economists such as Arthur Lewis in his two-sector model with his extensive studies of Latin American economies has examined the dual nature of developing economies whereby traditional, low-productive, informal and subsistence economic activities coexist with modern, urban, formal economic activities, as different from that of developed countries with a structure that reallocates labour from traditional to modern, urban sectors of the economy. Others provide models which highlight the determinants of dynamic structural change, employment and growth in a dual economy with abundant labour surplus (Rada 2007; Ocampo *et al.* 2009; Lavopa 2015).

Although the more advanced industrial countries have followed a similar pattern of structural transformation process as shown by the three-sector hypothesis, the realities of developing countries prove otherwise (Bah 2009). Many developing countries tend not be experiencing this conventional pattern of transformation. For instance, evidence from recent literature point to the peculiarity of the African transformation process compared with how most Asian countries caught up to the frontier developed countries. Amongst other things, the agricultural sector has remained pivotal in the economic development process of many African countries due to its employment generating potential and contribution to GDP per capita. An examination of changes in the output structure – agriculture, industrial and services sector – over two decades for selected sub-Saharan countries indicates that although many African countries have a relatively thriving modern sector with high contribution of services to GDP, agricultural employment remains dominant in many countries (Tomšík *et al.* 2015). For Ethiopia, structural changes experienced in cereal markets was attributed to economic and income growth, urbanization, improved road infrastructure, greater access to information technologies and better agricultural technology adoption (Minten *et al.* 2014).

The Latin American experience is one of divergence, while several other countries of the world experienced notable increases in labour productivity in recent years (Ferreira and da Silva 2015). Even so, there was an observed process of structural transformation and reallocation of labour across sectors in the region over the period 1950–2005. Ferreira and da Silva (2015) studied the relative productivity path of selected Latin American countries, measuring the contribution of various sectors to the productivity slows experienced in the region's development trajectory. The authors found that productivity slowdown in traditional services account for the aggregate productivity retardation experienced by several economies. The study indicates that the traditional services sector, which is usually characterized by low productivity and low-productivity growth, happens to be the sector with the greatest increase in employment during the process of labour reallocation in Latin American economies.

We also know that developing countries are not only late starters to industrialization; their speed of industrialization tends to be slower than the early industrializers. Machicado (2014) tested a model of industrialization which explains why countries industrialize at different periods and what accounts for the slow pace of industrialization. The model (Gollin *et al.* 2002) postulates that countries only begin the process of industrialization when they are able to satisfy their basic agricultural requirements. After this stage, resources move up from the agricultural sector to non-agricultural sector at the onset of industrialization. As such, agricultural productivity tend to increase in the time it takes a country to become agriculturally self-sustaining, thereby slowing the start time and pace of industrialization. Overall, such countries tend to remain at a relatively lower level of income per capita in global or regional perspective.

Using a sample of nine Latin American countries (Argentina, Bolivia, Brazil, Chile, Colombia, Ecuador, Peru, Paraguay and Uruguay) with similar colonial institutions and cultural background, the country with the highest agricultural productivity over the sample period (Argentina) was found to have the highest GDP per capita and began the process of industrialization ahead of all other countries in the sample. Similarly, findings of Restuccia *et al.* (2008) allude to the importance of agricultural productivity in addition to institutional factors for structural transformation. Human capital accumulation also determines the pace and pattern of labour migration from agricultural to non-agricultural sectors of the economy (Caselli and Coleman 2001).

5.2.1   *Industrialization policies and structural transformation*

Macroeconomic policies in general and trade policies in particular amongst other structural reforms have been noted to influence the structural change or de-industrialization experience of developing countries. In an analysis of the economic performance of a sample of East Asian, Latin American and African developing economies that had embraced structural reforms and trade liberalization measures, mixed results on the objectives of export expansion and diversification of manufacturing sector output are noted (Shafaeddin 2005). In East Asian countries, rapid export growth was accompanied by expansion of industrial capacity and industrial upgrading. It is pertinent to note that, prior to the reform, the Asian countries were characterized by considerable industrial base and capability in the export of manufacturing goods. On the other hand, majority of the low-income sample countries from Latin America and Africa experienced slow growth of exports, de-industrialization and increased economic vulnerability because of the overreliance of their manufacturing sector on imports from the external sector due to import intensity of production and consumption.

One of the reasons adduced for the differential impact of trade liberalization is that while in the East Asian countries trade liberalization was engaged gradually and selectively as a component of a long-term industrial policy after having achieved a certain level of industrialization and development, in the Latin American and African sample of countries, trade liberalization was employed as a tool in the process of structural reforms including uniform and across-board liberalization. Generally, the study showed that irrespective of their geographical location, countries at early stages of industrialization and development tend to be vulnerable to import competition as a result of trade liberalization (Shafaeddin 2005).

Using an input-output-based structural change decomposition method, an observation of the sources and pattern of growth during three phases of Indonesian economic development over the period 1975–2000 was carried out (Jacob 2005). The study examined how latecomer countries industrialize, which industries led their process of industrialization and what policies trigger successful industrialization experience. Amongst factors that contributed to the growth spurt and significant structural changes especially in manufacturing were selective industrial policies and overall favourable macroeconomic conditions. In the aftermath of the 1997 Asian financial crisis, appropriate attention to the technological foundations and human capital base of the economy were considered pivotal to recovery and sustained growth. Since capital accumulation fuels the development of the industrial sector in addition to implementation of selective industrial policies, South East Asian exemplars attracted foreign direct investment by setting up special economic zones and providing incentives for emergent industrial clusters innovation. Other efficiency gains resulted from improvements transportation, communication networks and human capital investments

Following the failed applications of the Washington Consensus model across the developing world, there are renewed debates on the essential role that industrial policy plays in stimulating manufacturing productivity. Manufacturing plays a unique role in generating increasing returns unlike any other sector of the economy. Through three main conduits, manufacturing changes the structure of an economy. First, by producing more proportionate output relative to inputs, it generates increasing returns at the firm level. Second, sector or cluster level productivity gains accrue as a result of the economies of propinquity of allied supplier and competitor firms and institutions. Third, through working with inputs from the primary sector, secondary and tertiary sectors, it stimulates economy-wide backward and forward linkages and multipliers. African countries engaged the Import Substitution industrialization strategy after independence. However, contrary to the results obtained through a similar adoption of the Import Substitution Industrialization (ISI) in Latin American countries, the policy failed to achieve desirable outcomes due to structural constraints in the domestic market of many African countries. Specifically, the low level of physical and human capital accumulation – prevalence of low literacy rates and unskilled labour – slowed the process of industrialization in African countries and increased their dependence on developed countries for manufactured goods (Mendes *et al.* 2014). On the policy front, Africa's failed industrialization can also be attributed to the inability of African policy initiatives to find the right balance between the state and the market (Rodrik 2015). Pre-independence manufacturing capacities which were built through the adoption of Import Substitution policies seem to have shrunk and account for a meagre proportion of GDP.

5.3   Empirical analysis

What follows this section is empirical analysis that relates the degree of industrialization with structural transformation. The degree of industrialization is measured here as a ratio of value added of manufacturing and services to the total value added by all sectors.

5.3.1   Africa

The chart below depicts the direction of movement of productivity in various sectors and growth of industrialization in sample African economies.

It can be seen from the figure that structural change in Botswana was marked by productivity growth in all the sectors during 1991 to 2013. As indicated in Chapter 1, the value added in all other sectors except mining in Botswana recorded a positive growth. The figure shows that the mining sector which is a part of the industrial sector experienced highest productivity growth. This could have resulted from workforce in mining moving to more productive sectors such as manufacturing and services, resulting in a decline in the value added and employment. However, the rate of decline in value added is much lower than in employment, leading to higher-productivity growth. It may be inferred that the structural transformation experienced by the Botswanan economy is in the right direction. The value-added share of low-productive sector declined over the last two decades. Not only did the share of high-productive sectors have increased, but productivity and employment have also increased. The industrialization indicator increased at the rate of 2.56 per cent annually. Consequently, it can be deduced that structural transformation has led to significant industrialization in Botswana's economy.

The figure shows that labour productivity in industrial and manufacturing sectors drastically declined, while services sector experienced a growth of 1.33

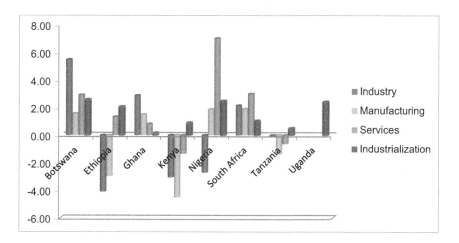

Figure 5.1 Industrialization and structural change in Africa

per cent annually. Although labour productivity in industrial and manufacturing sectors declined, value added increased at the rate of 8.82 and 7.33 per cent annually during 1991 to 2013. In the case of the services sector, the CAGR of value added was 8.72 per cent. The substantial growth rate in value added led to a higher degree of urbanization, which is reflected in the figure. The CAGR of industrialization was 2.04 per cent. It may be attributed to higher growth of value added in manufacturing and services sectors coupled with positive growth of labour productivity in the services sector.

Consequent to discussions in Chapter 4 that the Ethiopian government might be more concerned about employment than labour productivity growth, employment in all three sectors, that is, industry, manufacturing and services, has increased substantially during 1991 to 2013 at the cost of productivity growth in industry and manufacturing. This may be a deliberate policy of the government to focus on labour-intensive activities so that a large percentage of the workforce can be provided employment. The policy may be fine in the short run, but in long run, the government would have to pay due attention to labour productivity.

Conversely, the situation in Ghana is very different from that of Ethiopia. Despite the positive labour productivity growth of 1.49 and 0.83 per cent in manufacturing and services respectively, the growth of industrialization was marginal (CAGR: 0.15 per cent). In fact, the industrial sector witnessed the highest productivity growth of 2.88 per cent among all the sectors, and the growth of value added was highest (CAGR: 7.25 per cent) among all the sectors. On the other hand, the growth of value added in manufacturing and services sectors were 3.94 and 6.19 per cent respectively. It seems that the entire focus of the Ghanaian government has been on industry, which is dominated by natural resources, such as forest products leading to low growth of productivity and value added in urban sectors. Consequently, the Ghanaian economy witnessed low growth of industrialization.

Clearly, there has been improvements in productivity and employment in all the sectors, but it is unclear if policy alone has been responsible. Employment growth in industry, manufacturing, and services sectors were 4.62, 2.25 and 5.12 per cent respectively. In sum, the industrial sector, over that period experienced relatively better growth compared to the other two sectors. While the industrialization process has not been spectacular as with other African countries, productivity has risen in some sectors. This may signal improvements in the growth of the right type of skills that get the surplus workforce absorbed into high-productivity activities. This could well be a more sustainable industrial development process than merely focusing on employment growth at the cost of productivity.

Figure 5.1 shows that in Kenya, labour productivity in all the sectors declined over the period of time. The CAGR were –3.06, –4.52 and –1.35 per cent in industry, manufacturing and services respectively. Although labour productivity in all the sectors declined, the annual growth rates of value added were 3.12, 2.44 and 4.61 per cent respectively. On the other hand, the employment in these sectors grew at the rate of 6.70, 7.91 and 6.37 per cent, showing that the growth of employment and productivity was not commensurate. The higher growth of employment than value added resulted in negative productivity growth. Although productivity growth during 1991 to 2013 was negative as discussed in Chapter 4, it had been stagnant for the last one decade.

There are no suggestions that de-industrialization is taking place, but the growth of industrialization was marginal as the growth of value added in all the sectors were more or less similar leading to virtually no growth of industrialization. Another noticeable fact is that the growth of employment was much higher than value added. As with the case of Ethiopia, there has been more progress with employment growth than productivity growth. A balance needs to be found to ensure skill development policies equally promote productivity-enhancing higher value-adding activities. Economic and industrial policies in Kenya need to foster both skill development that leverage youth innovative energy and also promote rising productivity across sectors especially the continually growing albeit, low-productivity services sector.

The Nigerian case is very different from most of the African countries. The industrial sector registered a decline in labour productivity, while manufacturing and services sectors registered a positive growth at −2.72, 1.87 and 7.02 per cent respectively. The major reason behind the decline in labour productivity of industrial sector is the mining component of the sector. The share of value added of the mining sector was 52.61 per cent in 1991, which declined to 28.17 per cent in 2011. On the contrary, the services sector registered an impressive growth. Decline in value added of the mining sector and increase in the manufacturing and services sectors contributed to the growth of industrialization. It grew at the rate of 2.46 per cent preceding Botswana.

The Nigerian case is different in many ways. It is the only sample country in the continent where CAGR of labour productivity in agriculture was 4.67 per cent, much higher than that of the manufacturing sector. Although productivity of the industrial sector declined drastically, the average labour productivity was still the highest among all the sectors. As discussed in Chapter 3 that although productivity growth declined, employment registered a positive growth. Decline in productivity and increase in employment suggests that the economy might be losing high-productivity jobs in the sector. This unconventional trajectory of Nigeria's structural transformation tends to be by-passing industry into low-productive services sector tends to depress overall dynamism of the economy as a whole.

The type of structural transformation promoting a decline in the share of low-productive sector and an increasing share of high-productive sectors is considered the most desirable. Presently, in Nigeria, the share of low-productive primary sector, that is, agriculture has increased and that of industry has decreased. While the government of Nigeria did explicitly promote the policy of improving the agriculture sector, the growth of productivity in manufacturing improved only marginally, while services have risen far more disproportionally. The unprecedented growth of services sector has resulted in a greater degree of service-based industrialization, which is reflected in the figure.

The case of South Africa is similar to that of Ghana. From the figure, all the three sectors registered an increase in productivity growth accounting for 2.15,

1.90 and 3.0 per cent in industry, manufacturing and services respectively. Also, value added in the sectors registered a CAGR of 1.39, 2.71 and 5.45 per cent respectively. As well, the services sector registered the highest growth rate, not only in labour productivity, but also that of value added, resulting in a higher degree of growth in the industrial sector at the rate of 1.03 per cent. The low growth rate of value added by the industrial sector has also contributed to low degree of industrialization.

Employment was stagnant in all the sectors except the services sector, which witnessed an annual growth rate of 2.39 per cent. It appears that structural transformation of the South African economy has fostered greater productivity growth than employment in sectors other than services. The process of structural transformation of South Africa tends to follow in part the conventional pathway, whereby the share of low-productive primary sector, the agriculture sector is declining; while concomitantly, the share of a potentially high-productive sector, namely services, is increasing. However, the industrial sector which should equally be recording continuing dynamism tends to have stalled and is actually experiencing a premature decline.

The nexus of structural transformation and industrialization in Tanzania is similar to that of Kenya, where labour productivity in all the sectors declined during 1991 to 2013 accounting for –0.13, –1.41 and –0.63 per cent in industry, manufacturing and services respectively. Again, while value added in the sectors grew annually at the rate of 7.64, 6.60 and 5.61 per cent respectively, growth was similar in all the sectors resulting in low growth of industrialization. The figure shows that CAGR of industrialization was very low (0.49 per cent). While labour productivity in all the sectors declined, employment share grew substantially. The annual employment growth rate was 7.93, 8.13 and 6.39 per cent in industry, manufacturing and services. The decline in labour productivity and substantial growth in employment suggests a relatively strong focus on employment relative to productivity growth.

Due to lack of employment data, labour productivity of the Ugandan economy cannot be generated. Consequently, the growth of industrialization and labour productivity cannot be analysed.

5.3.2   Asia

The analysis of industrialization and structural change in selected Asian sample countries is presented in Figure 5.2. The figure shows that the pattern of structural transformation emerging from the Asian countries is very different from that of their African counterparts. Structural transformation in Asia unlike much of Africa is characterized by productivity growth in all the sectors in most of the sample countries. For instance, China, India, Philippines and Sri Lanka registered productivity growth in urban economic activities. Consequently, along with structural change, the countries have experienced growth of industrialization.

In China, labour productivity in all the three urban sectors registered a positive annual growth rate, manufacturing being the highest (9.99 per cent). Notably,

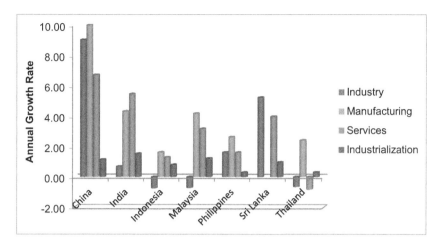

Figure 5.2 Industrialization and structural change in Asia

and in contradistinction to Africa's experience, the services sector which was dominant in Africa witnessed the lowest productivity growth (6.71 per cent) in China suggesting a different growth dynamic compared to African countries. The annual growth of value added in industry, manufacturing and services sectors were 11.82, 12.41 and 10.89 per cent respectively. Since value added in all the sectors grew with almost similar rate during 1991 to 2013, the growth of industrialization is not very high, as reflected in the figure with annual industrialization growth of 1.14 per cent.

Not only has productivity growth in urban sectors been positive, but employment has also grown positively with the highest growth rate (4.19 per cent annually) in services sector. China has for several years developed a robust industrial policy and made significant explicit investment on growing its industry. Not surprisingly, there has been growth in productivity and employment growth. The pattern of structural transformation taking place in the Chinese economy is a model of the conventional growth dynamic that could be emulated by other developing countries.

The model of structural change experienced by the Indian economy is different from that of China. Contrary to the Chinese case, productivity of the Indian services sector registered the highest annual growth rate (5.47 per cent), while that of the industrial sector was 0.68 per cent. The manufacturing sector productivity growth rate did not match that of China and was just 4.32 per cent. The annual growth rate of value added in industry, manufacturing and services sectors was 6.86, 6.65 and 9.22 per cent, respectively. Unlike China, value-added growth in the services sector was much higher compared to other two sectors leading to higher growth of industrialization in India, as depicted in Figure 5.2. It was the highest (1.53 per cent) among all the sample Asian countries.

The structural transformation of the Indian economy was accompanied by the positive growth of employment in all urban sectors with highest growth rate in the industrial sector (6.69 per cent). In sum, structural transformation in both China and India is productivity growth driven, leading to employment growth also. However, while the Indian economy is driven in large part by the services sector, the Chinese government has prioritised the manufacturing sector.

One of the reasons for growth in productivity and employment in urban sectors is the entry of private sector in higher education. For several years, India has invested in tertiary education through increased private sector participation. Consequently, a large number of private technical and management institutions have entered into the market. Due to intense competition in the sector, the private sector has tended to be always up-to-date in terms of teaching and training courses. This has resulted in the creation of skilled human resources equipped with the latest technical and managerial knowledge and abilities producing high value-added goods.

The Indonesian economy experienced a decline in productivity (–0.74 per cent) of the industrial sector during 1991 and 2013. Although the other two urban sectors witnessed a positive productivity growth rate, it was much less compared to China and India. The productivity growth in manufacturing and services sectors grew at the rate of 1.63 and 1.29 per cent annually. However, the annual growth rates of value added in these sectors were industry (2.55 per cent), manufacturing (3.29 per cent) and services (5.11 per cent). The dissimilar growth in value added has resulted in expected growth of urbanization but is constraint by the magnitude of value-added growth rates. Overall, industrialization has grown at the rate of 0.80 per cent annually.

Like many other Asian economies, the structural transformation in Indonesia has resulted in employment growth in all urban sectors, with highest growth in the services sector (3.92 per cent) and a comparable growth in the industrial sector (3.25 per cent). Structural transformation in the country has led to productivity and employment growth in manufacturing and services, resulting in greater degree of industrialization. However, decline in productivity needs to be a concern of the government. Significantly, the services sector as with majority of African countries, has recorded high growths of value added and employment. Although employment in the industrial sector has grown similar to that of services, the comparatively lower productivity growth in value added resulted in a decline in productivity in the industrial sector, which may be attributed to lack of appropriate skill-development policies.

The scenario in Malaysia is more or less similar to that of Indonesia. The decline of productivity in the industrial sector is by and large similar (0.72 per cent), but productivity growth in other two sectors is much higher. The highest productivity growth (4.18 per cent) was registered in manufacturing sector, while productivity in the services sector grew at a lower rate of 3.17 per cent. The annual growth of value added was 2.91, 5.87 and 7.11 per cent respectively, although the growth data suggest that urban sectors have witnessed varying degree of value-added growth. The growth rate of manufacturing and services sectors is much higher than the industrial, therefore, the growth of industrialization is expected to be higher. Malaysia registered the industrialization growth of 1.22 per cent annually, growing at a much faster rate than many sample Asian economies.

The varying degree of productivity growth resulted in a structural transformation that contributed positive growth to employment in all the urban sectors. It was 3.35, 1.49 and 3.70 per cent annually in industry, manufacturing and the services sectors. The lowest growth rate of value added and second highest growth rate of employment in the industrial sector resulted in decline in productivity in the sector. It may point to a situation that additional workforce might have been absorbed in low-productive activities of the sector. It could also suggest the prioritization of the services sector.

The pattern of structural change and degree of industrialization in the Philippines is similar to that of China, although it varies drastically in terms of magnitude. Like China, productivity growth was highest in the manufacturing sector (2.63 per cent), followed by industry (1.62 per cent) and services (1.61 per cent). The annual growth rates of value added in these sectors were 3.58, 4.13 and 5.75 per cent, respectively. Significantly, productivity growth and value-added growth are in reverse order. For instance, productivity growth in the services sector is the lowest (1.61 per cent), while value-added growth is highest (5.75 per cent). The lowest growth rate in one component of industrialization, that is, manufacturing has adversely affected the process of industrialization resulting in very low growth (0.30 per cent).

Structural transformation as a result of this kind of productivity growth had positive impact on employment. Employment in urban sectors grew at the rate of 2.59 per cent in industry, 1.01 per cent in manufacturing and 4.12 per cent in the services sector. Like most of the developing countries, Philippines also recorded high growth rates in the services sector. Consequently, not only did the sector achieve the highest productivity growth, but it also provided employment to a large segment of the population. The share of employment in the services sector in 2013 was highest (0.43 per cent). Although the concentration of one sector contributed significantly to productivity and employment growth, the neglect of the manufacturing sector resulted in a slow growth in industrialization. In order to achieve a higher degree of industrialization, the government reoriented its industrial policies and paid due attention to the manufacturing sector.

Unlike the other countries, data for Sri Lanka do not come from GGDC used for the other countries; therefore, they are not comparable. In the case of Sri Lanka, manufacturing sector was not reported separately. It was merged with the industrial sector. Therefore, industrialization has been measured as a ratio of value added of services and industrial sectors to the total value added. The figure shows that the country's productivity growth in industrial and services sectors were 5.24 and 3.99 per cent respectively. The growth of value added in both sectors was 6.14 and 6.24 per cent respectively. Such a high growth in value added in both sectors resulted in high rate of industrialization (0.97 per cent).

Structural transformation resulting from such productivity growth in both sectors resulted in positive employment growth. It was 1.29 and 2.21 per cent in the industrial and services sectors respectively. Like most of the sample countries, the dominant sector was services. The employment growth in the sector was better than the other sector, but at the cost of productivity growth.

Structural change emerging from productivity growth in Thailand is very different from other Asian countries. It is the only country where labour productivity in services sector declined at the rate of –0.84 per cent annually. The productivity in manufacturing sector grew at the rate of 2.41 per cent, while industrial sector also registered a decline (–0.66 per cent). On the other hand, growth of value added in all the sectors was positive. Highest growth was registered in manufacturing (5.22 per cent) followed by services (2.69 per cent) and industry (1.63 per cent). Although the growth of value added in both components of industrialization was higher than the industrial sector, the growth of agriculture sector (2.51 per cent) increased substantially resulting in low degree of industrialization in Thailand as it grew at the rate of 0.31 per cent.

The kind of structural change emerging from negative growth of productivity in the two urban sectors contributed to positive growth of employment, that is industry (2.20 per cent), manufacturing (2.76 per cent), and services (3.74 per cent). The findings suggest that the growth of employment and valued added in services are not proportionate resulting to a decline in productivity. Clearly, the manufacturing sector has thrived, whereby value added has grown substantially, albeit with limited growth of employment. It will seem that explicit investment is being made to develop skilled human resources suited to be employed at high value-added sub-sectors in the manufacturing sector. Productivity and employment growth in manufacturing is appreciable, but the decline in productivity in the services sector could be a concern to the Thai government.

5.3 Latin America

The level of industrialization in Latin American countries is much higher compared to their counterparts in Asia and Africa. Hence, a major change in the degree of industrialization is not expected in the sample countries. As presented in earlier sections, the highest productivity growth in Asian countries were almost two digits, while in Africa, it was around 7 per cent. The productivity and industrialization growth in Latin American countries are presented in Figure 5.3. The figure shows that the highest productivity growth (2.39 per cent) was attained in the manufacturing sector of Argentina.

From the figure, the industrial sector registered a decline in productivity (–0.46 per cent), while growth rate of productivity in the services sector was 1.44 per cent. The growth of value added in industry, manufacturing and services were 3.15, 2.54 and 3.85 per cent, respectively. Although the services sector experienced the highest value-added growth, the comparatively lower value-added growth of manufacturing compared to industry resulted in low growth (0.33 per cent) in industrialization.

Although productivity growth was very impressive in the manufacturing sector, employment in the sector almost remained stagnant (0.27 per cent growth rate).

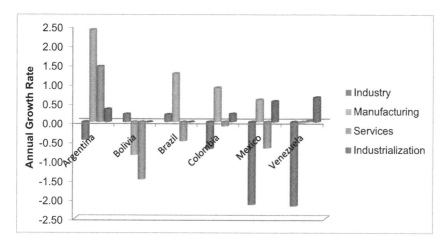

Figure 5.3 Industrialization and structural change in Latin America

Structural transformation in Argentina contributed significantly to employment growth in industry (3.40 per cent) and services (2.77 per cent). On one hand, the highest productivity growth and lowest employment growth in manufacturing could be attributed to the strategic decision of the country. It might be due to technological improvements or augmentation of productivity in the sector by providing skill upgrading opportunities to the existing workforce. On the other hand, the industrial sector has not been paid due attention and consequently, the additional workforce is absorbed in low value-added activities, resulting in highest employment growth and decline in productivity. While productivity and employment growth in services sector is appreciable, due attention needs to be paid to productivity growth in manufacturing to achieve higher degree of industrialization.

The economy of Bolivia is almost stagnant from the productivity growth and industrialization point of view. Labour productivity grew marginally in the industrial sector (0.20 per cent) and declined in manufacturing (−0.86 per cent) and services (−1.49 per cent). Although productivity growth is disappointing, the growth of value added is reasonably good accounting for 4.43, 3.70 and 3.71 per cent respectively. The highest growth rate of value added in the industrial sector and an impressive growth rate in agriculture resulted in decline (−0.1 per cent) in the degree of urbanization. Another reason for de-industrialization could be the already high contribution of the sector to GDP and relative level of industrialization, which was 66.74 per cent in 1991 – a level which many sample countries have not been able to achieve even in 2013.

As far as employment growth as a result of structural transformation is concerned, it has been very impressive. The annual employment growth in industry, manufacturing, and services were 4.37, 4.80 and 5.26 per cent, respectively. The high employment growth with declining or marginally increasing productivity growth suggests that additional workforce is employed in low value-added activities in the sectors. One of the possible explanations could be that high value-added activities are moving away from the country at the cost of low-value ones. This form of structural change may be good in short run (full employment situation), but could be detrimental in long run.

The scenario of industrialization and productivity growth in Brazil is somewhat better than Bolivia. In the services sector, productivity has declined at the rate of –0.49 per cent annually. The highest productivity growth of 1.26 per cent was achieved in manufacturing sector. On the other hand, the growth of value added was 3.77, 2.83, 2.97 and 2.54 per cent in agriculture, industry, manufacturing and services sectors, respectively. The lower growth rates in both the components of industrialization compared to agriculture and industry resulted in de-industrialization of the Brazilian economy. The prevalence of high degree of industrialization in the beginning of the study period may also be attributed to this phenomenon.

Despite the process of de-industrialization, the impact of structural change on employment growth has not been adverse. It has grown at the rate of 2.54, 1.64 and 3.19 per cent in industry, manufacturing and the services sector respectively. The noticeable fact is that the services sector registered a decline in productivity at the same time; the employment growth in the sector has been highest. It may be inferred that the Brazilian government is concentrating more on employment rather than productivity and consequently allowed low value-added activities in services sector to thrive. Alternatively, the observed lower productivity in the sector could be due to lack of appropriate skill development programmes to raise capabilities and produce high-value products in the sector. Whatever may be the case, the productivity of the highest contributing sector of the economy needs to foster industrial dynamism and subsequent economic development.

Like Argentina, productivity in the industrial sector declined (–0.70 per cent); while in manufacturing, it registered positive growth rate (0.89 per cent), whereas the services sector experienced decline in productivity (–0.11 per cent). However, there has been growth of value added in all the sectors; that is industry (2.86 per cent), manufacturing (2.78 per cent) and services (3.59 per cent). The higher growth of value added in the services sector resulted in slightly better industrialization compared to other Latin American countries. It grew at the rate of 0.21 per cent annually. Our findings suggest that the manufacturing sector that recorded growth in productivity realized the least value-added growth among all other urban sectors.

The structural change process resulting in the decline in productivity of the industry and services sectors did not contribute to decline in employment. Rather, employment in these sectors grew at the rate of industry (3.59 per cent), manufacturing (1.76 per cent) and services (3.84 per cent). It may be worth noting that although services sector achieved the highest growth in value added and employment, labour productivity in the sector declined during 1991–2013. In view of this sectoral behaviour, it would seem that employment and value-added growth was achieved at the cost of productivity. It might be that additional workforce provided employment at low value-added activities in the sector. Consequently, employment and value added grew, but productivity declined. The rise in value added certainly contributed to industrialization, but decline in productivity needs to be controlled. The growth of industrialization in Colombia is also constraint by its existing level in the beginning of the study period, which was substantially high.

The case of Mexico is very much similar to the Colombia. Productivity in the industrial and services sectors declined, while it grew moderately in the manufacturing sector. Like most of the sample countries, the value added in the urban sectors however experienced reasonable growth. It was 1.89, 2.12 and 3.20 per cent in the industrial, manufacturing and services sectors respectively. The higher value added by both components of industrialization compared to industrial sector significantly boosted the industrialization process. Consequently, it grew at the rate of 0.54 per cent, a growth rate much higher than all Latin American sample countries except Venezuela. The higher growth of industrialization could also be attributed to its lower level in 1991 compared to other sample countries in the region.

The impact of structural change on employment was similar to other sample economies. It grew at the rate of 4.12 per cent in industry, 1.47 per cent in manufacturing, and 3.99 per cent in the services sector. Like Colombia, the productivity in the manufacturing sector improved, but the growth of employment was lowest among the other urban sectors. The higher growth in productivity and lowest growth in employment may be attributed to technological changes in the sector. On the other hand, it appears that the Mexican government concentrated on the services sector and achieved high growth of value added and employment at the cost of productivity. It is appreciable from the growth of industrialization point of view, but decline in productivity of the highest contributing sector to the national income needs to be controlled.

Venezuela presents a unique scenario among other economies in the region. The labour productivity in industrial and manufacturing sectors declined at the rate of –2.18 and –0.03 per cent respectively, while the services sector registered a positive growth rate of 0.03 per cent. Apart from Argentina, Venezuela is another country where productivity in the services sector experienced positive growth. The growth of value added in urban sectors was as follows: industry (1.16 per cent), manufacturing (0.58 per cent) and services (3.48 per cent). The significantly higher growth of value added in the services sector led to a greater degree of industrialization. Consequently, it achieved the highest growth rate (0.64 per cent) among other sample countries in Latin America.

Like other countries, the type of structural change emerging from the varying degrees of productivity growth results in employment growth in all the sectors. It was 3.24, 0.52 and 3.52 per cent in industry, manufacturing and services sectors. It may be noticed that the growth of employment is similar to that of value added. In the services sector, not only has labour productivity increased, but also the growth of employment and value added was highest among all the sectors. Apparently, services emerged the dominant sector in the Venezuelan economy.

Another reason for higher degree of industrialization is the scope of its expansion. The level of industrialization in 1991 was the lowest among other sample economies in the region.

5.4   Comparative analysis

The chapter presents an analysis of the growth of industrialization resulting from structural transformation. It is clear from the analyses that it was affected by the historical path of productivity growth as well as by the initial conditions: both the level and degrees. In general, it was found that the level of industrialization in Latin American countries was higher compared to the two other regions of Asia and Africa during early 1990s. Consequently, the growth of industrialization has been moderate in the region.

Structural transformation in the African countries is marked by significant productivity shifts (growth or decline) in most of the economies. For instance, labour productivity in all the urban sectors in Botswana, Ghana and South Africa increased, while in Tanzania it decreased in all the sectors. However, productivity in the industrial and manufacturing sectors declined in Ethiopia and Kenya, whereas Nigeria witnessed a decline in productivity in industrial sector only. Kenya is the only country in the region where productivity in the services sector also declined. As far as the growth of industrialization is concerned, Botswana registered the highest annual growth of 2.56 per cent, followed by Nigeria (2.46 per cent). Despite productivity growth in all the sectors in Ghana, it did not contribute much to industrialization (grew at the rate of just 0.15 per cent). The contribution to industrialization has been mainly by the services sectors. In the countries where the services sector performed better, the degree of industrialization increased more than the others. For instance, the annual value-added growth in services sector in Botswana, Ethiopia and Nigeria were 7.09, 8.72 and 8.01 per cent, and industrialization grew at the rate of 2.56, 2.04 and 2.46 per cent respectively.

Structural change in the Asian countries was marked by clear productivity shifts (relative growth and decline) in most of the countries. In Indonesia, Malaysia and Thailand, productivity in the industrial sector declined with Thailand being the only country in which productivity in the services sector also declined. On the other hand, China, India, Philippines and Sri Lanka registered growth in productivity in all the sectors. However, the growth of industrialization was highest in India (1.53 per cent) followed by China (1.14 per cent). The services sector played an important role in industrialization in Asia also. The countries, in which the services sector performed well, experienced higher growth in industrialization. For instance, value-added growth in China, India and Malaysia was 10.89, 9.22 and 7.11 per cent, respectively, and these countries have experienced higher degree of industrialization (1.14, 1.53 and 1.22 per cent) compared to others. The contribution of manufacturing was relatively less compared to services in all other countries except China; where value-added growth in manufacturing (12.41 per cent) was higher than services.

The scenario in Latin America is very different than in Asia and Africa. Labour productivity in the services sector declined in all the sample countries except Argentina and Venezuela. In fact, de-industrialization has taken place in Bolivia and Brazil due to decline in productivity in both sectors in Bolivia and drastic decline in productivity in the services sector in Brazil. Although value-added grew positively in all the sectors of all the countries in the region, the magnitude of growth is less compared to their counterpart in Asia and Africa. One of possible reasons could be the saturation level in industrialization in Latin American countries as it was substantially high in the beginning of the study period. Despite the fact that the Mexican and Venezuelan economies have registered a high growth of industrialization (0.54 and 0.64 per cent respectively) comparatively, it appears that the Venezuelan economy is moving away from oil-based to manufacturing-based one. The manufacturing sector witnessed a growth of 3.48 per cent, much higher than other sectors.

Note

1 See Chapter 1 of this book for elaboration.

Bibliography

Amsden, A. H. (1989). *Asia's next giant: Late industrialization in South Korea.* Oxford: Oxford University Press.

Amsden, A. H. and Chu, W. W. (2003). *Beyond late development: Taiwan's upgrading policies.* Cambridge: MIT Press Books.

Bah, E. H. (2009). *Structural Transformation in Developed and Developing Countries,* online, available at http://econstor.eu/bitstream/10419/40244/1/42_bah.pdf (accessed on April 10, 2016).

Carmignani, F. and Mandeville, T. (2014). Never been industrialized: A tale of African structural change. *Structural Change and Economic Dynamics,* 31, 124–137.

Caselli, F. and Coleman II, W. J. (2001). The US structural transformation and regional convergence: A reinterpretation. *Journal of Political Economy,* 109(3), 584–616.

Dasgupta, S. and Singh, A. (2006). "Manufacturing, services and premature de-industrialisation in developing countries: A Kaldorian empirical analysis," ESRC Centre for Business Research, University of Cambridge.

Ferreira, P. C. and da Silva, L. F. (2015). Structural transformation and productivity in Latin America. *The BE Journal of Macroeconomics,* 15(2), 603–630.

Fourastié, J. (1949). Le Grand Espoir du XXe Siecle. *Progress Technique, Progress Economique, Progress Social.* Paris, Presses Universitaires de France, p. 224 (Reprinted in 1989 collection, Tel Gallimard).

Gollin, D., Parente, S. and Rogerson, R. (2002). The role of agriculture in development. *The American Economic Review,* 92(2), 160–164.

Jacob, J. (2005). Late industrialization and structural change: Indonesia, 1975–2000. *Oxford Development Studies,* 33(3–4), 427–451.

Krüger, J. J. (2008). Productivity and structural change: A review of the literature. *Journal of Economic Surveys,* 22(2), 330–363.

Kuznets, S. S. (1971). *Economic growth of nations*. Cambridge, MA: Harvard University Press.

Lavopa, A. (2015). "Structural transformation and economic development: Can development traps be avoided?" Doctoral dissertation, Maastricht University.

Lin, J. Y. (2011). New structural economics: A framework for rethinking development. *The World Bank Research Observer*, 26(2), 193–221.

Machicado, C.G., Rioja, F., Saravia, A. (2014) Productivity, Structural Change, and Latin American Development. *Review of Development Economics*, 18(3), 610–624.

McMillan, M. S. and Rodrik, D. (2011). "Globalization, structural change and productivity growth," National Bureau of Economic Research No. w17143.

Mendes, A. P. F., Bertella, M. A. and Teixeira, R. F. (2014). Industrialization in Sub-Saharan Africa and import substitution policy. *Revista de Economia Política*, 34(1), 120–138.

Minten, B., Stifel, D. and Tamru, S. (2014). Structural transformation of cereal markets in Ethiopia. *Journal of Development Studies*, 50(5), 611–629.

Ocampo, J. A., Rada, C. and Taylor, L. (2009). *Growth and policy in developing countries: A structuralist approach*. New York: Columbia University Press.

Rada, C. (2007). Stagnation or transformation of a dual economy through endogenous productivity growth. *Cambridge Journal of Economics*, 31(5), 711–740.

Restuccia, D., Yang, D. T. and Zhu, X. (2008). Agriculture and aggregate productivity: A quantitative cross-country analysis. *Journal of Monetary Economics*, 55(2), 234–250.

Rodrik, D. (2015). Premature deindustrialization. *National Bureau of Economic Research Working Paper No. 20935*, 21(1), 1–33.

Shafaeddin, M. S. (2005). Trade liberalization and economic reform in developing countries. *The IMF, World Bank and Policy Reform*, 155, 2–20.

Subramanian, A. (2014). Ideas and power in contemporary trade development. *Adelphi Papers*, 54(450), 39–60.

Tomšík, K., Smutka, L., Lubanda, J. E. and Rohn, H. (2015). Position of agriculture in Sub-Saharan GDP structure and economic performance. *Agris On-Line Papers in Economics & Informatics*, 7(1), 69–80.

6 Poverty

6.1 Introduction

The new structuralist economics attaches importance to the poverty-alleviation-led growth strategies. They accredit growth processes that enhance productive activities, productive employment, improved earnings and so on, as sustainable drivers of long-term development and poverty alleviation. Structural transformation is said to contribute to poverty alleviation when the changing sectoral distribution of GDP towards high-productivity sectors correspond to proportionate change in distribution pattern of the labour force. Implying that altering production structure from low to high productivity, while countenancing labour movement to high-productivity sector, may increase labour remuneration; hence improving standards of living and reducing poverty levels.

The World Bank defines poverty as deprivation in well-being; this may be viewed in varying dimensions including low incomes and the inability to acquire the basic goods and services necessary for survival with dignity. Poverty also encompasses low levels of health and education, poor access to clean water and sanitation, inadequate physical security, lack of voice, and insufficient capacity and opportunity to better one's life. It is a multifaceted concept, which includes social, economic, and political elements. Poverty may be measured as either absolute or relative. Absolute poverty or destitution refers to the lack of means necessary to meet basic needs such as food, clothing and shelter. The relative poverty takes into consideration individual social and economic status compared to the rest of society. Poverty reduction is the central objective of the international development agenda of many institutions. A number of key social development objectives have been agreed upon by the world leaders at the Millennium Summit 2015, and poverty reduction was considered most significant. It is believed that the global poverty rate has reduced, as income and wealth inequalities have increased in most countries, as well as inequalities based on gender, ethnicity and religion. As a recent United Nations progress report on the millennium development goals suggests that about 1 billion people are still in extreme poverty; persistent poverty in some regions and growing inequalities worldwide are stark reminders that economic globalization and liberalization have not created an environment conducive enough for sustainable and equitable social development.

The current approaches in reducing poverty have increasingly focused on "targeting the poor". However, when a substantial proportion of a country's population is poor, it makes little sense to detach poverty from the dynamics of growth and development. In short, poverty remains a major challenge because current dominant defy the evidence that a fall in poverty generally results from long-term processes of structural transformation, not from policies aimed at poverty. The shortcomings of such approaches to poverty reduction are a source of widespread concern. A substantial and sustained poverty reduction approach requires growth and structural change that generates productive employment, improves earnings and contributes to the welfare of the population.

The link between employment and poverty depend critically on how the employed and the economically dependent populations are organized in households. The employment structure of a household depends on the composition of dependants and earners as it directly influences the employment opportunities that translate into changes in poverty outcomes. Two sets of institutions are critical in shaping the employment-poverty linkage. These are the labour market and the household. The employment status is typically defined and analysed at the level of the individual or the job. Poverty, or income poverty in particular, is most commonly defined and measured at the household level. The relationship between poverty and employment is mutually reinforcing, implying that poverty tends to increase total household employment, often in more marginal activities, and particularly among women and children. However, it is also important to recognize that the additional employment income earned might be combined with other sources of household income, ultimately influencing the depth and incidence of poverty. If the burden of supporting the dependent population is unequally distributed, the result will be higher risks of poverty for certain segments of the population (United Nations Research Institute for Social Development [UNRISD] 2010).

There are a number of countries that have successfully dealt with poverty such as China, South Korea and Taiwan. In these countries, poverty alleviation was just one of the several goals prompting the introduction of social policies. Additionally, the most significant reduction in poverty has occurred in countries with comprehensive social policies that lean towards universal coverage. There are numerous reasons to invest in public, universal social protection policies in developing countries; since they protect people from income loss throughout the lifecycle in times of economic transition or crisis, enhance the productive capacities of individuals, groups and communities, and reinforce the progressive redistributive effects of economic policies.

For development strategies to generate the types of structural transformation and corporate behaviour conducive to equitable growth and poverty reduction, the states must possess certain capacities. They need to be able to overcome critical market failures; assist in the acquisition of new technologies; mobilize and channel resources to productive sectors; enforce standards and regulations; establish social pacts; and fund, deliver and regulate services and social programmes.

The states that can deliver growth-oriented and welfare-enhancing structural change need to be rule based, knowledgeable about their economy and society, and staffed by adequately paid and trained individuals. They also need to be able to mobilize domestic resources and strengthen capacities to influence and discipline investor behaviour. A few Asian countries did break out of poverty in a sustained way and emerged as economic giant, doing so under authoritarian political systems. A number of countries, namely Botswana, Brazil, Costa Rica, India, Kenya, Malaysia, South Africa and Taiwan Province of China with democratic regimes combined moderate growth with redistribution and achieved spectacular gains in social development (UNRISD 2010).

6.2   Review of literature

Poverty reduction has for so long been at the heart of development policies. Most economies strive to address poverty through accelerating economic growth owing to the long argument in favour of economic growth as a drive for poverty reduction. Different growth mechanisms have different effect on poverty; in this case, efforts will be concentrated on structural transformation and showing its impact on poverty. Economic growth is said to alleviate poverty when the poor are allowed to participate in economic activities and benefit from them. Growth accompanied by structural transformation may help reduce poverty if a proportionate share of employment is moved to manufacturing and/or services. However, when structural change is not geared to the right direction, it prevents the realization of poverty-reducing effect of economic growth. Job creation as a result of industrial expansion accompanied by redistributive policies is the way forward for poverty reduction. Despite the theoretical explanation in favour of the positive contribution of structural change in reducing poverty, limited empirical evidence has been provided on the direct causal relationship between structural transformation and poverty. This chapter discusses the link between structural change and poverty reduction on the assumption that the employment in high-productivity and value-added non-primary sectors would boost growth and eventually reduce poverty.

As indicated by Silva and Teixeira (2008), structural change is the change in distribution of economic activity and productive factors among various sectors of the economy. The seminal work by Matsuyama (1992) finds that low productivity of labour in the agriculture sector can fuel the industrialization process. The relationship between economic growth, employment and poverty reduction is thus a process in which output growth induces an increase in productive and remunerative employment, which in turn leads to an increase in the income of poor people, resulting in poverty reduction. A high rate of economic growth, associated with a high degree of employment intensity, is a necessary condition for poverty reduction, but may not be sufficient (Perry *et al.* 2006; OECD 2009). Various other studies have also highlighted the role of structural change in economic growth and poverty reduction.

Economic growth and structural change are mutually reinforcing phenomena. In such a two-way relationship, interlinkages lead to structural shifts and are inconceivable without them. Growth causes structural shift from agriculture to industry and then to services, (Kuznets 1966, 1971). As countries develop, they restructure away from agriculture and urbanize. However structural transformation and urbanization patterns differ substantially, with some countries fostering migration out of agriculture into rural off-farm activities and secondary towns, and others undergoing rapid agglomeration in megacities. Using cross-country panel data for developing countries spanning 1980–2004, Christiaensen and Todo (2014) found that migration out of agriculture into the missing middle (rural nonfarm economy and secondary towns) yields more inclusive growth patterns and faster poverty reduction than agglomeration in megacities. This suggests that patterns of urbanization deserve much more attention when striving for faster poverty reduction.

Antoci et al. (2015) studied the dynamics of a two-sector economy (with a natural resource-dependent sector and an industrial sector) characterized by free inter-sectoral labour mobility and heterogeneity of agents; that is, workers and entrepreneurs. The effects of deterioration of natural resources caused by the production activity of both sectors on inter-sectoral movements of the labour force (structural changes) on ecological dynamics and on the revenues of workers and entrepreneurs were analysed. The findings suggest that low productivity of labour in the resource-dependent sector can fuel the industrialization process. However, industrialization process may give rise to a reduction in workers' revenues (increased incidence of poverty) if the contribution to environmental depletion of the industrial sector, per unit of product, is higher than that of the resource-dependent one. Aggarwal and Kumar (2012) indicate that sectoral employment change from low-productivity to high-productivity sectors can contribute significantly to poverty reduction by raising income levels of those absorbed in more productive sectors. Moving out of less productive sector (generally agriculture) where poverty rates are often much higher than in more productive sectors may also relieve some of the pressure put on agricultural productivity and have some direct poverty-reducing effect through raising agricultural incomes. Such change in the structure of employment can have very large effects on poverty, as it may enable people to escape poverty traps.

Hasan et al. (2013) examined the relationship between growth in labour productivity and poverty reduction through the lens of structural change. They combined state-level data on poverty in India with state-level data on output and employment for 11 production sectors over 1987–2009. The study shows that the movement of workers from lower to higher-productivity sector is an important channel through which increases in aggregate productivity translate into poverty reduction. They also find that the importance of this channel of productivity growth varies across states, with indicators of financial development, pro-competitive business regulations and flexible labour regulations associated with larger reallocation of labour from lower to higher-productivity sectors.

Aggarwal and Kumar (2012) argue that structural change in India has substantially reduced poverty, in particular amongst the poorest, but the reduction of poverty slowed down after 2000 and there are indications that poverty has begun to increase again in the post-2007 period although rural poverty, in particular, remains high. Salih and Colyer (2000) found that Malaysia is one of the high-performing economies (HPE) in South East Asia. The country had experienced strong growth and development for the period between 1957 and 1995. The socio-economic planning, structural and trade adjustments, and adoption of pragmatic policies promoted agriculture as well as the manufacturing sub-sector resulting in higher productivities, incomes and standards of living.

Grootaert (1995) provides evidence that economic destabilization and the absence of managed structural change in an economy can be more harmful to the welfare of the poor than the process of adjustment itself. The findings are based on four consecutive years of household survey data from Côte d'Ivoire, spanning both a period of adjustment and destabilization. These constitute a unique database in Africa to assess the impact of structural change on the poor. The analytic methodology used is that of static and dynamic decomposition of poverty measures along policy-relevant dimensions.

Patroni (2004) argues that the most relevant and enduring implication of structural reforms in Argentina has been the consolidation of precarious work because of the new reality of employment for a very large segment of the working class. Neo-liberalism in the country performed effectively as a disciplining mechanism for the working class. Also, under the convertibility regime implemented for a decade since 1991, the wages were increased and working conditions improved under conditions that made reducing labour costs the critical variable in the adjustment of all sectors of the economy. The study is based on the transformation of Argentina over the last 25 years, following the period of military dictatorship since 1976 that was responsible for the first neo-liberal programme.

In order to evaluate the viability of Bolivia for attaining the MDG established in year 2000 and of halving extreme poverty by 2015, Buzaglo and Calzadilla (2009) examined the objectives in the country namely: policy autonomy, structural change and poverty reduction. They found that the MDG of halving extreme poverty by 2015 seemed a challenging, but attainable goal for Bolivia. Due to the expected debt reduction agreed with international creditors, the goal could be attained by a combination of investment and redistribution policies. Domfeh and Bawole (2009) examined poverty reduction at the local level in the Hohoe Municipality and Sefwi-Wiaso in Ghana using case study approach. The study found that although many poverty reduction initiatives have been undertaken in the country, their impact on the poor farming communities has been very minimal. The failure of these policies could be attributed to the non-involvement of local people in the process of policy formation.

Mustapha *et al.* (2015) examined the relationship between the industrial sector growth, inequalities and urban poverty reduction in Nigeria. The findings of the paper suggests that the industrial sector growth exert no significance on urban poverty, while the urban wholesale and retail services growth is found to be substantially strong in reducing urban poverty. The results also indicate that there is no statistically significant evidence to conclude that higher incidence of urban poverty was due to the high degree of inequalities. In the paper by Ncube *et al.* (2013), empirical results show that income inequality reduces economic growth and increases poverty in the region. The study presents the patterns of inequality, growth and income inequality in the Middle East and North Africa (MENA) region. Using a cross-sectional time series data of MENA countries for the period 1985–2009, they also investigated the effect of income inequality on key societal development, namely economic growth and poverty, in the region.

Structural change contributes to income generation, but this new income might be unequally distributed, which could derail the inclusive nature of growth. In this context, several authors (Wilkinson and Pickett 2010; Roháč 2012) argue that income inequality is among the most pressing current problems of our era and provide evidence that income inequality has a dramatic impact on people's everyday lives as greater inequality seems to lead to general social dysfunction. People trust each other less in more unequal societies and unequal societies tend to do worse when it comes to health, education and general well-being. In addition, homicide rates are lower, and children experience less violence in more equal societies.

Deininger and Squire (1998) and Son Le (2014) used cross-country studies, and have argued that on average, within country, inequality is stable over time, or changes too slowly to make a significant difference in poverty reduction. They found that the elasticity of inequality should always be positive since a decrease in inequality should decrease poverty. Shorrocks and van der Hoeven (2004) emphasized that poverty can be reduced at a faster rate when inclusive growth strategies are applied and when special income distribution policies are undertaken. Lustig and Arias (2000) argued that large increases in income inequality in countries in sub-Saharan Africa, Latin America and Central Asia over the 1990s, intensified the negative effects of growth on poverty.

Anyanwu (2013) on the empirical study of 43 African countries during 1980 to 2011 suggests that higher levels of income inequality, mineral rents, inflation and higher level of population tend to increase poverty in Africa and therefore prevent inclusive growth in the continent. Based on African data, Ali and Thorbecke (2000) found that poverty is more sensitive to income inequality than it is to income.

The use of development aid to alleviate poverty is debated in empirical studies. On one hand, Alvi and Senbeta (2012) suggests that aid has a significant poverty-reducing effect even after controlling for average income. Specifically, foreign aid is associated with a decline in poverty measured as the poverty rate, poverty gap index and squared poverty gap index. They also found that the composition of aid matters – multilateral aid and grants perform better in reducing poverty than bilateral aid and loans. Using data from 69 districts in Kenya, Oduor and Khainga (2009) shows that net Official Development Aid (ODA) has significantly reduced poverty in the country, emphasizing that net ODA disbursements have had stronger impacts on the poorest of the poor than on the rest of the poor. On the other hand, Connors (2012) finds that foreign aid does not exert a significant impact on reduction in poverty rates, suggesting that foreign aid as currently practiced, is ineffective at reducing poverty.

Ormonde (2011) examined the question of whether mineral resource rents have helped to reduce poverty rates in countries with an extensive mineral base in a cross-country case study analysis including Botswana, Nigeria, Zambia, Bolivia, Chile and Venezuela. The results indicates that Chile and Botswana have managed to utilize mineral rents to propel strong economic growth and reduce poverty, but inequality levels remain high in both countries. The levels of poverty are noticeably lowest in Chile, while Nigeria and Zambia, which have been unable to capitalize on their extensive mineral bases to reduce poverty rates, have the highest poverty rates among the countries.

Many believe that employment is a by-product of economic growth. But Cook (2011) in her study argues that economic growth or industrialization per se would not lead to sustained improvements in employment. Structural transformation can have many trajectories: situations of stalled industrialization and dualistic labour markets as in many Latin American and middle-income countries or service-led growth paths. The growth paths that are driven by low-productivity activities, where structural change is stuck in the primary sector, have produced highly segmented and unequal labour markets, and the poor are often locked out of dynamic growth sectors. Consequently, proper policy undertaken by the government is crucial for generating structural change that realizes better quality employment and poverty reduction outcomes. It can achieve employment-centred, socially inclusive structural change by – avoiding pro-cyclical policies during periods of slow growth; pursuing well-managed industrial and agricultural policies such as subsidies, tax credits, extension services and land redistribution; stimulating and maintaining an adequate level of labour demand; directing public investment in infrastructure and skill development of the population; and reducing vulnerability to commodity price and interest rate shocks.

Macroeconomic policy, financial institutions, the international structure of production, nature and composition of households, gender dynamics and social policy all influence employment outcomes and the potential for opportunities to translate into real differences in people's lives (Cook 2011). In the study, she indicates that social policy can contribute to economic growth as well as social welfare, and has been an integral part of the growth strategies of countries that have experienced far-reaching structural change and reduced poverty rapidly. The report argues that although structural constraints matter; neither are there prerequisites for social and economic policies that seek to eradicate poverty, nor are there stages of development through which countries must inevitably pass when introducing social policy. Typically, a fall in poverty has less to do with policies aimed at poverty per se than those aimed at much wider social objectives.

The following sections examine the linkages between poverty alleviation and structural transformation in sample countries of the three continents. The Gini index has been used as a measure of income inequality in the chapter. A zero value of Gini index expresses perfect equality, where all values are the same (for example, where everyone has the same income). A value of one (or 100 per cent) expresses maximal inequality among values (for example, where only one person has all the income or consumption, and all others have none). The five-year average of the Gini index and poverty indicators has been used in the chapter due to non-comparability of yearly data. Moreover, poverty-related data have been reported after five-year interval in most of the countries.

6.3   Africa

Figure 6.1 shows the income disparity in sample economies of Africa. It can be seen from the figure that income disparity in Ethiopia is lowest, while in Botswana and South Africa, it is very high. It is observed that income per capita and disparity are positively associated. The GDP per capita (constant at USD 2005) in Botswana and South Africa were USD 6,303 and 5,911, respectively in 2010, while the Gini index was 60.46 and 63.90 (higher disparity) during 2006–2010. On the other hand, GDP per capita in Ethiopia was USD 237.36, but the Gini index was 33.17 during 2006–2010, suggesting lower disparity. Hence, the findings shows that the higher the income per capita, the higher the income disparity. Thus high per capita income go alongside with high-income disparity.

Findings also show that disparity is increasing over time in many countries such as Ghana, South Africa, Tanzania and Uganda. Among the countries where disparity has declined, Ethiopia has seen the greatest decline with a Gini index that declined from 44.56 to 33.17 between 1991–1995 and 2006–2010.

Figure 6.2 depicts the percentage of people below poverty line of USD 1.90 (PPP, 2011) a day. Surprisingly, the poverty level has increased by almost 50 per cent in Kenya during 2001–2005 from that of 1996–2000. However, a noticeable positive fact is that poverty has a decreasing trend in all the sample countries

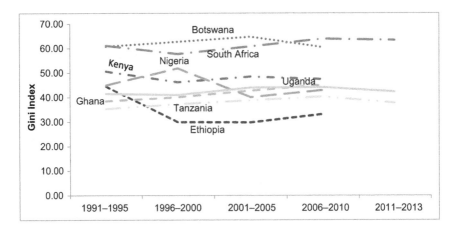

Figure 6.1 Gini index of African economies

Source: Based on WDI data

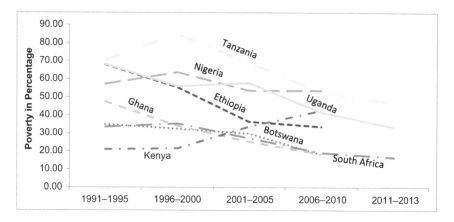

Figure 6.2 Poverty at USD 1.90 (PPP 2011) a day in Africa

Source: Based on WDI data

except Kenya. We can infer that poverty levels are low in high-income countries; for instance, GDP per capita in Botswana and South Africa was USD 6,303 and 5,911 respectively, with poverty levels of 18.24 and 19.10 per cent.

Figure 6.3 depicts the poverty gap based on an income level of USD 1.90 (PPP 2011) a day. It can be seen from the figure that trend in poverty gap is similar to that of poverty level. For instance, in Kenya, both the poverty gap and poverty level are lowest (5.59 per cent and 21.50 per cent during 1996–2000) in the same period. Figures also show that the poverty gap is low in high-income countries, while it is high in low-income countries as expected. For instance, in Tanzania with a GDP per capita of USD 578.67 in 2013, the poverty gap was 14.35 per cent during 2011–2013; while in South Africa with a higher income of USD 6,086.45 in 2013, the poverty gap was just 4.90 per cent.

Figures show that the poverty gap has declined in all sample countries except in Kenya, where it has increased from 7.16 per cent during 1991–1995 to 11.70 per cent during 2001–2005. The sharpest decline has been witnessed in Uganda, where poverty gap declined from 28.61 during 1991–1995 to 10.13 per cent during 2011–2013.

The data reveals that in Botswana's GDP per capita grew at the rate of 54.62 per cent, moving from USD 4,076 in 1995 to USD 6,303 in 2011. Along with increase of income, disparity was also reinforced. The Gini index recorded negative growth from 60.79 to 60.46 per cent point from 1995 to 2010, suggesting that income distribution became further distorted with the increase in income. Income rise had a significant impact on poverty with a reduction in poverty levels from 34.82 to 18.24 per cent during the same period. Regarding poverty gap, it also reduced from 13.49 to 5.78 per cent. However, the pace of poverty gap reduction is neither similar to increase in income levels, nor to the levels of poverty reduction.

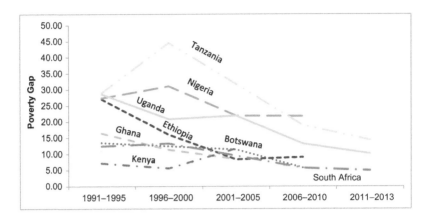

Figure 6.3 Poverty gap at USD 1.90 (PPP 2011) a day in Africa

Source: Based on WDI data

Although income per capita in Ethiopia is lowest among the sample economies, growth has been very impressive with 87.17 per cent increase from 1995 to 2010. The GDP per capita increased from USD 127 in 1995 to USD 239 in 2010. Despite this significant increase in income, the disparity in income distribution did not increase, but rather reduced at the highest pace among the sample countries. The Gini index changed from 44.56 to 33.13 percentage points (–11.39 per cent point). The levels of poverty also reduced drastically. The percentage of population below the poverty line reduced (–34.36 per cent points) from 67.90 in 1995 to 33.54 per cent in 2010. The poverty gap reduced (–18.03 per cent points) from 27.07 to 9.04 per cent. The data suggests that the pace of poverty gap reduction is much lower than that of poverty level reduction.

The GDP per capita income in Ghana rose from USD 405 to 606 during 1995 and 2010, with a growth rate of 49.60 per cent unlike Botswana and Ethiopia where income distribution further deteriorated. Consequently, Gini index increased (6.67 per cent points) from 38.44 to 45.11 percentage points during the same period. It may be inferred that additional economic opportunities were only appropriated by few, while many did not gain much economic benefits during 1995–2010. As a consequence, the population living below the poverty line changed, but not at the same pace as that of Ethiopia. The poverty levels changed from 47.38 to 18.32 per cent points during the same period. The reduction of poverty gap is much lower in Ghana (comparatively higher GDP per capita) than Ethiopia. It changed from 16.40 to 6.02 per cent.

The GDP per capita in Kenya increased merely by 13.83 per cent, changing from USD 514 to 585. This increase was lowest among the sample economies. The change in Gini index by –3.19 percentage points suggests that the income distribution has improved. More surprisingly, not only the poverty gap increased by 7.81 percentage points, from 7.16 per cent to 14.6 per cent, but also the poverty level with 21.58 percentage increase. The population below the poverty line significantly increased from 20.96 to 42.54 per cent. The increase in poverty gap and poverty levels suggests that the population at the bottom of the pyramid did not benefit from the economic gains during 1995–2010. Kenya might have suffered from WTO's ruling on apparel and garments manufacturing. According to Multi-Fibre Arrangement (MFA), the garments quota was abolished totally in 2005. Consequently, many foreign garments manufacturing firms operating from Kenya due to quota restrictions closed their operations from Kenya and started in their own countries. This led to a rise in unemployment and to reduction in the income of the workforce. This could be one of the reasons explaining the increase in poverty levels and poverty gap in Kenya.

On the other hand, the increase in per capita income in Nigeria has been the second highest after Ethiopia. In the case of Nigeria, the most noticeable fact is that the base-year income is much higher than that of Ethiopia and is comparable with most of other African countries. The income increased by 86.66 per cent, from USD 533 in 1995 to 996 in 2010. The income distribution also improved, which is captured by a decrease in Gini index by 2.01 per cent points. As a result of such increase in per capita income, the poverty levels and gap also decreased. Both the poverty levels and poverty gap decreased by 3.59 per cent and by 5.61 per cent respectively.

By comparing the economies with similar per capita income, one may notice that poverty level and gap are higher in Nigeria. For instance, in Ghana, the poverty level in 2010 was 18.32 per cent compared to 53.47 per cent in Nigeria. Similarly, poverty gap was 6.02 per cent in Ghana and 21.76 per cent in Nigeria. The income inequality reflected by the Gini index was 38.44 and 44.98 per cent in Ghana and Nigeria despite income levels of USD 606 and 996 respectively.

The per capita income in South Africa is comparable to that of Botswana, with USD 5,911 and 6,303 in 2010 respectively, although the base year income of Botswana was much lower than South Africa. Consequently, the growth of income in South Africa was 24.23 per cent, lower than that of Botswana but both countries differ in terms of income distribution. In Botswana, the income distribution improved, while in South Africa, it further deteriorated as income increased. From 1995 to 2010, the Gini index increased from 61.15 to 63.90, leading to an income disparity that was highest among all African sample economies. Although income distribution is most imperfect in South Africa, like Botswana, the poverty levels decreased from 33.43 to 19.10 per cent from 1995 to 2010 registering similar levels of decline in poverty as those of Botswana. The poverty gap also reduced from 12.42 to 5.70 per cent. In fact, the poverty gaps were similar to Ghana and Botswana in 2010.

Tanzania, whose per capita income was comparable with Kenya and Ghana in 2010 has seen a moderate growth of 56.53 per cent during 1995 to 2010. Moreover, the income distribution deteriorated. The Gini index increased from 35.29 in 1995 to 40.28 in 2010, thereby suggesting that economic gains during 1995 to 2010 only benefited a particular segment of the population. Despite the unequal distribution of income, the poverty level decreased by 17.69 per cent from 70.42 per cent in 1995. However, the poverty level still remains very high (52.73 per cent in 2010) in the country. Tanzania and Nigeria are the only two countries of the study where more than 50 per cent of the population is still below the poverty line. The poverty gap also decreased by 10 per cent from 28.95 per cent in 1995. The findings suggest that economic policies benefited all segments of the society, but high-income group received more benefits than the others leading to an increase in income inequality. Consequently, poverty gap and level both registered a declining trend.

Uganda having the second lowest GDP per capita in 2010 among the sample countries also registered a growth rate of 66.58 per cent. The per capita income increased from USD 234 in 1995 to 391 in 2010. Like its neighbouring country Tanzania, the income distribution became more skewed, resulting in increased Gini index by 2.77. It followed the trend of Tanzania related to poverty level and gap. The poverty level declined from 68.11 in 1995 to 41.46 per cent in 2010. On the other hand, poverty gap reduced from 28.61 in 1995 to 13.16 per cent in 2010. Economic policies in the country benefited more to high-income group of the population resulting in increased Gini index. Other segments of the society also benefitted leading to reduction in poverty level and gap. In fact, Uganda has achieved a great success in poverty alleviation as the poverty level as well as poverty gaps are lower than Nigeria, whose income per capita is almost 2.5 times of Uganda.

The association between poverty reduction as a result of structural change in Africa is presented in Figure 6.4.

The share of employment in high value-added sector is regarded as a measurement of structural change. The high value-added sectors include manufacturing,

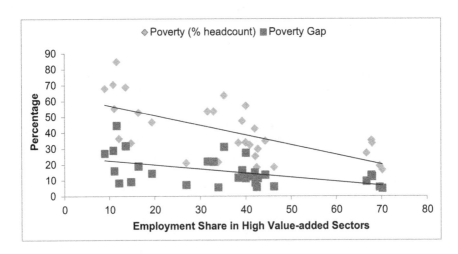

Figure 6.4 Skill of workforce and poverty in Africa

Source: Authors computation based on WDI and GGDC data

industry and services sectors. It can be seen from the figure that there is an inverse relationship between structural change and poverty level, as well as poverty gap. The trend for poverty level suggests that when the proportion of workforce employed in high value-added sectors increased, poverty level decreased. For instance, in South Africa, the share of employment in high value-added sectors was 69.59 per cent and only 19.10 per cent of population was below poverty line in 2010; while in Tanzania, the share of such employees was 11.68 per cent, and the poverty level was 84.74 per cent in 2000. It may be inferred from the findings that structural transformation offers potential to reduce poverty in Africa, which can be done by proper skill development programmes to enable employability of youths in high value-added sectors.

6.4 Asia

Figure 6.5 presents the trend in income disparity in sample Asian economies. Like Africa, there is a positive relationship between income disparity and GDP per capita. For instance, in Malaysia, where income per capita (USD 631 in 2010) was highest among sample countries, the Gini index (46.13 in 2006–2010) was also highest. On the other hand, in Indonesia with per capita GDP (USD 1,570.15 in 2010) the average Gini index during 2006–2010 was 34.84.

The Philippines is an exception, where income disparity was very high (Gini index 43.56 during 2006–2010), despite that, the per capita GDP (USD 1,403.38 in 2010) was the second lowest. The figure also shows that disparity in few comparatively high-income countries such as Malaysia and Thailand has decreased over time, which is a good sign of inclusive growth. On the other hand, income inequality is on the rise in several other countries such as China, India, Indonesia and

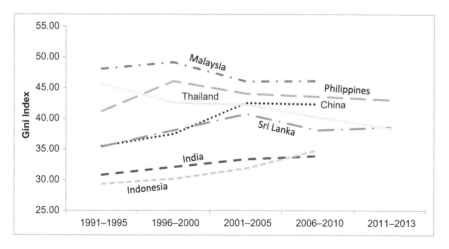

Figure 6.5 Gini index of Asian economies

Source: Based on WDI data

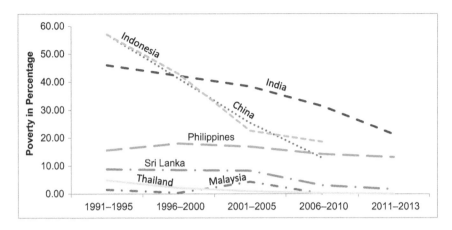

Figure 6.6 Poverty at USD 1.90 (PPP 2011) a day in Asia

Source: Based on WDI data

Sri Lanka, along with increasing GDP per capita. For instance, in China that has a fairly good GDP per capita (USD 2,891.08 in 2010), the Gini index significantly increased from 35.50 during 1991–1995 to 42.35 during 2006–2010.

The trend in poverty levels is presented in Figure 6.6. It can be seen from the figure that the population percentage earning less that USD 1.90 a day has declined in all countries. The sharpest decline was experienced by China followed by India. Poverty levels in China declined from 57 per cent during 1991–1995 to 12.92 per cent during 2006–2010; while in India, it declined from 46.06 to 31.43 per cent during the same period.

The association between income and poverty levels is on the expected lines. The poverty levels in relatively high-income economies are very low. For instance, in Malaysia and Thailand, it was 0.14 and 0.30 per cent during 2006–2010, respectively. On the other hand, in comparatively low-income countries such as India, Indonesia and Philippines, it was 31.43, 18.60 and 14.22 per cent, respectively during 2006–2010.

Figure 6.7 depicts the poverty gap in sample Asian economies. As expected, figures reveal that the relationship between poverty gap and income is similar to that between poverty levels and income. As shows in Figure 6.7, poverty gaps declined in all countries with the sharpest decline being in China. It reduced from 20.57 per cent during 1991–1995 to 3.27 per cent during 2006–2010. A substantial poverty gap has reduced in Indonesia (17.06 to 3.57 per cent), despite being a relatively low-income country. It may be due to a strong focus on inclusive growth rather than growth per se.

The figure also shows that the poverty gap in high-income economies such as Malaysia and Thailand has been very low. It further reduced from 0.16 to 0.002 per cent during 1991– 2010 in Malaysia; while in Thailand, it reduced from 0.83 to 0.04 per cent during the same period. The trend of poverty gap in Sri Lanka

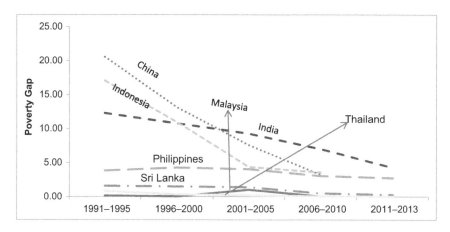

Figure 6.7 Poverty gap at USD 1.90 (PPP 2011) a day in Asia

Source: Based on WDI data

follows the similar pattern as that of Malaysia and Thailand, despite much lower GDP per capita.

It is well-known that China has been one of the fastest-growing economies for the last few decades. Its GDP per capita grew at the rate of 269.66 per cent from 1991 to 2010. The per capita income rose significantly from USD 782 in 1991 to 2,891 in 2010. But the growth in China cannot be labelled as inclusive as the Gini index deteriorated from 35.50 to 42.35 during this period, leading to higher income inequality. However, Chinese government did focus on poverty alleviation programmes. Consequently, not only did poverty levels experience drastic decline, but also poverty gap reduced substantially. The poverty levels reduced by 44.09 per cent, while poverty gap reduced by 17.31 per cent during 1991–2010. Despite such a drastic decline in poverty levels, it still remained 12.92 per cent in 2010.

Like China, the Indian economy has also experienced very high-income growth although much less than that of China. The GDP per capita in India grew at the rate of 119.73 per cent between 1991 and 2010, compared to 269.66 per cent in China. Apart from GDP growth, its magnitude is much lower than China's, as it was USD 1,031.56 in 2010 against 2,891.08 in China. But India is better placed than China in terms of income distribution point of view. Although the Gini index increased from 1991 to 2010, it still remained lower than that of China. It was 33.90 in 2010 against 42.35 in China. It may be inferred that India has been pursuing more of inclusive growth.

Concerning poverty level, it reduced from 46.06 to 31.43 per cent. It is worth noting that poverty level in India is highest among sample Asian countries. Although poverty gap also declined in India, its pace has been much lower than poverty level. The poverty level and gap decreased by 14.63 and 5.28 per cent respectively.

The income growth of other economies has been lower than that of China and India. In Indonesia, GDP per capita grew at the rate of 39.07 per cent. The Indonesian economy may be regarded as one of the slowest growing. One noticeable fact is that in 1991, the GDP in Indonesia was much higher than China (782) but became much lower in 2010. Like China and India, income distribution worsened: the Gini index increased from 29.31 to 34.84. Although income levels remained relatively stable in Indonesia, changes in poverty level and gap were similar to that of China. The poverty level changed from 57.06 to 18.60, while gap declined from 17.06 to 3.57 per cent.

The Malaysian economy has been very different from other sample economies in Asia. Its income in the base year itself (USD 4,348 in 1991) was very high. It grew at the rate of 45.34 per cent and attained USD 6,319 in 2010. Along with high income, inequality was also very high with Gini index of 48.09 in the base year. Unlike many other countries, this indicator slightly improved in 2010 (Gini index of 46.13) suggesting that of late, the Malaysian government is paying attention to inclusive growth. Although income disparity in Malaysia is still very high, poverty indicators were lowest among sample Asian countries. The poverty level reduced from 1.51 to 0.14 per cent, while poverty gap declined from 0.16 to 0.02 per cent.

The economy of the Philippines registered a moderate growth (41.31 per cent) in GDP per capita during 1991–2010. It changed from USD 993 to 1,403. Despite having such a low per capita income, income disparity is very high (Gini index of 41.17 during 1991–1995). Regarding the increase in income, it further deteriorated (Gini index of 46.13 during 2006–1910). Philippines is the only sample country where income inequality was at this high level despite having a very low GDP per capita. As a consequence of skewed income distribution, the poverty level did not change much. It declined marginally by 1.36 percentage points from 15.57 in 1991–1995 to 14.22 per cent during 2006–2010. Similarly, poverty gap also did not change much. It registered a decline of 0.78 percentage point from 3.83 per cent during 1991–1995.

The scenario of income growth and poverty alleviation in Sri Lanka is similar to that of several other sample countries. Its per capita GDP rose from USD 866 to 1,610 from 1991 to 2010, registering a growth rate of 85.82 per cent. Like other economies, income disparity also increased as income increased. This suggests that the attention of the Sri Lankan government is still on absolute growth rather than inclusive growth. Surprisingly, despite having such a low per capita income, the poverty statistics is similar to that of high-income countries such as Malaysia and Thailand. The poverty level in the base year was 8.85 per cent and reduced to 3.10 per cent during 2006–2010. The poverty level registered a decline of 5.76 per cent, while poverty gap declined by 1.12 per cent. The poverty gap during 2006–2010 was just 0.48 per cent.

The Thai economy is one of comparatively high-level economies with a GDP per capita of USD 3,164 in 2010. The base year income level itself was very high (USD 2,280), and it registered a growth rate of 38.78 per cent. Unlike most of the sample economies, the income disparity declined over a period of time.

The Gini index decreased from 45.67 to 40.20. It may be noted that the income levels and distribution are similar to that of China. But the poverty indicators are much better than that of China and are in fact comparable to that of Malaysia, whose per capita income is more than double in 2010. The poverty level declined by 4.62 per cent from 4.92 per cent during 1991–1995, while poverty gap declined marginally by 0.78 per cent from 0.83 per cent during 1991–1995.

Figure 6.8 presents the association between poverty reduction and structural transformation in Asian economies. As mentioned earlier, structural transformation is caused by the movement of workforce from low to high value-added sectors. Therefore, the percentage of workforce employed in manufacturing, industry and services has been used as a measure of structural change.

The figure shows the same trends as in the African context: an inverse relationship exist between poverty reduction and employment share in high value-added sectors which is being used as a proxy of structural change. For instance, share of employment in India for high value-added sectors was 29.11 per cent, and poverty level was very high at 46.06 per cent during 1991–1995. On the other hand, in Malaysia, with an employment share of 71.42 per cent during 2001–2005, merely 4.35 per cent of people were earning less than USD 1.90 a day. Although both poverty level and gap declined with the movement of workforce from low to high value-added sectors, the slope of poverty level trend line was steeper than that of the poverty gap. This suggests that more changes occur in poverty level than poverty gap with per unit change in labour movement from low to high value-added sectors. It also suggests that additional income due to structural change is unequally distributed among the poor with the marginal poor earning more than the poor at the bottom of the pyramid.

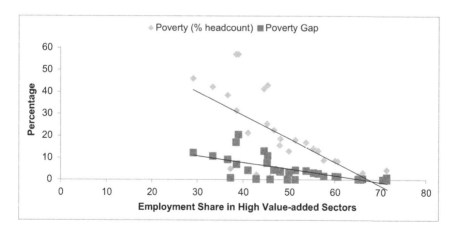

Figure 6.8 Skill of workforce and poverty in Asia

Source: Authors computation based on WDI and GGDC data

6.5 Latin America

This sub-section presents analyses of structural change, and its linkages with poverty alleviation in Latin American (LA) sample countries. Figure 6.9 depicts the income inequality of the economies in the region. It can be seen from the figure that the pattern of inequality in income distribution in the region is somewhat different than that of the economies of Africa and Asia. In general, the Gini index in all the countries with the exception of Mexico increased in the last decade of 20th century. The sharpest increase was in the case of Bolivia, changing from 49.11 during 1991–1995 to 59.57 per cent in 1996–2000. Income inequality has declined since then in all countries except in Argentina and Venezuela, but in these two countries, the Gini index started declining from 2001–2005.

Mexico is the only country where disparity has not only been low, but has declined since the beginning of the study period. It may be attributed to high per capita in the country and persuasion of inclusive growth policies. It may be noted that per capita GDP in Mexico was highest (USD 8,084.63) in 2010 among all the sample economies in Latin America. The figure also shows that considering the entire period, it is clear that income inequality has declined in most of the countries during 2011–2013 from the beginning of the study period, although it remained highest in Colombia and lowest in Argentina.

Figure 6.10 presents the trends of poverty reduction from 1991 to 2013. The poverty line has been defined as an income of USD 1.90 a day. It can be seen from the figure that trends are similar to that of income inequality. In all economies except Brazil, the percentage of people below the poverty line increased until 1996–2000. Brazil is the only country where percentage of poor people has been steadily declining. In Argentina and Venezuela, poverty continued to increase until 2001–2005.

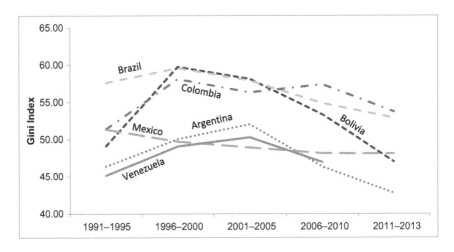

Figure 6.9 Gini index of Latin American economies

Source: Based on WDI data

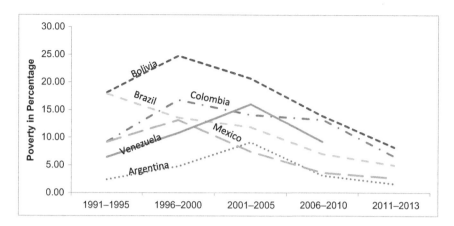

Figure 6.10 Poverty at USD 1.90 (PPP 2011) a day in Latin America

Source: Based on WDI data

It is worth noting that per capita income levels in LA countries is much higher than sample countries of Africa and Asia. In addition, LA economies are more integrated to the world economy than Asian and African economies. The increase in poverty levels in 1990s may be attributed to the fact that multi-national corporations (MNCs) moved away to cheaper locations, in Asia particularly as the Asian economies started opening up in early 1990s. This phenomenon might have created substantial unemployment, resulting in increase in poverty levels. The LA economies rebounded in the beginning of the century and consequently poverty saw a declining trend in all economies. The association of poverty levels with income per capita is on expected lines. The poverty levels are low in high-income countries such as Mexico and Argentina, while they are high in low-income countries such as Bolivia and Colombia.

Poverty gap in sample LA economies is depicted in Figure 6.11. It can be seen from the figure that pattern of change in poverty gaps is similar to that of poverty levels. As mentioned earlier, poverty levels increased during 1990s, and so did the poverty gap in all countries. Subsequently, the poverty gap also started reducing.

The changes in poverty level and gap are strongly associated with income levels. During the later part of 1990s and early 2000s, most of LA economies experienced a decline in per capita income and hence an increase in poverty level and gap. For instance, GDP per capita of Argentina was USD 5,835.11 in 1998 and declined to USD 4,930.87 in 2003. Similarly, GDP per capita in Mexico changed from USD 7,689.01 in 2000 to 7,461.06 in 2003.

Analysing each country in detail, it is found that GDP per capita in Argentina changed from USD 5,105 to 7,294 with a growth rate of 42.86 per cent. The change in income did not have any impact on disparity of income distribution. The Gini index (46.38 per cent) during 1991–1995 did not change. The poverty level and gap in Argentina was very low due to high income in the base year itself.

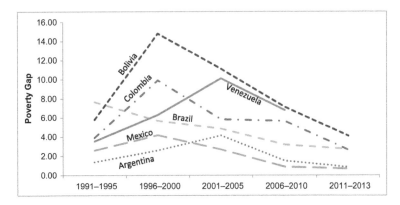

Figure 6.11 Poverty gap at USD 1.90 (PPP 2011) a day in Latin America
Source: Based on WDI data

With the increase in income, the poverty level and gap in the country did not reduce, but rather increased marginally. The poverty level and gap increased by 0.13 and 0.74 per cent respectively.

Bolivia, having the lowest GDP per capita among the sample LA countries, witnessed a growth rate of 29.77 per cent, with income levels of USD 1,177 in 2010. This change in income adversely affected the income distribution. The Gini index further deteriorated from 49.11 per cent during 1991–1995 to 53.35 during 2006–2010. Consequently, poverty levels increased from 5.80 during 1991–1995 to 7.14 per cent during 2006–2010. Although poverty level increased during this period, poverty gap registered a decline. It reduced by 4.22 per cent from 18.13 during 1991–1995. Bolivia is one of the LA countries where poverty level and gap were still very high compared to other countries in the region.

Brazil, being a prosperous economy relatively in the region, registered income growth of 31.98 per cent. The GDP per capita in 2010 was USD 5,678. Despite being prosperous, the income disparity is quite high. The Gini index which was 57.62 per cent during 1991–1995, slightly improved to become 54.85 per cent during 2006–2010. Surprisingly, despite having more than four time the income of Bolivia, the poverty indicators were similar in Brazil during 1991–1995, although the rate of poverty alleviation has been much faster than Bolivia. The poverty level declined by 4.48 percentage points, while the poverty gap reduced by 10.89 per cent. It seems that Brazil has more focussed on inclusive growth rather than growth per se for the last two decades.

The Colombian economy grew at the rate of 24.69 per cent during the study period. The GDP per capita increased from USD 3,159 in 1991 to 3,939 in 2011. This increase in GDP did not result in reducing income disparity; rather, it further deteriorated. The Gini index changed from 51.39 to 57.38 per cent, reaching the highest level among all LA countries from the sample. It seems that the additional income was appropriated by rich people resulting in further increase in poverty level and gap. The poverty level increased from 3.91 to 5.67 per cent, while gap increased from 9.21 to 13.13 per cent. This is the only sample economy where poverty has increased despite the increase in per capita GDP. The poverty indicators were relatively similar to that of Bolivia whose income is around one-third. This might have been due to the fact that the country has been successful in creating employment in very high value-added activities but failed to provide employment to a large segment of people resulting in job losses for many. Consequently, additional income became unequally distributed leading to worsened Gini index and increase in poverty.

Mexico, on the other hand, is the richest economy among the sample LA countries. Its per capita income grew at the rate of 23.77 per cent. It attained GDP per capita of USD 8,085 in 2010. As income increased, its distribution slightly improved. The Gini coefficient decreased from 51.33 per cent during 1991–1995 to 48.12 per cent during 2006–2010. The impact of an increase in income on poverty can be easily seen as the poverty level reduced by 1.71 per cent to reach a poverty level of 0.88 per cent, the lowest among the LA sample countries during 2006–2010. Similarly, poverty gap reduced by 5.53 per cent from 9.16 to 3.63 per cent during 2006–2010.

Venezuela, which is an economy predominantly based on natural resource export, registered meagre growth rate of 7.45 per cent. Its income per capita increased from USD 5,594 in 1991 to 6,010 in 2010. It is worth noting that Venezuela and Argentina had similar levels of per capita income in 1991. The slow growth of the Venezuelan economy could be attributed to global oil demand. With little change in per capita income in the country, the income disparity also remains at the similar level. The Gini index slightly increased from 45.17 to 46.94 per cent. With almost no growth in GDP per capita, the poverty level and gap further deteriorated by increasing by 3.26 and 2.81 per cent respectively. This could be attributed to oil-export-led characteristics of the economy. The additional income from the export was only appropriated by a few and added unemployment, resulting in increase in poverty level and gap.

Figure 6.12 presents the association between structural change and poverty alleviation in LA countries.

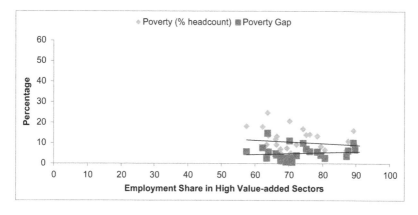

Figure 6.12 Skill of workforce and poverty in Latin America

Source: Authors computation based on WDI and GGDC data

It can be seen from the figure that the nature of the association is similar to that of economies of Africa and Asia. The employment in high value-added sectors is inversely related to poverty. For instance, the employment percentage (57.47 per cent) in high value-added sectors in Bolivia with lowest per capita income was very low, resulting in high levels of poverty (18.13 per cent) in 1991–1995. On the other hand, with 87.66 per cent employment ratio in high value-added sectors, the poverty level in Venezuela was just 10.80 per cent. Although, the trend is similar to other countries, the slopes of trend line are different. The trend lines are much less steep in LA compared to other countries. Less steep trend lines mean that poverty reduction is less sensitive to further structural change. It is very obvious in LA countries as poverty levels are lower compared to the two other continents, and further per unit change in income is unlikely to have similar impact on poverty.

6.6   Summary and conclusion

This chapter analyses the association between structural transformation and income inequality with poverty alleviation. It found that per capita GDP and income disparity are positively associated in Asia and Africa. For instance, in 2010, the per capita GDP was USD 6,303 and 5,911 in Botswana and South Africa respectively, and the disparity was also very high with a Gini index of 60.46 and 63.90 per cent. More surprisingly, in most countries, income inequality has increased alongside increase in income. Similarly in Malaysia, Thailand and China, per capita income in 2010 was USD 6,319, 3,164 and 2,891 respectively, and the Gini index was 46.13, 40.20 and 42.35 respectively. On the other hand, low-income countries in Asia such as India (GDP per capita in 2010, USD 1,032) and Sri Lanka (GDP per capita USD 1,610) had much better Gini index than that of India (33.90) and Sri Lanka (38.09).

The scenario in LA countries is different from the other two continents. Income disparity has not been associated with the level of income. For instance, high-income countries such as Argentina (USD 7,294) and Mexico (USD 8,085) had less income inequality with 46.33 and 48.12 per cent Gini index respectively in 2010. On the other hand, low-income countries such as Bolivia (USD 1,177) and Colombia (USD 3,939) had highly unequal income distribution. The Gini index in these countries were 53.35 and 57.38 per cent respectively. Therefore, income disparity may be attributed to the level of income to some extent, but more depends on country-specific policies related to inclusive growth.

The association between poverty and income is on the expected lines with few exceptions. Income and poverty are inversely related. High-income countries such as Botswana and South Africa had poverty levels of 18.24 and 19.10 per cent respectively in 2010. On the other hand, low-income countries such as Ethiopia (USD 239) and Uganda (USD 391) had 33.54 and 41.46 per cent of poverty levels. The exception is Tanzania with an income of (USD 521), but a high poverty level of 52.73 per cent. Similarly, in Asia, high-income countries such as Malaysia and Thailand had 0.14 and 0.30 per cent poverty levels respectively, while low-income countries such as India and Indonesia had 31.43 and 18.60 per cent of poverty level. In Asia also, few exceptions were observed, such as Sri Lanka with 3.10 per cent poverty level and China with a high income (USD 2,891) but a fairly high incidence of poverty (12.92 per cent).

The poverty levels in LA are generally very low compared to the other two continents. It varies from 0.88 in Mexico to 7.14 per cent in Bolivia in 2010. The income and poverty association holds true in LA as per capita income is high when poverty is low in Mexico and vice-versa in the case of Bolivia but the elasticity of poverty alleviation in LA countries with respect to change in income is much lower than the countries of the other two continents. The findings are on the expected lines: the linkages between poverty gaps and income follow the similar trend as that of poverty levels. When comparing the poverty levels with structural transformation, it is found that poverty is very strongly associated with ST in Asia and Africa, while in LA the trend is less steep. The percentage of workforce employed in high value-added (HVA) sectors has been used as a proxy of ST. Another distinguishing aspect noticed in LA is the magnitude of poverty levels and gaps in 2010.

The poverty level varies from 18.24 in Botswana to 52.73 per cent in Tanzania, while in Asia, it varies from 0.14 in Malaysia to 31.43 per cent in India. And poverty variation in LA ranged from 0.88 in Mexico to 7.14 per cent in Bolivia. It may be noticed that poverty levels are very high in Africa and very low in LA. These poverty levels are highly associated with ST. The employment share in HVA in Africa varies from 14.81 in Ethiopia to 69.59 per cent in South Africa. It varies from 38.59 in India to 71.40 per cent in Malaysia; while in LA, the lowest HVA employment share (67.55 per cent) was in Argentina and the highest (89.74 per cent) was in Venezuela. It is striking that the larger the structural change, the lower the poverty levels and this holds true for all the regions. The association of poverty gap is very much similar to that of poverty level. Hence, findings suggest that structural transformation is the way forward for poverty eradication and the key tool to prioritise for poverty eradication.

Bibliography

Aggarwal, A. and Kumar, N. (2012). Structural Change, Industrialization and Poverty Reduction: The Case of India. *ESCAP Development Papers 1206*, Unites Nations Economic and Social Commission for Asia and the Pacific, online, available at http://www.unescap.org/sites/default/files/SSWA_Development_Paper_1206_Nov2012.pdf (accessed on February 15, 2016).

Ali, A. A. and Thorbecke, E. (2000). The state and path of poverty in Sub-Saharan Africa: Some preliminary results. *Journal of African Economies*, 9(Supplement 1), 9–40.

Alvi, E. and Senbeta, A. (2012). Does foreign aid reduce poverty. *Journal of International Development*, 24(8), 955–976.

Antoci, A., Galeotti, M., Iannucci, G. and Russu, P. (2015). Structural change and inter-sectoral mobility in a two-sector economy. *Chaos, Solitons & Fractals*, 79, 8–29.

Anyanwu, J. C. (2013). Determining the Correlates of Poverty for Inclusive Growth in Africa. African Development Bank Working Paper No. 181. Tunis, Tunisia: African Development Bank.

Buzaglo, J. and Calzadilla, A. (2009). Towards a new consensus: Poverty reduction strategies for Bolivia. *International Journal of Development Issues*, 8(1), 18–39.

Christiaensen, L. and Todo, Y. (2014). Poverty reduction during the Rural-Urban Transformation- The role of the missing middle. *World Development*, 63, 43–58.

Connors, J. (2012). Foreign Aid and Global Poverty. Duke University Working Paper no. 17 Department of Political Science.

Cook, S. (2011). "Combating Poverty and Inequality: Structural Change, Social Policy and Politics," online, available at http://www.unicef.org/socialpolicy/files/May2011_ChildPovertyInsights_EN.pdf (accessed on Feb 12, 2016).

Deininger, K. and Squire, L. (1998). New ways of looking at old issues: Inequality and growth. *Journal of Development Economics*, 57, 259–287, online, available at http://citeseerx.ist.psu.edu/viewdoc/download?doi=10.1.1.194.8608&rep=rep1&type=pdf (accessed on February 17, 2016).

Domfeh, K. A. and Bawole, N. (2009). Localising and sustaining poverty reduction: Experiences from Ghana. *Management of Environmental Quality: An International Journal*, 20(5), 490–505.

Grootaert, C. (1995). Structural change and poverty in Africa: A decomposition analysis for Côte d'Ivoire. *Journal of Development Economics*, 47(2), 375–401.

Hasan, R., Lamba, S. and Sen Gupta, A. (2013). "Growth, Structural Change, and Poverty Reduction: Evidence from India," ADB South Asia Working Paper Series, 22. Asia Development Bank, online, available at http://www.adb.org/sites/default/files/publication/31214/south-asia-wp-022.pdf (accessed on February 08, 2016).

Kuznets, S. (1966). *Modern Economic Growth,* New Haven, CT: Yale University Press.

Kuznets, S. (1971, January). *Economic Growth of Nations: Total Output and Production Structure.* Cambridge, MA: Harvard University Press.

Lustig, N. and Arias, O. (2000). Poverty reduction: Latin America and the Caribbean. *Finance and Development*, 37(1), 30–33.

Matsuyama, K. (1992). Agriculture productivity, comparative advantage, and economic growth. *Journal of Economic Theory*, 58(2), 317–334.

Mustapha, A. B., Said, R. and Sidique, S. F. (2015). Urban poverty, inequality and industry in Nigeria. *International Journal of Development Issues*, 14(3), 249–263.

Ncube, M., Anyanwu, J. C. and Hausken, K. (2013). "Inequality, Economic Growth, and Poverty in the Middle East and North Africa (MENA)," AfDB Working Paper Series No. 195, African Development Bank, Tunisia.

Oduor, J. and Khainga, D. (2009). "Effectiveness of Foreign Aid on Poverty Reduction in Kenya," Working Paper No. 34, GDN Working Paper Series. Global Development Network.

OECD. (2009). "Promoting Pro-poor Growth: Employment and Social Protection," online, available at http://www.oecd.org/dataoecd/63/8/43514582.pdf (accessed on Feb 13, 2016).

Ormonde, P. (2011). "The Relationship between Mineral Rents and Poverty: Evidence from Sub-Saharan Africa and South America," online, available at http://dalspace.library.dal.ca/bitstream/handle/10222/14226/Ormonde,%20Pamela,%20MDE,%20ECON,%20August%202011.pdf?sequence=2 (accessed on Feb 21, 2016).

Patroni, V. (2004). Disciplining Labour, Producing Poverty: Neoliberal Structural Reforms and Political Conflict in Argentina. In Paul Zarembka (ed.) *Neoliberalism in Crisis, Accumulation, and Rosa Luxemburg's Legacy (Research in Political Economy, Volume 21,* pp. 91–119), Bradford, UK: Emerald Group Publishing Limited.

Perry, G. E., Arias, O. S., Lòpez, J. H., Maloney, W. F. and Servèn, L. (2006). *Poverty Reduction and Growth: Virtuous and Vicious Circles.* Washington: World Bank.

Rohác, D. (2012). *Does Inequality Matter?* London: Adam Smith Institute.

Salih, T. and Colyer, D. (2000). A case study of structural transformations, trade and poverty in Malaysia's socioeconomic development, 1960–95. *International Journal of Commerce and Management,* 10(1), 24–47.

Shorrocks, A. and van der Hoeven, R. (eds.). (2004). *Growth, Inequality, and Poverty: Prospects for Pro-Poor Economic Development.* Oxford: Oxford University Press.

Silva, E. G. and Teixeira, A. C. (2008). Surveying structural change: Seminal contributions and a bibliometric account. *Structural Change and Economic Dynamics,* 19(4), 273–300.

Son Le, M. (2014). Trade openness and household welfare within a country: A microeconomic analysis of Vietnamese households. *Journal of Asian Economics,* 33, 56–70, online, available at http://viet-studies.info/kinhte/TradeOpenness_August14.pdf (accessed on February 10, 2016).

UNRISD. (2010). "Combating Poverty and Inequality: Structural Change, Social Policy and Politics," online, available at http://www.unrisd.org/unrisd/website/document.nsf/(httpPublications) (accessed on Feb 13, 2016).

Wilkinson, R. and Pickett, K. (2010). *The Spirit Level – Why Equality is Better for Everyone.* London: Penguin.

7   Role of the state and policy

7.1   Introduction

This book examines the process of structural transformation and the inter-connections with the myriad and complex drivers of economic change, notably industrialization, employment, poverty and urbanization. Clearly, the most successful countries in our sample have undergone sustained and gradual transition from agrarian economies into high-productivity agricultural and industrial sectors. In the long-term evolution of countries, some have made the shift through rural-urban divide to achieve sustained urbanization. For example, China's stellar economic performance has been driven in large part by sustainable and well-managed urbanization and dynamic industrialization. A poignant demonstration of the impact of urban dynamics is the fact that the top 10 cities in China account for 20 per cent of the country's GDP (Cadena *et al.* 2012). The country has industrialized in the context of several urban economic hubs that boast of modern infrastructure fostering technological change and innovation within very competitive milieu. In sum, there is a close connection between industrialization and sustainable urbanization aptly demonstrated in this book. Where these two dynamic processes are positively connected, we find strong employment and sustained economic growth, progressive rise in living standards and lowering of poverty.

Conventional structural transformation is underlined by a systematic shifting of the production structures, whereby agriculture through higher productivity provides food, surplus labour with skills, and even savings to the process of urbanization and industrialization. This book has explored these issues at length across regions and countries. At a general level, our analyses sought to understand the factors that explain the differentials in the ways countries transit to sustained economic growth by looking at the different pathways taken by selected Asian and sub-Saharan African countries.

The first set of issues to examine is the role of governments and the policies (industrial and urban for example) the states enacted with the ways in which these helped to shape economic transformation. Industrial policy is defined as a "concerted, focused, conscious effort on the part of government to encourage and promote a specific industry or sector with an array of policy tools" (UNCTAD 2015). From the perspective of the World Bank, industrial policy is an explicit tool used as "government efforts to alter industrial structure to promote productivity-based growth." However, industrial policy does not limit itself to the industrial sector; it could also be applicable in its impact to manufacturing, as well as agricultural or services sectors. In the context of structural transformation, the way we view industrial policy is that it connects closely with other policies such as urban and economic policies in ways to achieve multiple objectives. In this book, our findings show the complementarities of rapid urbanization, industrialization undergirded by productivity growth, and with long-term implications for changes in living standards. The book provides ample evidence that sectoral shifts and the differential performances are an outcome of policy decisions arising from political constituencies shaped by the mediation of both internal and external factors, and it is for this reason we provide a few case studies.

A second major issue that calls for a more nuanced understanding is the rise in the contribution of the services sector to GDP in Africa in a way that the structural transformation process in nearly all countries tended to have "skipped" the industrial phase leading to "premature service growth," and in some countries, early onset of de-industrialization. We will treat this phenomenon at some length to understand the reason for its dominance at the expense of the industrial sector.

Much of East Asia has become fully engaged in global trade in manufacturing and value-adding services, while Africa's engagement is largely through supply of raw materials. We hypothesize that this is due to the weak industrial and technological capabilities of African countries, and the poor planning of African cities that do not support the formation of productive cities leading in large part to "consumptive cities." For this reason, the direction of raw materials exports has shifted towards Asia, while considerable export of manufactures is now on the reverse route to Africa. Manufacturing is fueling growth in the Asian continent, but it seems this may well be at the expense of nascent domestic manufacturing capacity.

This chapter is organized in four sections. The next section sets out a brief discussion on states and policy with a narrative of a few examples followed by the discussion on the services sector. We end the chapter with policy implications drawing on the various chapters.

7.2   The roles of governments and policies

The academic literature is replete with widespread and deep discussions on the role of governments and policies too vast and far outside the scope of this chapter. We will only briefly touch on the subject to provide a scaffold for our narrative. For example, the role of governments in the process of reform and economic development could consist of five broad categories: (1) manager of the economy, (2) promoter of economic growth, (3) distributor of income, (4) regulator of industry and (5) protector of citizen and business (Kuotsai 1998). Historically, governments have taken the initiative to promote economic growth through direct participation in economic investment, and indirectly through the formulation of policies and establishment of economic institutions. Another form of state participation is through industry-augmenting investment in public utilities such as power and water, funding of university research and manpower training; however, direct intervention in industry and other productive sectors was a relatively common feature in developing countries particularly in the 1970s to the 1980s. In other words, the state could be an entrepreneur, a producer or a regulator of the economy. The state also manages conflict because any form of structural change will lead to internal conflict; governments therefore require the capacities to resolve conflicts and manage the fallouts of conflicts. Hence this section will examine the role of states and policy in some African, Asian and Latin American countries with a view to determine the extent to which the state and its policies has driven the economic development and industrialization.

A review of the academic literature shows that states can be considered "strong" or "weak" derived from a diverse set of criteria points to results in superior social and economic efficiency and performance. A strong developmental state has long been associated for example with countries of East Asia that achieved very fast economic progress. On the contrary, African countries tend to be associated with weak or no state capacity, which explains their backwardness in the first place (Oyelaran-Oyeyinka 2015). Our empirical work on latecomer countries strongly supports the view that state capacity is an important prerequisite of sustainable development (Oyelaran-Oyeyinka and Gehl-Sampath 2010). The implicit assumption in this book is that governments play important roles in the formulation of policies and this promote structural transformation.

According to UNCTAD (2006), "an economic transformation process can take place only if an enabling policy is put in place that would bring about the process of capital accumulation, structural change and technological progress." To bring about this, conventional wisdom stresses the need for a strengthening of the capabilities of governments to enable them achieve structural change (Ohno and Ohno 2012). According to these authors, the "weak policy capability (faced by African countries) was common in today's successful East Asian countries; but they overcame the problem through focused hands-on endeavors to achieve concrete objectives which we call dynamic capability development" (Ohno and Ohno 2012: page 242). A large literature cites the East Asian experience as evidence to take seriously, the role of "institutions" and state capacity. These various sources emphasize the need to learn lessons from successful cases that led to capital formation and the promotion of technological capability accumulation.

Throughout the book, we conceptualize structural transformation as development in the broadest term; to mean a shift away from agriculture, to production of high-value manufactured goods. This implies rising productivity driven by the emergence of skilled manpower (technicians, engineers and scientists). In other words, where manufacturing is absent or weak, one might not see the sort of transformation that brings about sustainable development. This chapter seeks to interrogate a few case studies to understand the specific actions taken by the governments in some of the countries here analysed.

7.3   Government policy interventions – case studies

This book demonstrates unconventional growth patterns of structural transformation across developing countries, notably that countries particularly in

Africa are skipping industrial manufacturing and transiting directly into the services sector. This section presents selected case studies to understand the role played by the states in these widely different economic performance outcomes. Past and current policies formulated by governments are highlighted in an outline form with a particular attention given to initiatives directed towards industry and services. This is in an attempt to explain sectoral shifts and particularly the striking dominance of the services sector in the sample economies. Overall, this chapter builds on our empirical findings to provide policy recommendations in order to achieve structural transformation leading to a successful growth.

South Africa

South Africa has since independence adopted several initiatives and industrial policies aimed at promoting industrialization (a list of policies are presented in Appendix – Table 7.4). After the apartheid era in South Africa, most of the economic development policies initiated by the government were directed at the privatization of state assets, a set of policies built on liberal economic reform ideology which eventually failed in the realization of long-term investment, growth and employment. In 2007, a National Industrial Policy framework and Industrial Policy Action Plan were launched by South Africa's Department of Trade and Industry (DTI) in order to foster diversification, generate employment and increase the GDP. Conversely, during the consensus of these policies, South Africa's level of industrialization improved in comparison with the rest of African countries. The country is an outlier in terms of level of industrialization from the rest of sub-Saharan African countries.

However, the country is currently experiencing de-industrialisation which has led to continuous decline in manufacturing sector value-added contribution to GDP from 19.2 per cent in 2004 to 12.4 per cent in 2012 (Table 7.1). Its sectoral contribution to GDP in agriculture declined from 3.1 per cent in 2004 to 2.6 per cent in 2012. During this period, only the services sector had positive contribution to GDP from 65.6 per cent in 2004 to 69 per cent in 2012. As such, although South Africa has a comparatively higher manufacturing contribution to GDP, there are indications that it may be experiencing a services-sector-led growth.

Table 7.1 Values added per sector (current USD and percentage of GDP): South Africa

Sector added value	2004		2008		2012	
	USD	%GDP	USD	%GDP	USD	%GDP
Agriculture	6,113	3.1	7,329	3	8,859	2.6
Industry	61,517	31.3	79,319	32.3	98,112	28.4
Manufacturing	37,768	19.2	41,232	16.8	42,764	12.4
Services	129,067	65.6	158,806	64.7	238,351	69

Source: World Development Indicators (WDI); intracen.org.

Industrialization in South Africa during the Apartheid regime was dominated by mining linked activities and harnessing of mineral resources, but not much attention was paid to developing value-adding labour-intensive manufacturing sector. Despite this, the agro-processing, metal fabrication automotive and capital equipment sectors facilitated development of techno-managerial skills. These specialized skills contributed greatly to the country's economy as is the case when a country goes through this phase in the structural transformation model described before.

Kenya

In the case of Kenya, during 1960s and 1970s, economic development policy was driven largely by import substitution industrialization strategies which later resulted in export-led industrialization. The government provided an enabling platform through the provision of incentives for increase in exportation through the establishment of Export Promotion Council (EPC) and Export Processing Zones (EPZ) Authority in 1992 and 1996 respectively. In order to foster efficiency, privatization and liberal economic reforms were launched through a Structural Adjustment Program in the 1990s, which in retrospect contributed very little to economic performance in the subsequent years. As a result, further economic recovery strategies were formulated during 2003–2007 with a view to improve competitiveness in manufacturing and transform the country from a low-income country to an industrialized middle-income country (Table 7.5 in Appendix).

Kenya's current industrial policy was put in place since 2007 within its National Development Strategy christened Vision 2030 towards achieving sustainable economic growth, employment creation and poverty alleviation; while promoting performance of manufacturing, agriculture and services sectors. Although Kenya has a diverse output base, agriculture still accounts for a major share in output and productive employment. Thus, within its broad development vision, Kenya strives through its industrial policies to improve investment, as well as further diversify exports (Marti and Ssenkubuge 2009).

However, manufacturing contribution to GDP declined from 11.2 per cent in 2004 to 10.4 per cent in 2012. The services sector in Kenya, similar to South Africa, also contributes the largest share (over 50 per cent) of Kenya's total output, maintaining an average contribution of 53 per cent to the GDP from 2004 to 2012 (Table 7.2). Agriculture is the second largest contributor to GDP in Kenya, and although its value added fell from 28 per cent in 2004 to 25.8 per cent in 2008, it rose again to 29.3 per cent in 2012.

Nigeria

Nigeria's economic development plans evolved through three phases from post-independence until the current period. The first stage (1960–1985) featured Import Substitution Industrialization (ISI) Strategies with a view to foster technological advancement, reduce imports and increase foreign exchange. During this period, the Indigenization Decree (1972) was enacted and it was targeted at promoting

Table 7.2 Value added per sector (current USD and percentage of GDP): Kenya[1]

Sector added value	2004		2008		2012	
	USD	% GDP	USD	% GDP	USD	% GDP
Agriculture	4,012	28	6,942	25.8	9,686	29.3
Industry	2,608	18.2	5,311	19.8	5,742	17.4
Manufacturing	1,610	11.2	3,300	12.3	3,437	10.4
Services	7,688	53.7	14,610	54.4	17,585	53.3

Source: World Development Indicators (WDI); intracen.org.

Note: Added value is USD expressed in million, GDP USD and "6,976 to be read 6'976" (6,976 is to be read in billion).

indigenous participation in productive sectors of the economy. However, this plan did not succeed in import displacement and in achieving positive shift of the sectors from agriculture to industry. The second phase (1986–1999) witnessed the launch of Export-Led Strategies and Structural Adjustment Programme, which aimed to improve value addition in the primary sector by ensuring that commodities were processed before exportation. Trade policies were also instituted to promote exportation of locally manufactured goods. In addition, the dominant policy strategy in this era was privatization and liberalization, which in the course of time encouraged product dumping thereby adversely affected the production capacity of domestic industries. Evidently, the adoption of Structural Adjustment Programme (SAP) resulted in premature de-industrialization and widespread unemployment in Nigeria. In addition, it led to the decline in manufacturing contribution to GDP from 9.9 per cent in 1983 to 4 per cent by 1993. The third phase of economic reform in Nigeria included foreign private sector led initiatives to attract investment and deepen technological capability and as well increase the contribution of the manufacturing sector to GDP. Several policies were put in place to accomplish this, including outright bans on importation of goods with adequate local substitutes, formulation of legal framework for local content in the industrial sector and creation of sustainable programmes for small and medium enterprises (SMEs).

Nigeria became Africa's largest economy in 2014 and the 26th in the world due to rebasing of its GDP. It is Africa's largest oil exporter with the largest natural gas reserves. The agricultural, trade, telecommunications, manufacturing and entertainment industries contribute significantly to the economy's growth (Table 7.6 in Appendix). Although Nigeria has enjoyed impressive growth rates of GDP over the last decade, the pathway it took in respect of its structural transformation and industrialization has been unconventional. Presently, over 60 per cent of the labour force is engaged in low-productivity agriculture, and oil remains the mainstay of the Nigerian economy (International Trade Center [ITC] 2014). Nonetheless, the narrative on the state of manufacturing sector in Nigeria cannot be concluded without recourse to the role of industrial policy employed at various points in the development history of the country.

Of the three case countries examined, Nigeria is the least diversified with exports concentrated in minerals. In 2010, the contribution of agriculture recorded the largest share at 37.69 per cent and like the other African countries, the services sector recorded positive growth rate. The transport and trade services achieved CAGR of 7.08 and 2.54 per cent respectively, while share of financial services has been fluctuating with overall CAGR of −0.45 per cent. It may be worth mentioning that the contribution of transport sector was at the level of 2.14 per cent in 2010, which is lowest among services sector. As with other African countries, analysis of the Nigerian economy suggests that the country is *skipping the manufacturing phase* of development and jumping right into the services sector, while agriculture has regained some level of significance but is still unable to bridge the wealth and employment gaps.

Overall, there is a need for greater policy emphasis on manufacturing, which has served as the engine of growth in several countries.

China

For the last two decades, Asian countries have experienced massive economic transformation. The performance of different sectors of the Asian economies shows that institutional structure and policy initiatives helped in achieving high economic performance across countries. Until 1980, the growth of the Chinese economy was not so remarkable. After this period, economic reforms initiated steadily boost growth and investment in the country. Consequently, the export performance improved drastically (Table 7.3).

In 1952, China Council for the Promotion of International Trade (CCPIT)[2] was established in order to promote Chinese trade. Due to the establishment of CCPIT and initiatives taken in the country, China's foreign trade has grown faster than its GDP in the past 25 years. A key source of growth of the Chinese economy is the huge state investment in infrastructure and heavy industry such as iron and steel, that is deeply rooted in the manufacturing sector. It has been the dominant sector of the economy and provided the platform for the country's

Table 7.3 Export of major manufactured goods in China[3]

Product	Values in USD 100 Million					
	2008	2009	2010	2011	2012	2013
Chemicals and related products	793.46	620.17	875.72	1,147.88	1,135.65	1,196.18
Light textile, industrial products, rubber products etc.	2,623.91	1,848.16	2,491.08	3,195.60	3,331.41	3,606.06
Machinery and transport equipment	6733.29	5902.74	7802.69	9017.74	9643.61	10385.34
Miscellaneous products	3,359.59	2,997.47	3,776.52	4,593.70	5,356.72	5,812.49

economic transformation. It is the main channel for employment in the many cities and towns and embodiment of international competitiveness.

India

The Indian manufacturing sector has transited through various phases of development over the period being examined. It has evolved from the initial phase of building an industrial foundation in the 1950s to early 1960s, to the license–permit "Raj" in the period between 1965 and 1980.

More recently, the government of India launched various economic development policies concentrating on the manufacturing sector in order to overcome the problem of poverty and unemployment facing the country. Some of these policies include Ease of Doing Business, Industrial Infrastructural Upgrading Scheme, Scheme for Investment Promotion, Small and Medium Enterprises Development Act, Credit Linked Capital Subsidy, Invest India, National Policy on Electronics (Table 7.7 in Appendix). Currently, the Indian economy has become more competitive leading to significant increase in overall output of the industrial sector due in large part to successful implementation of these policies.

Like China, India's manufacturing sector is growing at a fast rate and contributing significantly to the country's GDP. The government of India has enacted various developmental policies to promote growth of the manufacturing sector since 1991. These instruments have boosted sub-sectors like chemicals and chemical products, computer, electronic and optical products, electronic equipment, textile and pharmaceuticals, among others. The chemicals and chemical products group has the highest total output of 7.14 per cent in 2008–2009, 7.53 per cent in 2010–2011, 8.04 per cent in 2011–2012 (highest) and a drop to 7.85 per cent output in 2012–2013. This product registered an increasing growth rate of 19.49 per cent in 2009–2010 to 31.76 per cent in 2011–2012. It dropped to 1.89 per cent growth rate in 2012–2013. The transport equipment sub-sector however had the highest growth rates of 35.08 per cent in 2010–2011.

7.4 The role of policies in driving industry and services

Structural transformation and industry

The conceptual underpinning of structural transformation shows the central roles that industry, manufacturing and agriculture play in economic transitions towards sustainable growth. Industrialization has over the years, been the change agent for economies of the world; it has bridged the divide between the rich and the poor, enabled technical advancements to spread across the globe and is accounting for emerging economies' growth due to their cheap labour force which supports the manufacturing activities. Industrialization is pivotal to domestic capability building and a country's ability to export and trade and is measured by the outcome of:

$$\frac{\text{manufacturing employment}}{\text{output share}} \div \frac{\text{total employment}}{\text{output}}$$

Notably, developing countries with high per capital incomes invariably have relatively high share of manufacturing in GDP with equally high levels of nonfarm employment. At a higher level of functioning, the more successful countries move to production of more complex and higher value manufactures for both domestic and export markets. Countries at a lower level of wealth on the contrary record high levels of agricultural labour force and low manufacturing contribution to GDP. Second, industrializing developing countries record higher living standards that is, higher GDP per capita that correlates with higher shares of manufacturing. This is because productivity is higher in the manufacturing sector than in the agricultural sector (Fei and Ranis 1964; Syrquin 1984, 1986; Szirmai 2009). Structural transformation attended by positive industrialization pathway results in the shift of resources from agriculture to manufacturing; and this process continues for as long as the share of manufacturing continues to rise in overall GDP (Oyelaran-Oyeyinka 2015). Third, unlike agriculture, development path through industrial manufacturing provides a faster road to capital accumulation; this is particularly so in manufacturing clusters (spatial agglomeration) compared with agricultural activities that are spatially dispersed. Capital intensity is equally high for sectors linked closely to manufacturing such as mining, utilities, construction and transport, and much lower in agriculture and services.

In sum, manufacturing, unlike other sectors has the ability to generate increasing returns and this makes its contribution to any economy unique. Also, it has the power to change economic structures in three ways:

1   At the firm level, it generates increasing returns by enabling proportion of outputs to be proportionate if not higher than inputs.
2   At the cluster or sector level, it fosters collaborative interactions among suppliers and competitors because they are all in the same production vicinity
3   Economy-wide backward and forward linkages are stimulated as a result of transactional exchanges between the primary, secondary and tertiary sectors.

As a country develops, it experiences a rising share of resources especially surplus labour in the manufacturing sector suggesting an intensification of industrialization. De-industrialization is the natural successor of industrialization and leads to changing contributions by the sectors reflected in a declining share of employment and wealth. Negative de-industrialization is characterized by a decrease in output, declining or stagnant labour productivity, reducing manufacturing employment and a resultant increase in services sector employment. As highlighted in this book, most African countries have experienced exactly this phenomenon. Early industrializers did not face the challenges brought about by the negative aspect of de-industrialization (faster reduction of industrialization opportunities at much lower levels of income), which late industrializers such as African countries today are facing. However, the sort of de-industrialization that follows the natural order tend to have positive impacts such as increasing or constant manufacturing output, higher labour productivity, accompanied by the natural decrease in manufacturing employment share complimented by an increase in service employment share. However, this order of progress is observed mostly in advanced industrial societies that have industrialized over a long period of time possessing the skills and capabilities for innovation.

An examination of Africa's structural transformation shows that the countries are not following conventional pathways of growth given the premature dominance of services and its significant and disproportional contribution to GDP and employment over the last decade. Evidence across most countries in Africa presented in the various chapters of this book indicates that economic growth has been steered essentially by growth in the services sector, indicating the possibility of a services-led structural transformation, in addition to income surges resulting from increase in commodity trade across borders.

Overall, manufacturing activities play the key role of an engine of growth by fostering increasing returns. Agriculture and natural resource extraction are examples of primary sector activities that can stimulate increases in output; however, they are not inclusive or sustainable for the long term. Pursuing them alone can result in growth, but not structural transformation which, as seen before, is important for sustainable development and growth of any economy. In order for full structural transformation to occur, one that benefits the economy in the best possible way, industrialization as an important phase and must be undertaken.

The positive impacts of industrialization clearly outweigh the negatives, making it an integral component of the transition that should drive structural transformation for sustainable growth and development. Within the right institutional context, the right techno-managerial capacity, and well thought-out industrial policy, a country could drive the transitional process to ensure the smooth and eventual transition from industry to services.

Structural transformation and services

The services sector plays an important role in satisfying customer needs: it enables and supports technological progress and in turn boosts productivity. An efficient and productive services sector could provide support to other sectors of the economy, which in turn improves the overall economic performance of an economy (Mann 2003). In a series of models that tested for the importance of agriculture, manufacturing and services on real economic growth, it found that growth in services value added is the only variable that is statistically significant (Gehl-Sampath and Oyelaran-Oyeyinka 2015). This confirms that the services sector is an important driver of Africa's real economic growth. Compared to other sources of growth such as agriculture and manufacturing value added, services value added has by far been the largest driver of real economic growth in sub-Saharan Africa in the last three decades.

Deriving from various case studies of the African economies, modernization and structural transformation are mainly driven by the following five factors, which also double as benefits experienced by an economy with a strong services sector:

1   Telecommunication services – facilitating efficient communication across all economic units
2   Education and training services – provide a labour force that has the required skill set

3   Energy infrastructure and services – ensure production flow is continuous and efficient
4   Transportation systems and services – ensure transfer of goods, services and labour force in a timely and efficient manner
5   Financial services sector – driven by innovation and IT, it supplements all other sectors with required financial support and services, thereby increasing their efficiency

In other words, moving towards and eventually developing a strong services sector creates more economic opportunities, offers livelihood and stimulates foreign investments as well as domestic and private one. Services can thus be seen as key contributors to development and in fact facilitate structural transformation. The services sector can be instrumental in generating inclusive growth, creating employment opportunities and enabling better regional integration of economies (UNCTAD 2015).

Africa's services sector growth rate was 4.6 per cent during 2009–2012, a factor which facilitated growth in several services sub-sectors. Intra-African expansion of service industries can be seen in the following examples: Uganda's education service industry, Egypt's telecommunication industry, Nigeria and Mauritius's financial and banking service industries and South Africa's commercial and cargo services airport industry.

It is important to note that even during the 2008–2009 global economic crisis, the growth of Africa's services sector maintained its pace and sustained any volatility for the most part. This suggests that an efficient and growing services sector could serve as an absorber of global economic shocks and also as a buffer.

Good examples of economies benefiting and growing as a result of thriving services sector are the two Asian giants: China and India. Both countries have displayed increasing trends in economic growth and development as a result of the growth in their respective services sectors. China has experienced a rapid growth in the services sector, which has made growing contributions to the overall economy seen during the 1991–2013 period when China also experienced increasing GDP. Over this period, not only has the services sector's contribution to GDP increased, but has also caught up with the contribution made by the manufacturing sector. In 2012, the top three (wholesale and retail, finance and real estate) out of a total of 14 services sub-sectors alone made a total contribution of 20.7 per cent to the GDP showing what a great impact this sector is having in improving the GDP of China (Wang 2013).

Similar growth trends were seen in the Indian economy, where a study by Chahal (2015) confirms that India's services sector has grown significantly over the years as compared to other sectors and again this compliments the growth in the overall GDP. India's growth in services sector output has mostly come from the fast paced developments seen in the IT and professional services sub-sectors. The compounded annual growth of India's services sector between 1991 and 2014 totals 8.37 per cent, showing the increasing trend which is mimicked by the overall economic growth in the country, while other sectors' growth (agriculture and manufacturing) have been on the decline at the same time. This and the example of China clearly suggest that the growth and development of a strong services sector truly has the power to promote overall economic growth for a country.

Services seem to be a sector of great potential for countries on the path of economic development and growth. However, findings of a set of service-led growth studies show that for a services-led growth to be sustainable, it must be accompanied by manufacturing growth as it creates the necessary forward and backward linkages in the economy (Hansda 2005). The analyses in this book of structural transformations occurring across Africa shows that African countries are not following conventional pathways of growth; rather, they have experienced premature emergence and dominance of the services sector instead of the all-important industrialization phase which should precede it. The services sector in African countries has been making significant and disproportional contributions to national GDP over the past decade, which as mentioned earlier, is not sustainable if not backed and supported by a strong manufacturing sector. Skipping the industrialization phase in the process of structural transformation and "jumping" right into a services sector directly has many negative implications, including structural underemployment and unemployment. The main reason that services-led growth may not be as sustaining as manufacturing-led growth is because of the high skill-intensive nature of tradable services. This being said, services-led growth can be self-sustaining in one special scenario: the case where technical skills and available technological capabilities are specifically targeted and developed to supplement the services sector labour which would have otherwise been achieved by a functional manufacturing sector (Ghani 2010; Gehl-Sampath and Ayitey 2015).

7.5 Analysis of differential pathways and policy implications

This last section summarizes important empirical evidences and points out some of the new insights from our findings into the process of structural transformation. It equally outlines a guide for policy-making in order to properly link structural transformation, employment, industrialization, productivity growth, urbanization and poverty reduction.[4]

The relationship between services and economic growth suggested in this book and in previous work found a clear but varying dependence between real GDP per capita growth and services value added; this has been the strongest in sub-Saharan Africa in the past three decades. The relationship of real GDP per capita growth and manufacturing value added, as well as that of agriculture value added and agricultural exports, has been positive but weak. The linkages between services exports and manufacturing exports have been similarly strong.

Both agriculture value added and manufacturing value added, as well as their exports, are important drivers of real economic growth; however, the effects of manufacturing value added on real economic growth has been weaker than that of services in Africa, confirming the findings in this book that sub-Saharan Africa might be "jumping" the manufacturing phase of development.

Structural transformation and employment

Our findings show differences across regions when we relate employment, wealth and structural transformation. In Africa, while structural change contributes significantly to wealth creation, it does not necessarily guarantee employment creation. Economists generally distinguish between three different types of unemployment. Frictional unemployment exists when a lack of information prevents workers and employers from becoming aware of each other. It is usually a side effect of the job-search process and may increase when unemployment benefits are attractive. Structural unemployment occurs when changing markets or new technologies make the skills of certain workers obsolete. And finally, cyclical unemployment is a result of the cyclical nature of the economy and occurs whenever there is a general downturn in business activity. Structural unemployment which prevails in the African context can create a higher unemployment rate over the long term; if ignored by policymakers, it can even lead to a higher natural employment rate.

Incidence of jobless growth was found in Ethiopia and Botswana for instance, the same pattern was observed in Asia. On the contrary, the relation between structural change and employment was positive in Latin America sample countries, where there is no association between structural transformation and wealth creation.

The most important element explaining the lack of relationship between structural change and employment is the fact that the labour force does not have the appropriate skills to work in these newly high value-added activities resulting from structural change. For augmenting productivity and generating employment in any sector, commensurable skill formation is extremely critical.

An important finding is that compared with the two other sectors, the services sector in sub-Saharan Africa has been driven largely by the presence of low-skill and less technology-intensive manufactures rather than by exports of knowledge-intensive medium and high-technology manufactures, including telecommunication equipment. In other words, Africa's services sector is not driven by skill-based performance, but rather the sector is operating within low-cost, low-value telecom and other segments, which suggest that services value added and its effects on real economic growth might not be sustainable. The sector exists on low-skill manufactures categorized as less knowledge based and less technology intensive. The products include office and stationery supplies, musical instruments and parts, records, tapes and similar low-value telecom products.

The dominance of services and the stagnation of industry results in Africa's persistent structural unemployment, which is mainly due to the lack of industrial skills demand. In the region, the weakness of the industrial sector has been a major source of structural unemployment. Our analysis reveals deep-seated obstacles or inefficiencies in African urban labour markets, such as a mismatch between the characteristics of labour demand and supply in terms of necessary skill sets. It may result from shifts in the composition of urban economies from industry to services, or from low-skilled to highly skilled occupations, and may require a combination of demand and supply-side policy responses.

In the Indian context, the process of structural change is different from that of China. The major reason could be the lack of appropriate human development and economic policies. It seems that India lacked skilled labour force and consequently, the performance of services and manufacturing sectors have not met their potential.

Moreover, governments should promote skills development programmes that particularly target the youth as this age group constitutes the future generation of workers and the potential actors of change. Therefore, policymakers should expand access to education at all levels and adapt technical, vocational and higher education to changing labour market requirements.

Structural transformation and productivity growth

Structural transformation in a conventional sense is accompanied by productivity growth, but recent empirical evidence suggests that this could take place without much change in labour productivity; this is the case with many African countries. One of the reasons for this phenomenon is the peculiar urban dynamics that occurs with little change in economic structures that ordinarily accompany transitions observed in more advanced industrial settings but is caused largely by the export of natural resource-based products which Africa tends to specialize in.

There are broad differences in the growth of productivity in Asia and Africa. In Africa, the contribution of structural change to productivity growth was always positive in a few countries, namely Ghana, Nigeria and Tanzania. In the case of Asia, the pattern of productivity growth and the contribution of structural change are similar in all countries, although the level of productivity growth is much higher than that of Africa. China and India are good examples of this positive relationship between structural transformation and productivity growth. The findings of this book suggest a need for specific policies that facilitate productivity growth. A distinguishing characteristic of the Asian countries is that explicit economic and industrial policies have been implemented to ensure the absorption of surplus labour from agriculture into other sectors leading to high value-added jobs. Consequently, the productivity growth in other sectors was positive, thereby preventing the phenomenon of jobless growth. This will involve an array of policies sometime difficult to coordinate involving economic actors that often do not collaborate.

However, in some countries, there is no link between structural change and higher productivity. This can also be due to the lack of skills relevant to these newly high value-added activities. It is not sufficient to favour high-value activities to raise productivity, but it is also crucial to develop the skills needed by these value-added activities. For example, in Tanzania, productivity growth in the majority of sectors was negative, except for few years (2007 to 2011). Similarly, in Ethiopia, annual productivity growth in manufacturing was positive only in 2012, based on estimated data. The Tanzanian and Ethiopian governments therefore need to embark on policies to augment labour productivity in various sectors through proper human development policies. This would notably enable youth to be absorbed in high value-added jobs.

Structural transformation and urbanization

As with the other key development drivers analysed in this book, empirical findings that relates structural transformation to urbanization points to the need for specific policies to leverage the relationship. It was found that urbanization correlates strongly with wealth generation at the early stages of development, but this relationship weakens beyond urbanizations levels of over 70 per cent. This indicates that high levels of urbanization alone are not sufficient for generating high levels of prosperity. Clearly, initiatives are required to leverage appropriate urban policy, planning, design, management and governance; as well as the existence of institutions capable of addressing the challenges associated with rapid urbanization.

Our empirical analysis also reveals that the relationship between structural transformation, urbanization and development is positive in all countries across the three developing regions, except in the Philippines and Sri Lanka, where the definition of urban areas changed. However, in some cases, urbanization is accompanied by economic development only up to a point. This was the situations in Botswana and Ethiopia. In general, it was found that the rapid urbanization in sub-Saharan Africa is not accompanied by the same economic progress seen in other regions. For Asian countries, the analysis suggests that urbanization and economic development are positively correlated without any threshold at which the relationship weakens. However, this is not the case of Thailand where the contribution of urbanization to economic development was very marginal until it even disappears, which can be explained by the decline in productivity in the industrial sector. Therefore, governments should formulate policies to help raise urban productivity levels. China is a striking example of a country where structural transformation is strongly positively correlated with urbanization. Unlike several African economies, the surplus of labour coming from agriculture was not absorbed in low value-added activities, but rather in highly productive sectors. This explains the economic success of the country as with Malaysia with high levels of urbanization that has gone along with declining employment level in agriculture.

This book validates what we know: that structural transformation does not occur without urbanization but not all urbanized countries experienced high economic development and structural transformation. This suggests that not all types of urbanization are beneficial, but only sustainable urbanization. Urban areas should be properly managed to raise urban productivity in ways to take advantage of agglomeration economies and economies of scale that cities offer. Explicit policies are needed to nurture the growth of highly productive activities particularly manufacturing and its connection to services.

The strategy to create "urban engine of growth" includes the adoption of sustainable urban plans and legislation; the promotion of urban industrial agglomerations to build productive cities; the implementation of policies stimulating high growth rate of manufacturing output; and the adoption of policies raising the share of employment in industry, which leads to high per capita incomes.

Structural transformation and industrialization

Our findings show that the progress of countries will depend in large part on the productivity of urban areas and the extent to which urban growth are managed to nurture the growth of high-productivity activities through agglomeration economies. However, a number of African countries have become highly urbanized without significant changes in their sectoral structures towards manufacturing and in most cases directly skipping to services.

The study reveals that the more dynamic Asian countries that achieved long-term growth are characterized by urban sectors that are driven by manufacturing and services led the growth. In developing countries, 86 per cent of growth in value-added between 1980 and 1998 came from the urban sector – manufacturing and services (Montgomery *et al.* 2003). Sustainable urban and structural shift come about through proper planning and is supported by enforceable legal mechanisms. When properly managed alongside industrialization and planned urban space, it leads to higher productivity and eventually, rising living standards and better quality of life.

From our analysis, structural transformation in Africa and Asia is marked by significant productivity shifts in most countries. Labour productivity increased in all sectors in Botswana, Ghana, South Africa, China, India, the Philippines and Sri Lanka. Our findings show that the services sector has been very important in the industrialization of Asia. However, unlike Africa, where services activities are characterized by low-value activities, the sector in Asia is built on high value-added services.

The growing dominance of the services sector requires policy attention to ensure that the sector contributes effectively to long-term economic growth. One option is to progressively raise the capabilities of the sector through explicit investment in manpower and skills development. In the medium and long term, African countries will have to build up the capacity of their manufacturing sector to support the services sectors. In other words, the two sectors will have to develop in tandem for sustained long-term benefits of the economy.

Clearly, the economic progress associated with emerging economies led by China is largely due to the maximization of relatively cheaper but skilled-labour inputs in the manufacturing sector. China has, for several years developed a robust industrial policy and made significant explicit investment on growing its industry. Not surprisingly, this had led to both productivity and employment growth. The pattern of structural transformation that took place in the Chinese economy is a model of the conventional growth dynamic that should be considered by other developing countries.

Structural transformation and poverty

We analysed the changes in poverty levels in the process of structural transformation; it was found that both factors are strongly and negatively associated in Asia and Africa. This association between poverty reduction and structural transformation was the clearest result across all regions in this analysis. However, the trend lines are much less steep in Latin America, which suggests that poverty reduction is less sensitive to further structural change. It is because in Latin America, poverty levels are lower compared to the other two continents, and further improvement in the per unit income have less impact on poverty.

In Africa, there is an inverse relationship between structural change and poverty level as well as poverty gap: when the proportion of workforce employed in high value-added sectors increased, poverty level decreased. For instance, in South Africa, the share of employment in high value-added sectors was 69.59 per cent, and only 19.10 per cent of population was below poverty line in 2010, while in Tanzania, the share of such employees was 11.68 per cent, and the poverty level was 84.74 per cent in 2000. Our findings imply that structural transformation offers a great potential to reduce poverty in Africa.

In Asia, although both poverty level and gap declined with the movement of workforce from low to high value-added sectors, the slope of poverty level trend line was steeper than that of the poverty gap. This suggests that additional income due to structural change is unequally distributed among the population and do not benefit the poorest as much as it benefits the richest. Governments should pay attention to this increasing inequality.

This study also suggests ways of thinking about the informal sectors and slums, which are the physical manifestations of poverty. About 70 per cent of the total population in large metropolis lives in slum communities. Our research reveals a negative correlation between informal employment and GDP per capita; hence, informal growth tends to be growth-reducing in developing countries. Thus, informal workers tend to be less well-off than those who work and live in more formal settings. Significantly, the emergence of unplanned cities tend to come with informality, illegality and slums, which is why urban growth in poorer developing countries is strongly associated with slum growth. This can be remedied with appropriate planning and delivery of affordable housing and urban basic services. Urban and economic policies will do well to address urban inequality that has arisen as a result of differentiated wealth concentration in cities.

Overall, in developing countries, the growth paths that are driven by low-productivity activities, where structural change is stuck in the primary sector, have produced highly segmented and unequal labour markets, and the poor are often locked out of dynamic growth sectors. Consequently, the right labour policy is crucial for fostering the types of structural change that realizes better quality employment and poverty reduction outcomes. It should aim to achieve employment-centred, socially inclusive structural change by avoiding pro-cyclical policies during periods of slow growth; pursuing well-managed industrial and agricultural policies such as subsidies, tax credits, extension services and land redistribution; stimulating and maintaining an adequate level of labour demand; directing public investment in infrastructure and skill development of the population; reducing vulnerability to commodity price and interest rate shocks; and managing a sustainable urbanization.

Appendix

Table 7.4 Trade and development strategies: South Africa (2001–2011)

Year	Strategy	Objective	Sector
2011	Industrial Policy Action Plan 2011	The plan constitutes a central tool in applying the job creation strategy.	Advanced manufacturing; agro-processing industry; automotive components, medium and heavy commercial vehicles
2011	National Development Plan	The plan outlines the national South African strategy.	
2011	National Strategy for Sustainable Development and Action Plan	The strategy envisages the sustainable transformation in South Africa.	
2011	New Growth Path	The plan aims at creating 5 millions jobs by 2020.	
2011	Southern Africa ADB Regional Integration Strategy Paper		
2011	Strategic Plan for the Department of Agriculture, Forestry and Fisheries	To improve service delivery of the Department of Agriculture	
2010	A South African Trade Policy and Strategy Framework	To achieve the objectives of upgrading and diversifying South Africa	
2010	Industrial Policy Action Plan 2010		Advanced materials, aerospace industry, agro-processing industry, automotive components
2007	National Industrial Policy Framework	The National Industrial Policy Framework aims at diversifying the economy.	
2007	UNDAF South Africa 2007–2010	To assist South Africa in achieving the MDGs; it is aligned with the other local national policies.	
2001	The Strategic Plan for South African Agriculture	To reshape the agricultural sector in order to increase wealth creation, employment and exports; reduce poverty and inequalities; improve farming efficiency; improve business climate and attract foreign investments	

Table 7.5 Kenya's development strategy and sectoral focus (2003–2010)

Year	Strategy	Objective	Sector
2010	Agricultural Sector Development Strategy	To reduce unemployment and poverty and achieve an average growth of 7 per cent for agric sector between 2010 and 2015; to increase productivity, commercialization and competitiveness of agricultural products and firms.	Aquaculture, food crops, forestry, horticulture, industrial crops, livestock, wildlife
2008	UNDAF (United Nations Development Assistance Framework) Kenya 2009–2013	It is aligned with Kenya Vision 2030 and prioritizes the following fields: improvement in governance and human rights enforcement; economic empowerment and reduction of disparities and vulnerabilities; promotion of equitable and sustainable growth.	
2007	Kenya Vision 2030	A long-term Kenyan development plan; it aims at ensuring an economic growth rate of 10 per cent per annum till 2030.	Agriculture (fisheries, food crops, horticulture, industrial crops, livestock), business services, outsourcing, financial services, manufacturing, tourism, wholesale and retail trade
2004	Poverty Reduction Strategy Paper – Kenya 2003–2007	Designed to meet the ERS medium-term objectives, it focuses on economic growth, inequality and poverty reduction, as well as promotion of good governance.	
2003	Economic Recovery Strategy for Wealth and Employment Creation (ERS)	Recovery based on four pillars of (1) macroeconomic stability; (2) strengthening of institutions and governance; (3) rehabilitation and expansion of physical infrastructure; (4) investment in human capital of the poor	Agriculture, fisheries, forestry, information, broadcasting and film, livestock, mining industry, mining industry, tourism
2003	National Export Strategy	The National Export Strategy looks at Kenyan past and current export performance.	Apparel and clothing, beverage industry, commercial crafts, fish products, fisheries, food industry, horticulture, ICT, livestock and livestock products, tea, textile industry, tourism, transport services

Source: Adapted from International Trade Centre

Table 7.6 Sectoral diversification in products for Nigeria's exports

Sector	Average share of sector in country's exports 2009–2013	Share of top three detailed products (HS6) in sector's exports		Sector's leading exported product HS6
		2009	2013	
Minerals	89.1%	97.7%	97.7%	Petroleum oils and oils obtained from bituminous minerals, crude
Fresh food	6.5%	79.4%	67.4%	Cocoa beans, whole or broken, raw or roasted
Leather products	1.2%	75.0%	72.7%	Leather further prepared after tanning or crusting
Transport equipment	0.8%	80.6%	79.9%	Floating or submersible drilling or production platforms
Processed food	0.6%	81.1%	72.0%	Cigarettes containing tobacco
Basic manufactures	0.4%	55.0%	79.0%	Aluminium unwrought, alloyed
Chemicals	0.3%	54.2%	59.5%	Urea, wthr/nt in aqueous solution in packages weighing more than 10 kg
Miscellaneous manufacturing	0.1%	31.1%	35.2%	False beard, eyebrows and the like, of synthetic textile materials
Non-electronic machinery	0.1%	48.7%	44.4%	Gas turbines of a power exceeding 5000 KW
Wood products	0.1%	83.6%	94.6%	Wood charcoal, including shell or nut charcoal, whether or not agglomerate
Textiles	0.1%	58.3%	73.0%	Cotton yarn, ≥ 85%, single, uncombed, 714.29 > dtex ≥ 232.56, not put up
IT and consumable electronics	0.0 %	56.8 %	55.6 %	Machines for the reception, conversion and transmission or regeneration
Electronic components	0.0%	53.4%	70.2%	Waste scrap of prim cell
Unclassified products	0.0 %	99.9%	99.8%	Commodities not elsewhere specified
Clothing	0.0%	33.5%	37.6%	Pullovers, cardigans and similar articles of man-made fibres, knitted

Table 7.7 Indian policy in brief

Year	Initiative	Objectives
2001	Ease of Doing Business	Involves introduction of ICT in governance to make the process of applying for Industrial License (IL) and Industrial Entrepreneur Memorandum (IEM) more efficient and effective. This had led to ease of filing applications and online payment of service charges.
2001	North East Industrial Investment Promotion Policy	It is meant for the North Eastern region (NER) of India, with an objective to promote industrial development of the NER by subsidizing eligible industrial units.
2002	Pharmaceutical Policy	Ensures the availability of essential drugs of mass consumption at reasonable prices within the country; strengthening the indigenous capability for cost-effective quality production and exports of pharmaceuticals by reducing trade barriers, etc.
2003	Industrial Infrastructure Upgrading Scheme	The features include upgrading of infrastructure in industrial estates/parks/areas, supporting new projects in backward areas, including North Eastern region, priority to upgrade infrastructure in existing clusters over new cluster, etc.
2004	Scheme for Investment Promotion	To promote India as an attractive and credible destination for FDI, various activities at GtoG, GtoB and BtoB level; it involves capacity building, monitoring and evaluation, establishment of G2B Portal/e Biz Pilot Project and setting up of country focus desks to promote investment.
2006	Micro, Small and Medium Enterprises Development (SME) Act	To enhance the competitive strength of such enterprises, address the challenges of competition and avail of the benefits of the global market.
2007–2008	Credit Linked Capital Subsidy Scheme (CLCSS)	Aims at facilitating technology upgradation by providing upfront capital subsidy to SMEs, including tiny, khadi, village and coir industrial units, on institutional finance (credit) availed by them for modernisation of their production equipment (plant and machinery) and techniques.
2012	National Policy on Electronics	It is a holistic, investor friendly and market-driven initiative towards creating a conductive environment to attract global and domestic companies to invest in growing Electronics System Design & Manufacturing (ESDM) sector in India.
2014	Invest India	To facilitate foreign investors by providing support for all investment queries and for providing handholding and liaising services, quality input and support services to them

Notes

1 http://www.intracen.org/country/kenya/Income/#sthash.Atn119G6.dpuf (accessed on April 12, 2016).
2 http://www.ccpit.org.cn/ (accessed on Jan 24, 2016).
3 http://www.stats.gov.cn/tjsj/ndsj/2014/indexeh.htm (accessed on Jan 26, 2016).
4 This final section is supplemented by key findings coming out of recent empirical analysis (Gehl-Sampath and Oyelaran-Oyeyinka 2015).

Bibliography

Cadena, A., Dobbs, R. and Remes, J. (2012). The Growing Economic Power of Cities. *Journal of International Affairs*, 65(2), 1–18.

Chahal, M. (2015). An Analysis of Services Sector in Indian Economy. *International Journal for Research in Applied Science & Engineering Technology*, 3(V), 147–151.

Fei, John C. H. and Ranis, G. (1964). *Development of the Labour Surplus Economy: Theory and Policy*. Homewood, IL: Tichard A. Irwin, Inc.

Gehl-Sampath, P. and Ayitey, D. (2015). "Challenges and Opportunities to Structural Transformation: Africa's Service Sector," in P. Gehl-Sampath, and B. Oyelaran-Oyeyinka (eds.), *Sustainable Industrialization in Africa: A New Development Agenda* (pp. 46–65), London: Palgrave Macmillan.

Gehl-Sampath, P. and Oyelaran-Oyeyinka, B. (eds.). (2015). *Sustainable Industrialization in Africa: Toward a New Development Agenda*. London: Palgrave Macmillan.

Ghani, E. (2010). "Is Service-Led Growth a Miracle for South Asia?" in Ejaz Ghani (ed.), *The Service Revolution in South Asia* (pp. 35–102), New York: Oxford University Press.

Hansda, S. (2005). *Sustainability of India's Services-Led Growth: An Input Output Analysis of the Indian Economy*, online, available at http://129.3.20.41/eps/ge/papers/0512/0512009.pdf (accessed on April 10, 2016).

International Trade Centre. (2014). *ITC by Country Report. ITC by country – Trinidad and Tobago*, online, available at http://www.intracen.org/layouts/downloadcountryreport (accessed on April 08, 2016).

Kuotsai, T. L. (1998). *Managing Economic Reforms in Post-Mao China*, London: Praeger.

Mann, C. (2003). "Globalization of IT Services and White Collar Jobs: The Next Wave of Productivity Growth," Institute for International Economics, International Economic Policy Briefs, December.

Marti, D. F. and Ssenkubuge, I. (2009). "Industrialisation and Industrial Policy in Africa: Is It a Policy Priority?" The South Centre, Research Paper 20, online, available at http://www.southcentre.int/wp-content/uploads/2013/05/RP20_Industrialisation-and-Industrial-Policy-in-Africa_EN.pdf (accessed on April 10, 2016).

Montgomery, M. R., Stren, R., Cohen, B. and Reed, H. E. (eds.). (2003). *Cities Transformed: Demographic Change and Its Implications for the Developing World*. Washington, DC: National Academies Press.

Ohno, I. and Ohno, K. (2012). "Dynamic Capacity Development: What Africa Can Learn from Industrial Policy Formulation in East Asia," in A. Noman *et al.* (eds.),

Good Governance and Growth in Africa: Rethinking Development Strategies (Ch. 7, pp., 221–245), Oxford: Oxford University Press.

Oyelaran-Oyeyinka, B. (2015). The State and Innovation Policy in Africa. *African Journal of Science, Technology, Innovation and Development*, 6(5), 481–496.

Oyelaran-Oyeyinka, B. and Gehl-Sampath, P. (2010). *Latecomer Development: Innovation and Knowledge for Economic Growth*. London and New York: Routledge.

Syrquin, M. (1984). "Resource Reallocation and Productivity Growth," in M. Syrquin, L. Taylor, and L. E. Westphal (eds.), *Economic Structure and Performance, Essays in Honor of Hollis B. Chenery* (pp. 75–102), Florida: Academic Press.

Syrquin, M. (1986). "Productivity Growth and Factor Accumulation," in H. Chenery, S. Robinson, and M. Syrquin (eds.), *Industrialization and Growth: A Comparative Study* (pp. 229–262), Oxford: Oxford University Press.

Szirmai, A. (2009). "Industrialisation as an Engine of Growth in Developing Countries, 1950–2005," UNU-MERIT Working Paper, 2009–10. The Netherlands: United Nations University.

UNCTAD. (2006). "Least Developed Countries Report 2006: Developing Productive Capacities," online, available at http://unctad.org/en/Docs/ldc2006_en.pdf (accessed on April 21, 2016).

———— (2015). *Economic Development in Africa Report 2015: Unlocking the Potential of Africa's Services Trade for Growth and Development*. Geneva: United Nations Conference on Trade and Development.

———— (2015). "World Investment Report 2015: Reforming International Investment Governance," online, available at http://unctad.org/en/Publications Library/wir2015_en.pdf (accessed on April 20, 2016).

Wang, W. (2013). "Features, Restrictions, and Policy Recommendations in the Service Sector of the People's Republic of China," in Donghyun Park and Marcus Noland (eds.), *Developing the Service Sector as an Engine of Growth for Asia* (pp. 232–259). Manila: Asian Development.

Index

For Product Safety Concerns and Information please contact our EU
representative GPSR@taylorandfrancis.com Taylor & Francis Verlag GmbH,
Kaufingerstraße 24, 80331 München, Germany

Printed and bound by CPI Group (UK) Ltd, Croydon, CR0 4YY
08/05/2025
01864331-0003